ORDEAL
BY
FIRE

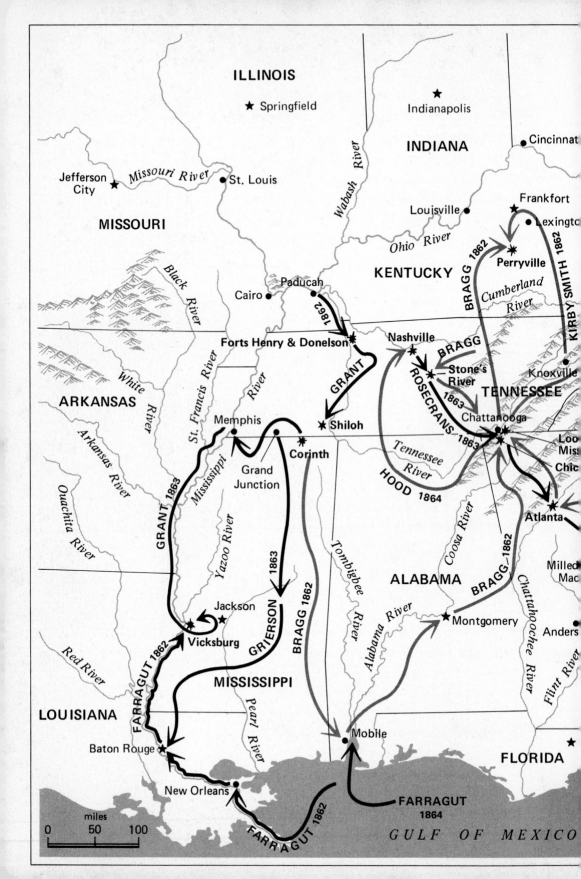

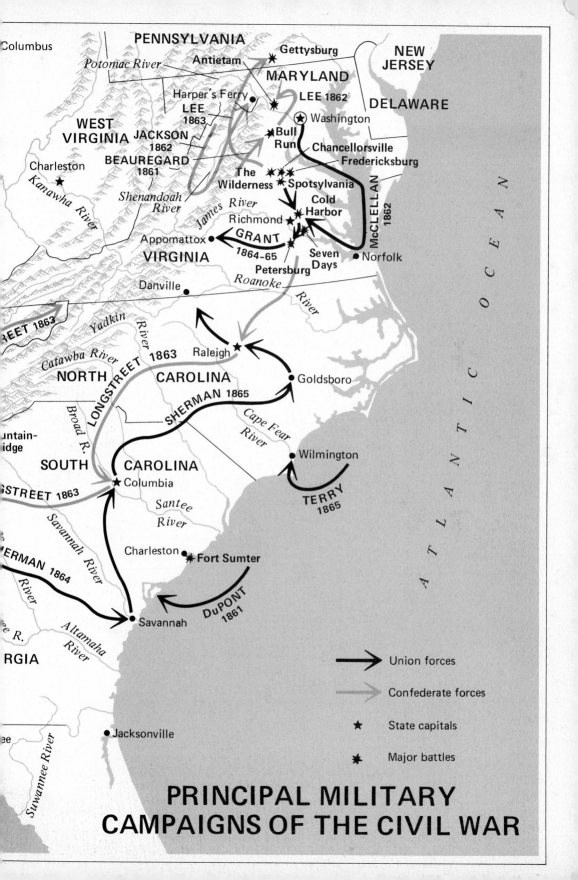

PRINCIPAL MILITARY
CAMPAIGNS OF THE CIVIL WAR

ORDEAL BY FIRE

VOLUME III
RECONSTRUCTION

James M. McPherson
Princeton University

Alfred A. Knopf ⌖ New York

THIS IS A BORZOI BOOK
PUBLISHED BY ALFRED A. KNOPF, INC.

First Edition

98765432

Copyright © 1982 by Alfred A. Knopf, Inc.

Library of Congress Cataloging in Publication Data

McPherson, James M.
  Ordeal by fire.
    Bibliography: p.
    Includes index.
    1. United States—History—Civil War, 1861–1865—Causes. 2. United States—History—Civil War, 1861–1865. 3. United States—History—1865–1898. 4. Reconstruction. I. Title.
E468.M23   973.7   81-11832
ISBN 0-394-35813-9 (pbk.: v. 3)   AACR2

Manufactured in the United States of America

Design by James M. Wall

For Jenny

A Note on This Paperback Edition

This volume is part of a separate printing of *Ordeal By Fire*, not a new or revised edition. Many teachers who have used the full edition of *Ordeal By Fire* have suggested the publication of each of its three parts—"The Coming of War"; "The Civil War"; and "Reconstruction"—as separate volumes for adaptation to various types and structures of courses. This edition, then, is intended as a convenience for those instructors and students who wish to use one part or another of *Ordeal By Fire* rather than the full edition. The pagination of the full edition is retained here, but the table of contents, bibliography, and index cover only the material in this volume.

Preface

In 1869 the Harvard historian George Ticknor, who had been born during George Washington's presidency, wrote that the Civil War and its aftermath had left "a great gulf between what happened before it in our century and what has happened since, or what is likely to happen hereafter. It does not seem to me as if I were living in the same country in which I was born." Four years later, in their novel *The Gilded Age*, which gave a name to the era, Mark Twain and Charles Dudley Warner described the Civil War and Reconstruction as having "uprooted institutions that were centuries old, changed the politics of a people, transformed the social life of half the country, and wrought so profoundly upon the entire national character that the influence cannot be measured short of two or three generations."

The greatest changes witnessed by Ticknor, Twain, and Warner were embodied in the Thirteenth, Fourteenth, and Fifteenth Amendments to the United States Constitution: the emancipation of four million slaves and the granting of equal civil and political rights to the freed people. These Amendments formed the framework for "reconstruction" of a Union shattered by secession and civil war. They legislated the most radical changes in American history. Yet a century later, more than one historian has questioned whether Reconstruction really accomplished any "fundamental changes" in "the antebellum forms of economic and social organization in the South. . . . Real freedom for the Negro remained much more of a promise, or a hope, than a reality for more than a century."

This book examines the promise and the reality of Reconstruction. As Volume 3 of a trilogy on America's *Ordeal By Fire,* this volume is intended for use in college courses in American history. It can be assigned in conjunction with

Volume 1: *The Coming of War,* and Volume 2: *The Civil War.* Or it can be
assigned separately in courses on the Civil War and Reconstruction, on the South,
in the survey course, or in other courses.

For a few years after the Civil War the reality of Reconstruction almost
measured up to the promise. But a "retreat from Reconstruction" in the 1870s
led to a restoration of white supremacy and the creation of an American version
of apartheid. The issues of Reconstruction, and its consequences, still confront us
today: relations between whites and blacks, nation and states, North and South.
The purpose of this book is to aid in understanding the historical roots of these
continuing concerns.

Princeton, New Jersey   James M. McPherson

Acknowledgments

A good many people and institutions have helped me produce this book. Students, colleagues, and lecture audiences over the years have knowingly or unknowingly helped to shape my knowledge and understanding of this era. The resources and staffs of the Princeton University Library and the Henry E. Huntington Library were indispensable. I am especially indebted to Martin Ridge, the late Ray Allen Billington, James Thorpe, Virginia Renner, and Noelle Jackson for making my year of research and writing at the Huntington so pleasant and productive. Thanks must also go to the National Endowment for the Humanities and to Princeton University, which provided the funds and a leave for my year at the Huntington.

Several colleagues and friends read drafts of these chapters and made fruitful suggestions for improvement. For their careful and honest reading, I am indebted to Richard N. Current, George M. Fredrickson, Michael F. Holt, and Peyton McCrary. I also owe thanks to members of the editorial staff at Alfred A. Knopf, especially to David C. Follmer, who as history editor for the college department first suggested the project from which this book grew and who faithfully supported it from the beginning, to his successor Christopher J. Rogers, who has shepherded this paperback edition to completion, and to James Kwalwasser, who gave the project more editorial time, effort, care, and enthusiasm than the most demanding author could expect. I am grateful to Louis Masur for his checking of quotations and references, and to my wife Patricia for her time and patience in helping me with the tedious task of reading proofs. Writing this book has been an intellectually rewarding experience, and all of these people have helped in various ways to enrich the experience.

Contents

———

ORDEAL
BY
FIRE

VOLUME III
RECONSTRUCTION

Twenty-six

The Problems of Peace

THE AFTERMATH OF WAR

The South in 1865 presented a bleak landscape of destruction and desolation. Burned-out plantations, fields growing up in weeds, and railroads without tracks, bridges, or rolling stock marked the trail of the conquering Union armies. The collapse of Confederate authority left large areas without law and order. Roaming bands of guerrillas and deserters plundered defenseless homes. Hundreds of thousands of black freedmen and white refugees suffered from disease, exposure, and hunger. As just one example of the horrors left by the war, a pile of sixty-five horses and mules killed by Sherman's army lay unburied near Columbia, South Carolina, for six weeks because the troops had carried off all spades and other implements.

Having swept through the South as destroyers, Yankees remained there as restorers. Into the vacuum of devastation and chaos moved the occupation forces, the Freedmen's Bureau, and Northern relief agencies. The 200,000 occupation troops functioned as the main source of law and order. The army placed the ex-Confederate states under martial law. Military courts punished criminals, and Freedmen's Bureau courts regulated relations between former slaves and their former masters. Army hospitals treated thousands of Southern civilians both black and white. During the summer of 1865, the Freedmen's Bureau issued 150,000 daily rations (one-third of them to white refugees), and the army fed at least as many more Southern civilians. The Freedmen's Bureau continued to provide food relief even after the postwar crisis eased; between 1865 and 1870 the Bureau issued nearly twenty-two million rations.

But not every agency of the government contributed to rehabilitation. The Treasury Department sent special agents into the South to seize whatever Confederate cotton had survived the war. However honest these agents may have been

493

when they left Washington, several of them succumbed to temptation when they reached their destinations. At prices of $200 a bale or more, cotton still exercised its wartime power to corrupt. Some Treasury men and army officers seized privately owned cotton, stamped it "C.S.A.," and sold it on their own accounts or extorted bribes from the owners not to do so. In this way, sizable amounts of the South's only remaining form of liquid wealth were siphoned away. In 1865, Congress levied a tax of 2.5 cents a pound on cotton and in 1866 raised it to 3 cents. Although the purpose of this tax, like that of similar taxes on Northern products, was to help pay the cost of the war, the impost appeared vengeful to the South. It also retarded the region's economic recovery. Congress finally repealed the cotton tax in 1868.

The Attitudes of Southern Whites

Contradictory appraisals of the Southern mood were sent North by army officers, government officials, and the multitude of journalists who flocked southward after Appomattox. Stories of continued defiance toward Yankees and violence against freedmen mingled with reports of submission and docility.

Southerners were a proud people who had staked all and lost all. Hatred of their conquerors was a natural response. "Day by day and hour by hour does the deep seated enmity I have always had . . . for the accursed Yankee nation increase & burn higher," wrote a young planter late in the war. "They have slaughtered our kindred . . . destroyed our prosperity as a people & filled our whole land with sorrow. . . . I have vowed that if I should have children—the first ingredient of the first principle of their education shall be uncompromising hatred & contempt of the Yankee." An innkeeper in North Carolina told a Northern journalist in 1865 that the Yankees had killed his soldier sons, burned his house, and stolen his slaves. "They've left me one inestimable privilege—to hate 'em. I git up at half-past four in the morning, and sit up till twelve at night, to hate 'em."[1]

Observers agreed that such attitudes were less prevalent among Confederate soldiers than among noncombatants, especially women. The soldiers had had enough of defiance, at least for the time being.* The experience of fraternization across the lines with Billy Yank and the liberal surrender terms, which protected Confederate soldiers from punishment for treason, also worked for the reconciliation of veterans to defeat. But noncombatants had endured the suspense and agony of war with no outlet for their anger. Many of them had been forced to watch helplessly as the invaders destroyed their property. After the fighting ended, their pent-up bitterness exploded in expressions of hatred and often in violence. The freed slaves and Southern white Unionists sometimes became surrogate victims of attacks by frustrated Southerners who did not dare to assault the real symbols of their humiliation, Yankee soldiers. For Southern white women, behavior such as the following incident in July 1865, described by a Northern reporter, provided an outlet for repressed rancor:

---

*Two or three years later, however, Confederate veterans would play a dominant role in the Ku Klux Klan and similar organizations.

A day or two ago a Union officer, yielding to an impulse of politeness, handed a dish of pickles to a Southern lady at the dinner-table of a hotel in this city [Savannah]. A look of unspeakable scorn and indignation met him. "So you think," said the lady, "a Southern woman will take a dish of pickles from a hand that is dripping with the blood of her countrymen?"[2]

During the early postwar months, however, many Southerners experienced successive waves of shock, despair, and apathy before feeling anger, which is a sign of reviving spirits. *"We give up to the Yankees!"* wrote a shocked woman when she learned of Lee's surrender. "How can it be? . . . Have we suffered all—have our brave men fought so desperately and died so nobly for this?" In June 1865, the daughter of a Georgia planter looked forward to nothing more than "a joyless future of probable ignominy, poverty, and want [with] God alone knowing where any of us will end a life robbed of every blessing and already becoming intolerable."[3] A South Carolina planter told a Northern journalist: "We are discouraged: we have nothing left to begin anew with. I never did a day's work in my life, and don't know how to begin." Many years later, an Alabama ex-slave recalled the return home of Confederate soldiers after the war: "I seen our 'Federates go off laughin' an' gay; full of life an' health. Dey was big an' strong, asingin' Dixie an' dey jus knowed dey was agoin' to win. I seen 'em come back skin an' bone, dere eyes all sad an' hollow, an' dere clothes all ragged. Dey was all lookin' sick. De sperrit dey lef' wid jus' been done whupped outten dem."[4]

While this mood of despondency lasted, Southern whites might have submitted to almost any terms of reconstruction the government had seen fit to impose. "They expected nothing," wrote a Northern journalist; "were prepared for the worst; would have been thankful for anything. . . . They asked no terms, made no conditions. They were defeated and helpless—they submitted." In many cases, to be sure, this submissiveness barely concealed the underlying hatred. Nevertheless, even South Carolinians admitted that "the conqueror has the right to make the terms, and we must submit."[5]

The Attitudes of Northern Whites

But the conquerors could not agree on what terms they wished to impose. Contradictory and shifting moods chased each other across the Northern landscape. In the immediate aftermath of Lincoln's assassination, a cry for the punishment of traitors rent the air. The new President seemed to endorse the demands for a draconian policy. "Treason is a crime and must be made odious," said Andrew Johnson. "It is a crime before which all other crimes sink into insignificance. . . . Traitors must be impoverished. . . . They must not only be punished, but their social power must be destroyed."[6]

Johnson, like Lincoln, was a self-made man of humble background. The death of his father, a tavern porter in North Carolina, left the family in poverty and made necessary the apprenticeship of young Andrew to a tailor. The apprentice learned the trade, moved to the mountain country of east Tennessee, married a shoemaker's daughter (who taught him to write), and scrambled up the ladder of success. Johnson acquired a farm and slaves. He served as state legislator, governor,

President Andrew Johnson *(Reproduced from the Collections of the Library of Congress)*

congressman, senator, vice president, and finally, by an accident of history, as president of the United States. A Jacksonian Democrat and a self-proclaimed champion of the common people, Johnson never lost his fierce plebeian pride. "Some day I will show the stuck-up aristocrats who is running the country," he had vowed early in his Tennessee career. "A cheap purse-proud set they are, not half as good as the man who earns his bread by the sweat of his brow."[7]

As President, Johnson now had his chance to show the Southern aristocrats— whom he blamed for secession—who was running things. He investigated the possibilities of indicting leading Confederates for treason and of confiscating their property under the 1862 Confiscation Act. Radical Republicans who had opposed Lincoln's reconstruction policy were gratified that Providence had "trained a Southern loyalist in the midst of traitors, a Southern democrat in the midst of aristocrats, to be lifted at last to the presidency of the United States, that he might be charged with the duty of dealing punishment to these self-same assassins of the Union."[8]

As the postassassination furor subsided, however, the mood toward traitors softened. Johnson gave no more speeches branding treason an odious crime. The joyous Northern celebrations of victory and the grim reports of Southern destitution purged vengeance from the hearts of many Yankees. A spirit of magnanimity toward a fallen foe began to manifest itself. "We want true union and concord in the quickest possible time," declared the influential *Springfield* (Mass.) *Republican* on June 10, 1865. "Are these ends to be gained by reproaches and invectives; by prolonging the spirit and the evils of the war after the war itself has terminated?"

But this sentiment coexisted uneasily with a conviction that the "fruits of victory" must not be sacrificed by premature leniency. Magnanimity must be tempered by justice. What were these fruits of victory? For most Republicans they included, at a minimum, absolute repudiation of secession, guarantees for the freedom and civil rights of emancipated slaves, security and political power for Southern Unionists, and at least temporary political disqualification of leading ex-Confederates.

Northern attitudes toward the problem of reconstruction ranged across a spectrum of alternatives. At one end of the spectrum was the Democratic alternative of self-reconstruction. Such a policy would have allowed the existing Southern state governments to proclaim their loyalty to the Union, to supervise the election of new congressmen and senators, and then to carry on as if the war had never occurred. Self-reconstruction would have met none of the minimum Republican conditions. It would have preserved ex-Confederates in power, shut out Unionists, jeopardized the rights of the freedmen, and perhaps periled their freedom itself —since the restored legislatures would have had the option of not ratifying, and therefore defeating, the Thirteenth Amendment.

At the opposite end of the spectrum was the radical vision of reconstruction as revolution. Radicals desired to overthrow the power of the Southern ruling class by disfranchisement and confiscation. They wanted to enfranchise the freedmen and grant them confiscated land. They wished to reshape the South in the Republican image of the free-labor North. Congressman George W. Julian of Indiana, one of the most radical of the Republicans, described his vision of the new South: in place of "large estates, widely scattered settlements, wasteful agriculture, popular ignorance, social degradation, the decline of manufactures, contempt for honest labor, and a pampered oligarchy," Republicans would plant "small farms, thrifty tillage, free schools, social independence, flourishing manufactures and the arts, respect for honest labor, and equality of political rights."[9]

Between these two extremes lay options ranging from partial to full enfranchisement of the freedmen, temporary to long-term disfranchisement of varying categories of ex-Confederates, and an assortment of proposals for economic assistance to freed slaves, including government loans to enable them to buy land. For two years after Appomattox, moderate Republicans struggled to forge a policy somewhere in the middle of this spectrum while President Johnson moved toward the Democratic position and broke with the party that had put him in office.*

PRESIDENTIAL RECONSTRUCTION, 1865

Although Johnson initially seemed to agree with radicals on the need to punish Rebels, his fundamental convictions clashed with Republican ideology in two crucial respects. A Jacksonian Democrat to the core, Tennessean Andrew Johnson

*The Republicans had nominated Johnson, a War Democrat from an occupied Confederate state, for vice president in 1864 in an attempt to broaden their appeal beyond the Republican electorate and to fit their new appellation as the "Union party." (See p. 407)

shared Tennessean Andrew Jackson's suspicion of banks, corporations, bondholders, and New England. He opposed the Whig/Republican policy of using government to promote economic development. His enemies list included both the
plantation aristocracy and the "bloated, corrupt aristocracy" of the commercial-
industrial economy emerging in the Northeast.

The President also proved to be hostile toward the Republican vision of the
freedmen's place in society. Although in 1864 Johnson had told Tennessee blacks
that he would be their "Moses" to lead them out of bondage, he never subscribed
to the liberal tenets of antislavery ideology. He had owned slaves himself, and he
was committed to white supremacy. When a fellow Tennessean had commented
during the war that the government was turning the conflict into a crusade to free
the slaves, Johnson exclaimed: "Damn the negroes! I am fighting these traitorous
aristocrats, their masters." In 1866 a delegation of blacks headed by Frederick
Douglass visited the White House to urge the merits of black suffrage as a
condition of reconstruction. The President parried their arguments and afterwards
remarked to his secretary: "Those d——d sons of b——s thought they had me
in a trap! I know that d——d Douglass; he's just like any nigger, and he would
sooner cut a white man's throat than not."[10]

These differences between Johnson and the Republicans only gradually became
clear to the latter. In the meantime, attention focused on the reconstruction
process. The President decided not to call Congress into special session during the
long interval between March and December 1865. Johnson, like Lincoln, conceived of reconstruction (which he preferred to call restoration) as primarily an
executive function. He also believed in Lincoln's theory of indestructible states.
The rebellion had been one of individuals, not states, said Johnson, and although
the individuals might be punished, the states retained all their constitutional rights.

On May 29, 1865, the President issued two significant proclamations. The first
offered amnesty and restitution of property, except slaves, to all who would take
an oath of allegiance, with the exception of several categories. These categories
included Confederate civil and diplomatic officials; army officers above the rank
of colonel and naval officers above the rank of lieutenant; all who had resigned
as congressmen, federal judges, or military officers to join the rebellion; state
governors under the Confederacy; those who had mistreated prisoners of war or
were under arrest for other military crimes; and all persons owning taxable property with an estimated value of more than $20,000. The last-named exemption,
which had been absent from Lincoln's amnesty proclamation of December 8,
1863, was Johnson's way of humbling the purse-proud aristocrats. Johnson's proclamation offered those in the exempted categories the opportunity to apply for
individual pardons.

Johnson's second proclamation named a provisional governor for North Carolina and directed him to call an election of delegates to frame a new state
constitution. Only white men who had taken an oath of allegiance and had
received amnesty could take part in this process. In subsequent weeks, Johnson
issued similar proclamations for six other Southern states. He also recognized the

Frederick Douglass
*(Reproduced from the
Collections of the Library of
Congress)*

Lincoln-sponsored governments of Louisiana, Arkansas, and Tennessee, and designated the wartime loyalist government that had administered the part of Virginia under Union military control as the official government of that state.

The provisional governors appointed by Johnson had opposed secession in 1861, though most of them had subsequently chosen to go with their states. The President hoped that these governors would build a new party in the South composed of Unionists and lukewarm Confederates. Most of the delegates elected to the state constitutional conventions in 1865 had indeed been conditional or outright Unionists in 1861. Up to this point, Johnson's policy seemed to be working as intended. As the conventions met, the President made clear the minimum conditions they must fulfill (despite the inconsistency of such conditions with his theory of unimpaired state rights): the abolition of slavery, the nullification of secession, and the repudiation of all state debts incurred during the period of the Confederacy (on the grounds that, secession being illegal, all obligations incurred in its behalf were null and void).

Republican Responses to Presidential Reconstruction

Most Republicans initially supported Johnson's actions. But many abolitionists and radicals immediately criticized the President's policy. They feared that the restriction of suffrage to whites would open the door to oppression of the freedmen and restoration of the old power structure. Charles Sumner considered the President's proclamations to be "madness." "Nothing since Chancellorsville," he wrote privately, "has to my mind been so disastrous to the National Cause." Radicals noted that the abolition of slavery automatically gave the South a dozen more congressmen by nullifying the three-fifths compromise and counting the entire black population in the basis for representation. Thus Johnson's policy would reward rebellion by increasing the South's power in national politics—unless blacks were enfranchised to offset the Rebel vote. "Is there no way to arrest the insane course of the President?" lamented Thaddeus Stevens in June 1865.[11]

Most Republicans did not yet share Stevens's and Sumner's alarm. Although a majority of them probably believed that black men should participate to some degree in the reconstruction process, they were not yet ready to condemn the President's policy. They looked upon that policy as only a beginning—an "experiment" that could be expanded or modified to include black suffrage at a later stage. Just as Johnson was requiring Southern states to abolish slavery and to repudiate the Confederate debt, so he would recognize the wisdom of requiring them to extend at least a limited franchise to blacks. "Loyal negroes must not be put down, while disloyal white men are put up," wrote a moderate Republican. "But I am quite willing to see what will come of Mr. Johnson's experiment." If Southern states did not voluntarily enfranchise freedmen, said another moderate, the President "will then be at liberty to pursue a sterner policy."[12]

In an attempt to arouse Northern opinion and to put pressure on Johnson, radicals organized a "Universal and Equal Suffrage Association" and launched a barrage of speeches, pamphlets, and editorials. Johnson did respond to the pressure, but not in a manner calculated to ease anxieties. On August 15 he telegraphed Provisional Governor William L. Sharkey of Mississippi, who presided over the first state convention to meet under Johnson's plan. The President suggested that if the new constitution were to enfranchise literate blacks and those who owned property worth $250, "you would completely disarm the adversary and set an example the other states would follow. This you can do with perfect safety, and . . . as a consequence, the radicals, who are wild upon negro franchise, will be completely foiled."[13]

This was a revealing telegram. It showed that Johnson already viewed the radicals as "adversaries" to be "foiled" by a token measure. Scarcely one in nine adult black males in the South could have qualified to vote under these criteria. Such a small number of black voters would pose no immediate threat to white supremacy. And Johnson was probably correct in his belief that their enfranchisement would satisfy moderate Republicans of the South's good intentions. It would also put the South on a higher plane than the North, where only six states allowed

blacks to vote on any terms. Johnson's communication to Sharkey invites comparison with Lincoln's letter to the reconstruction governor of Louisiana a year earlier
(see pp. 404–405). Both presidents tried the same tactic of noncompulsory persuasion; but Lincoln had made no reference to adversaries, and his suggested inclu-
sion of black soldiers would have nearly doubled the potential black electorate.
Johnson excluded soldiers because he knew that they were the most humiliating
symbol of Southern defeat and the most provocative threat to white supremacy.

In any case, Southern whites paid no more attention to Johnson's suggestion
than they had to Lincoln's. None of the conventions made any provision for black
suffrage in their new constitutions. The provisional governor of South Carolina
explained why: "This is a white man's government, and intended for white men
only. . . . The Supreme Court of the United States has decided [in the Dred Scott
case] that the negro is not an American citizen."[14] Johnson made no more
gestures in the direction of black enfranchisement. He stated that voting qualifications were a state matter and that it was beyond his constitutional right to
interfere. But his radical critics pointed out that under the Constitution the
president had no right to appoint provisional governors either, or to require states
to abolish slavery and repudiate debts. He had taken these extraconstitutional
steps because the Constitution prescribed no process for the unforeseen task of
restoring states after a civil war. Thus, to require black suffrage as a condition of
reconstruction would be no more unconstitutional than these other actions. But
Johnson refused to budge, and Republicans grew discouraged about the prospects
for success on the suffrage issue.

The Black Suffrage Issue in the North

Their discouragement was deepened by the outcome of three Northern state
referendums in the fall of 1865. The legislatures of Connecticut, Wisconsin, and
Minnesota placed on the ballot constitutional amendments to enfranchise the few
black men in those states. Everyone recognized that, in some measure, the popular
vote on these amendments would serve as a barometer of Northern opinion on
black suffrage. Democrats mounted an antisuffrage campaign that exploited race
prejudice in the usual manner. Republican leaders worked for passage of the
amendments but fell short of success in all three states. The results were subject
to conflicting interpretations. In each state a switch of about 5 percent of the votes
would have reversed the outcome.* A large majority of Republican voters had cast

---

*The referendum votes on black suffrage were:

Conn. (Oct. 2, 1865)   Wis. (Nov. 7, 1865)
  For: 27,217 (45%)   For: 46,588 (46%)
  Against: 33,489 (55%)   Against: 55,591 (54%)
Minn. (Nov. 7, 1865)
  For: 12,170 (45%)
  Against: 14,840 (55%)

Assuming that in each state virtually or nearly all the Democrats voted against black suffrage, the percentage
of Republicans in each state who voted for it can be calculated, using the 1864 presidential election as a base

their ballots for the amendments. This could be interpreted as a Republican mandate for black suffrage. On the other hand, the defeat of the amendments could be seen as a mandate against black suffrage by a majority of Northern voters. This was how most contemporaries interpreted it. Moderate Republican congressmen were therefore unwilling to force a showdown with the President on the issue. Even radicals conceded that the cause of black suffrage as a condition of reconstruction had suffered a setback. "We feel humiliated and ashamed" by the Connecticut vote, confessed one. "It jeopardizes—at least delays—the permanent settlement of the questions in dispute in the rebellious States."[15]

The Revival of Southern Defiance

At the same time, however, alarming signs in the South began to convince even moderate Republicans that Johnson's program was not working well. Reports filtered northward of a growing number of assaults on freedmen and Unionists. The old-time "secesh" manners of defiance and haughtiness seemed to have replaced the earlier docility of ex-Confederates. In September 1865, a leading Alabama politician scoffed at Republican insistence on guarantees of Southern loyalty and good behavior. "It is you, proud and exultant Radical, who should give the guarantees, guarantees that you will not again . . . deny to any portion of the people their rights." Two months later Wade Hampton, one of the antebellum South's richest planters and a Confederate war hero, said that "it is our duty to support the President of the United States *so long as he manifests a disposition to restore all our rights as a sovereign State*" (italics added).[16] This sounded like 1860 all over again. Little wonder that some Republicans began to question whether the South had learned anything from the war.

Political events in the South added to Republican concern. Ex-Confederates in Louisiana reorganized the Democratic party and wooed the governor (elected as lieutenant governor under Lincoln's policy in 1864) over to their side. He began to replace appointive Unionist officeholders with former Confederates. Louisiana Unionists, now allied with the Republican party, complained in alarm to Washington. "Hatred of the Government and to the Union men," reported one, "is now more intense than it was in 1860 & 1861, and were we without the Protection of the Federal troops in this State the union men would be persecuted and driven out of the country."[17]

Similar reports came from other Southern states in the fall of 1865. Johnson's own provisional governor of North Carolina wrote the President: "I regret to say that there is much of a rebellion feeling still in this state. In this respect I admit I have been deceived. In May and June last these rebellious spirits would not have dared to show their heads even for the office of constable; but leniency has emboldened them."[18] At the state constitutional conventions held during the fall,

---

to determine the proportion of each state's voters who were Republican. The Republicans voting for black suffrage amendments were, therefore, approximately as follows: Connecticut 85 percent, Wisconsin 80 percent, and Minnesota 75 percent.

delegates spent a great deal of time quibbling over the details of Johnson's requirements. Several states repealed rather than repudiated their secession ordinances, thereby yielding no principle; Mississippi and South Carolina refused to repudiate their Confederate debt; Mississippi and Texas failed to ratify the Thirteenth Amendment; Georgia reserved the right to seek compensation for emancipated slaves.

These actions did not sit well with the North—or with Johnson. But the President seemed unable to do more than plead ineffectively with Southerners to be more circumspect. And worse was yet to come. In the first elections held under the new constitutions, the voters elected to the United States Congress no fewer than nine Confederate congressmen, seven Confederate state officials, four generals, four colonels, and Confederate Vice President Alexander Stephens. An even larger number of prominent ex-Rebels won election to state offices. To apprehensive and angry Republicans, it appeared that the Rebels, unable to capture Washington in war, were about to do so in peace.

Johnson and the South

Although these developments distressed Johnson, he bore much of the responsibility for them. In August, Provisional Governor Sharkey had taken steps to reorganize the Mississippi militia, using Confederate veterans as a nucleus. The professed reason for this action was to curb an outbreak of robberies and assaults. But the true reason seems to have been a desire to reassert states' rights and to bring pressure on the federal government to reduce the number of occupation troops, most of whom were black. The commander of the occupation forces, General Henry W. Slocum, issued an order prohibiting the militia organization. Sharkey thereupon bombarded Washington with imperious telegrams insisting on the need for a state police force. The President, who had initially disapproved of Sharkey's action, meekly backed down. He endorsed the militia and sent a telegram reproving Slocum and General Carl Schurz, who was in Mississippi on an inspection tour and had supported Slocum. "The [Southern] people must be trusted with their Government," the President lectured the generals, "and if trusted my opinion is they will act in good faith and restore their former constitutional relations with . . . the Union." This spectacle of a president yielding to a provisional governor—and in the process humiliating two major generals who had fought gallantly at Gettysburg and elsewhere—delighted Southerners and outraged Republicans. A Southern friend told the President: "Your endorsement of [Sharkey's] militia call, electrified the whole South. From that day to this, I have met with no man who has not a kind word to say of President Johnson." But a Republican paper warned that "if rebels in Mississippi are to be thus armed, then also will they be in every state. . . . What can be hatched from such an egg but another rebellion?"[19]

Johnson's action in this affair was only one of several presidential signals that encouraged Democrats to think of him as one of their own. Southern Democrats who had once denounced the President as a renegade and demagogue now praised him fulsomely as the man "who had the courage to place himself as a breakwater between the Radicals of the North and the prostrate people of the bleeding South." Northern Democrats similarly flattered Johnson. Their only chance for political power lay in a revival of the antebellum alliance with Southern Democrats. Johnson's policy promised to facilitate such an alliance. Democratic newspapers began to hint that Johnson could receive the party's presidential nomination in 1868. Every Northern Democratic state convention that met in 1865 passed resolutions of "cordial and hearty approval" of the President's course. A veteran Jacksonian advised Johnson: "The Democracy of the North look to the South to reinstate them in power. If you so act, towards the South, as to command their confidence and support you will carry the Democratic party and unite the North West and South in your support."[20]

This was a heady prospect. Johnson was after all a Democrat, even though he had been elected to his office by Republicans. The President indeed hoped to construct a new political coalition, composed of Northern Democrats and conservative Republicans plus Southern Unionists. Excluded from this coalition would be radical Republicans on one extreme and "traitors" on the other. But something was going wrong with the Southern part of the plan. The purse-proud aristocrats and traitors had gotten into the coalition and were elbowing aside the genuine Unionists, with Johnson's apparent blessing. On September 11, 1865, a delegation from nine Southern states called on the President to express their "sincere respect" for his "desire and intention to sustain Southern rights in the Union." In his reply, Johnson waxed eloquent on his "love, respect, and confidence" toward the Southern people and his intent to be "forbearing and forgiving" toward their past sins.[21]

What explains this transformation from the Johnson of April, who spoke menacingly about the crime of treason, to the Johnson of September, who spoke of forgiveness? For one thing, the President was a Southerner. He had no more liking for the radical Yankee ethos than most Southerners had. Moreover, his experiences during the summer and fall of 1865 convinced him that the Southern whites, including ex-Confederates, were his real friends. They praised his policy and flattered his ego, while radical Republicans criticized him openly and moderates exchanged worried words in private.

Of special significance in this respect was the matter of presidential pardons for those excluded from the amnesty proclamation. The White House was thronged day after day with supplicants for pardon or their tearful female relatives or "pardon brokers." The President felt a deep sense of gratification when members of the haughty Southern ruling class whom he had once vowed to show "who is running this country" humbly confessed the error of their ways and promised to be good. To one group of Southerners, Johnson said that their expression of loyalty "excites in my mind feelings and emotions that language is totally inadequate to express." "I remember the taunts, the jeers, the scowls with which I was treated," the President continued. He was happy to "have lived to see the realization of my predictions and the fatal error of those whom I vainly essayed to save from the results" of secession.[22]

In this mood, Johnson bestowed pardons liberally—an average of a hundred a day in September 1865. Altogether he granted 13,500 special pardons out of about 15,000 applications. With pardons in their pockets, ex-Confederates seemingly faced no further obstacles to a bid for a return to power in their states. But this was too much for even conservative Republicans to swallow. Since the Republicans controlled Congress, they could exercise their right to exclude Southern representatives and senators, pending further consideration of the whole reconstruction question. *Their determination to do so was intensified by evidence of a Southern intention to restrict the freedmen to a twilight zone of quasi-freedom.

LAND AND LABOR IN THE POSTWAR SOUTH

The news of freedom came to slaves in many different ways. Because the Thirteenth Amendment was not finally ratified until December 1865, some uncertainty persisted until then about the precise legal status of slavery. But in the spring of 1865, Union army officers and Freedmen's Bureau agents had announced the abolition of slavery in the occupied South and warned that planters who thenceforth refused to pay wages to their black workers would be subject to confiscation of property. Owners called their slaves together and announced, with varying degrees of civility or surliness, that they were free. Where owners failed to do so, Yankee officers or freedmen from a neighboring plantation brought the news. In one way or another, emancipation had penetrated to the most remote corners of the South by the fall of 1865.

Many freedmen stayed to work as wage earners on the same plantation where they had formerly worked as slaves. But for others, leaving the old place was an essential part of freedom. In slavery times, the only way to become free was to escape from the plantation, and the impulse persisted after the war. "You ain't, none o' you," a black preacher told his flock, "gwinter feel rale free till you shakes de dus' ob de Ole Plantashun offen yore feet an' goes ter a new place whey you kin live out o' sight o' de gret house."[23]

Freed people also left the plantations to search for relatives separated from them in slavery, to accept offers of higher wages elsewhere, or to seek protection and rations at army posts or Freedmen's Bureau offices. The latter were usually located in cities and larger towns, and much of the black migration in the early postwar months was from country to city. Southern whites viewed this urban influx as a serious health, welfare, and crime problem. The movement away from plantations also created a labor shortage at a time when the South desperately

*Article I, Section 5 of the Constitution states that each house of Congress "shall be the Judge of the Elections, Returns, and Qualifications of its own Members." The Republican majority of Congress, therefore, could use this power to exclude Southerners until they met qualifications established by Congress. The words "readmission," "restoration," and "reconstruction" were used interchangeably by contemporaries to designate the process by which the former Confederate states would resume their place in the Union on an equal basis with other states. Once "restored," these states would be represented in Congress, would have their electoral votes counted in presidential elections, and would exercise the normal functions of state governments free of extraordinary intervention by the U. S. army or by federal courts.

needed to plant crops and repair war devastation. The occupation forces shared the concern of Southern whites for recovery and labor stability. The army urged and sometimes forced unemployed blacks to sign contracts for farm labor. Sensitive to charges in both the Northern and Southern press that the Freedmen's Bureau was fostering a welfare ethic among ex-slaves, some Bureau officers cut off rations to able-bodied blacks to compel them to work. City officials invoked vagrancy laws for the same purpose. By the fall of 1865, many footloose freedmen had returned to their old plantations or to others in the same county. But mobility remained a hallmark of freedom; when it came time to sign contracts for the new year, more than a few blacks left their old employers in search of better opportunities elsewhere.

The Issue of Land for the Landless

They would, of course, have preferred to work for themselves rather than for white folks. Many freedmen believed that only the ownership of land could make their freedom real. "What's de use of being free if you don't own land enough to be buried in?" asked one black man. "Might juss as well stay slave all yo' days." A black army veteran said: "Every colored man will be a slave, & feel himself a slave until he can raise him own *bale of cotton* & put him own mark upon it & say dis is mine!"[24] Freed slaves who had managed to save a little money tried to buy land in 1865. Demobilized black soldiers purchased land with their bounty money, sometimes pooling their resources to buy an entire plantation on which several black families settled. But for most ex-slaves the purchase of land was impossible. Few of them had money, and even if they had, whites often refused to sell or even to rent them land for fear of losing a source of cheap labor or of encouraging notions of independence.

If they could not buy land, many freedmen in 1865 expected the government to grant or lease them land. This hope—for "forty acres and a mule"—was no delusion of ignorant minds. By June 1865 the Freedmen's Bureau had placed nearly ten thousand families on almost half a million acres of plantation lands abandoned by planters who had fled Union armies along the coastal rivers in Georgia and South Carolina. General William T. Sherman had assigned this land to the freedmen in his famous Order No. 15. Sherman also turned over to the freedmen horses and mules captured from the enemy. Elsewhere in the South, the Freedmen's Bureau controlled nearly a million acres of abandoned or confiscated land, part of which it leased to the freedmen. The Bureau also provided some freedmen with tools and draft animals, to be paid for with the proceeds from their crops.

If these actual examples of forty acres and a mule were not enough to encourage the freedmen's hopes, many Bureau agents and Union soldiers—especially black troops—circulated rumors that the government intended to give blacks their former masters' land. Reports came from the North of powerful Republicans who favored the confiscation and redistribution of plantations. In a speech at Lancaster, Pennsylvania, on September 6, Thaddeus Stevens urged the confiscation of

Thaddeus Stevens
*(Reproduced from the
Collections of the Library of
Congress)*

land owned by wealthy ex-Confederates. Stevens proposed to allocate forty acres
of this land to each adult freedman and to sell the remainder to finance war
pensions and repay the war debt. "Strip a proud nobility of their bloated estates,"
said Stevens in a later congressional speech; "send them forth to labor, and teach
their children to enter the workshops or handle the plow, and you will thus humble
the proud traitors."[25]

The freedmen, therefore, seemed to have good reason to hope for government
assistance in obtaining land. But President Johnson's amnesty proclamation and
the failure of Congress to pass effective legislation dashed most of their hopes.
Presidential amnesty and pardon included the restoration of property. By midsummer 1865, pardoned planters were returning home to claim estates held by the
Freedmen's Bureau or under cultivation by freedmen. General Oliver O. Howard,
commissioner of the Freedmen's Bureau, refused to honor the planters' claims
without a direct order from the President to do so. Howard considered the
amnesty proclamation inapplicable to abandoned or confiscated property "which
by law has been set apart [for use] by refugees and freedmen."[26] Annoyed at this
unauthorized interpretation of his policy, the President on August 16 ordered
Howard to restore the property of all pardoned Confederates. But Howard and
several of the Bureau's assistant commissioners continued to stall and delay. They
hoped to retain as much land as possible until Congress met in December, when
new legislation might confirm the freedmen's possession of at least some of the
land under Bureau control.

Meanwhile, the pardoned owners of plantations affected by Sherman's Order No. 15 also clamored for restoration of their property. The Bureau's assistant commissioner for South Carolina was General Rufus Saxton, a native of Massachusetts and an abolitionist sympathizer. On the grounds that Sherman's order was "as binding as a statute," Saxton refused to give up plantations occupied by freedmen. But Andrew Johnson rejected this argument and directed the return of the properties to their former owners. With the support of Howard and the tacit encouragement of Secretary of War Edwin M. Stanton, Saxton dragged his feet to give Congress time to confirm the freedmen's title to these plantations. Senator Charles Sumner introduced a bill for this purpose in December 1865, but it failed to get out of committee. In the meantime Johnson cracked down on the Bureau, removed Saxton from office, and forced the return of the land. Some freedmen refused to give up their farms until the army compelled them to do so at bayonet point. Blacks protested eloquently against this betrayal of a promise, but in the absence of legislation by Congress there was little they or the Bureau could do about it.

In February 1866, Congress did pass a bill that extended the life of the Freedmen's Bureau and included a provision confirming the freedmen's possession for three years of lands occupied under the Sherman order. But Johnson vetoed the bill and Congress failed to pass it over the veto. Republicans finally managed to enact a revised Freedmen's Bureau bill over the President's veto in July 1866, but this law did not include the section confirming the Sherman grants. Instead, it offered the freedmen who had been dispossessed of these properties the opportunity to buy government-held land (at a price below market value) on the South Carolina and Georgia offshore islands. In this way more than two thousand dispossessed freed families obtained title to land; but this achievement marked a sad denouement to the high hopes of 1865. By the end of 1866, nearly all the arable land once controlled by the Freedmen's Bureau had been returned to its ex-Confederate owners.

Congress made one other effort to place freedmen on land of their own: the Southern Homestead Act of June 21, 1866. This law set aside forty-four million acres of public land in five Southern states (Alabama, Arkansas, Florida, Louisiana, and Mississippi) for individual grants of eighty acres to settlers who resided on and cultivated the land for five years. To give the freedmen and Unionist whites first chance at this land, the law stipulated that no one who had supported the Confederacy could file a claim before January 1, 1867. Generous in conception, the Southern Homestead Act was largely a failure in practice. Most of the remaining public land in these states was of poor quality. And few freedmen possessed the capital to settle on land distant from their homes, to purchase seed, tools, livestock, and building materials, and to support themselves while waiting for the first crop to mature. General Howard ordered Freedmen's Bureau agents to provide settlers with transportation to their claims, but many agents were indifferent or sluggish about complying. Fewer than seven thousand freedmen claimed homesteads, and only a thousand of these fulfilled the requirements for final ownership.

Land reform did not become a part of Reconstruction. Thaddeus Stevens's confiscation bill got nowhere in Congress. Despite the warnings of abolitionists that "to give [the slaves] only freedom, without the land, is to give them only the mockery of freedom which the English or the Irish peasant has," confiscation was too radical for most Republicans. The constitutional prohibition against bills of attainder that forfeited property beyond the lives of offenders was a major stumbling block. Moderates who wished to win the heartfelt loyalty of Southern whites to a restored Union could hardly expect to do so by taking away their land. Many Republicans expressed doubts about the ethics as well as the legality and expediency of confiscation. "People who want farms work for them," declared the *New York Tribune*. "The only class we know that takes other people's property because they want it is largely represented in Sing Sing."[27]

The free-labor ideology envisaged upward mobility through hard work, thrift, and the other Protestant ethic virtues. Many Northern proponents of this ideology believed that the freedmen would gain more by working and sweating to buy land than by having the government grant them special favors. But radicals who wanted confiscation insisted that the freedmen had already "earned" the land by their lifetime of toil in slavery. Whatever the merits of this argument, it did not prevail in the 1860s. Most freedmen did not achieve the economic independence they had hoped for. Instead, they had to work for white landowners, who in many cases were their former masters.

The "Labor Question" and the Freedmen's Bureau

Some of these former masters still perceived their workers as slaves in all but name. "They esteem the Negro the property of the white man by natural right," wrote a Freedmen's Bureau agent in September 1865, "and however much they may confess that the President's Proclamation broke up the relation of the individual slaves to their owners, they still have the ingrained feeling that the black people at large belong to the whites at large." Slavery had been a form of compulsion, and "three fourths of the [white] people assume that the negro will not labor except on compulsion," wrote a Northern reporter. "The whites seem wholly unable to comprehend that freedom for the negro means the same thing as freedom for them."[28]

This should not have been surprising. Proslavery convictions held for a lifetime could hardly be overcome in a few months. In the process of reorganizing their labor force, some planters tried to replicate slavery as closely as possible—even to the extent of hiring overseers, who punished recalcitrant workers with whippings. When freedmen refused to work under these conditions or walked away from the plantation to seek better terms elsewhere, planters complained of a labor shortage and said in an "I told you so" manner that such behavior proved blacks would work only under compulsion.

Into this uncertain situation stepped the Freedmen's Bureau. As Commissioner of the Freedmen's Bureau, General Oliver O. Howard had his headquarters in Washington. Army generals were assigned as assistant commissioners for each former slave state, with headquarters in the state's capital or in its largest city. Most of the Bureau's 550 local agents were junior army officers from middle-class Northern backgrounds. Some of them had taken a job with the Bureau because they were interested in the freedmen. Others were only marking time until they could make long-term plans for their future civilian careers. Their racial attitudes ranged from radical to conservative, though most felt some degree of liberal sympathy for the freedmen. The Bureau also appointed some civilian agents, including a few black men. Although the number of agents was too few to reach every corner of the South, these agents—backed by the army's occupation troops —nevertheless had considerable potential power to shape postwar Southern labor relations.

Once it became clear that no large-scale land redistribution would take place, the Bureau proceeded to patch together a new relationship between planters and the freedmen. Agents encouraged or required planters and laborers to sign written contracts that specified the amount and kind of work to be done, the wages to be paid, and other conditions of employment. Wages ranged from eight to fifteen dollars a month plus food, housing, and sometimes clothing and medical care. Payment took the form of cash or a share of the crop. Planters came to prefer the latter, both because money was scarce and because share wages, which could not be paid until after the harvest, gave laborers an interest in the crop and deterred them from breaking their contracts.

The Bureau tried to protect freedmen from exploitation. Its agents adjudicated thousands of disputes concerning the interpretation or violation of contracts, crimes by or against freedmen, and the like. After Southern states passed laws allowing the freedmen to testify in civil courts, the Bureau allowed these courts to handle such disputes—under the watchful eyes of agents. Some of the agents did not like what they saw. "The admission of Negro testimony will never secure the Freedmen justice before the courts of this state when that testimony is considered valueless by the judges and juries who hear it," wrote one agent. "It is of no consequence what the law may be, if the majority be not inclined to have it executed." None of the reconstruction governments in 1865–1866 allowed blacks to serve on juries. After two months of watching the Mississippi courts function, the assistant commissioner of the Bureau in the state reported that their rulings "with reference to the freedmen are a disgrace."[29]

On the strength of these and similar reports, General Howard urged Congress to create "Freedmen's United States Courts" to supersede the state courts. The revised Freedmen's Bureau bill, passed over Johnson's veto in July 1866, empowered the Bureau to establish special courts to function as military tribunals until Congress declared the rebellious states restored to the Union.* These "courts," which in most cases consisted only of a Bureau agent, remained in existence until

---

*The Supreme Court's decision in *ex parte Milligan* (April 1866) ruled that military courts could not try civilians in areas remote from a war theater. President Johnson believed that this decision rendered the Bureau courts invalid. But congressional Republicans insisted that the war was not over until Congress said so, and in the meantime the South was a war zone where military tribunals could dispense justice.

1868. But state courts continued to handle many cases concerning freedmen because some Bureau commissioners and military commanders, guided by Johnson's continuing hostility to the Bureau, were reluctant to override civil courts.

Not surprisingly, Southern whites denounced the Bureau as "a curse," a "ridiculous folly," a "vicious institution." Wade Hampton wrote in 1866: "The war which was so prolific of monstrosities, new theories of republican government, new versions of the Constitution . . . gave birth to nothing which equals in deformity and depravity this 'Monstrum horrendum informe ingens.' " Planters insisted that they could "make the nigger work" if the interfering agents would only leave them alone. "The Bureau doesn't seem to understand the possibility of a white man's being right in a contest or difference with a negro," complained one Southerner. Another added: "The fairest minded of all these [Bureau] officials seemed not to be able [to] comprehend the difference between the 'nigger' freedman and the white northern laborer."[30]

These complaints reflected a dislike of the Bureau more for what it symbolized —conquest and emancipation—than for what it did. In reality, the Bureau often functioned as an ally of planters by getting idle freedmen back to work and by enforcing contracts whose terms often favored employers. While publicly abusing the Bureau, a good many Southerners privately admitted that without it the postwar labor situation would have been even more chaotic. In late 1865, many freedmen refused to sign contracts for the next year because they expected soon to get their forty acres and a mule. This led to a short-lived but intense "Christmas insurrection" scare among whites. To the Freedmen's Bureau fell the unhappy task of disabusing the freedmen about land redistribution and of compelling them to sign contracts. In 1867, a Bureau official summed up his experience with the contract system: "It has succeeded in making the Freedman work and in rendering labor secure & stable—but it has failed to secure to the Freedman his just dues or compensation."[31]

The Bureau's enforcement policies varied greatly according to the priorities and convictions of individual commissioners and agents. In 1865 the assistant commissioners in South Carolina, Louisiana, Mississippi, and Tennessee demonstrated more sympathy for the freedmen than did those in Alabama and Georgia. In 1866, President Johnson removed some of the most liberal commissioners and appointed conservatives in their places. Some Bureau agents mixed socially with local whites and soon adopted the latter's viewpoints. Despite all this, however, agents appear to have tilted toward the freedmen in most disputes that came before them. A historian who studied a sample of 286 cases handled by fifteen Bureau courts in eight states found that 194 (68 percent) of them were decided in favor of the freedmen.[32]

The Black Codes

The Bureau also overruled or suspended the more oppressive features of the "black codes" adopted by Southern states in 1865–1866. One of the first tasks facing legislatures elected under Johnson's reconstruction program was the passage of laws to regulate the new status of blacks. Much of this legislation was unexceptionable: it authorized freedmen to own property, make contracts, sue and plead in the courts, and contract legal marriages. Under pressure from the Johnson administration and the Freedmen's Bureau, Southern states also permitted black testimony in court cases where blacks were parties. But the codes excluded blacks from juries and prohibited racial intermarriage. Some of them required segregation in public accommodations. Several also prescribed more severe punishment of blacks than whites for certain crimes. These provisions raised an outcry from abolitionists. But the North as a whole was in no position to condemn them, for numerous Northern states excluded blacks from juries, banned racial intermarriage, permitted discriminatory law enforcement, and allowed or required segregated accommodations and schools; and several Northern states until recently had denied blacks the right to testify against whites in the courts.

The provisions of the black codes relating to vagrancy, apprenticeship, labor, and land, however, provoked Republican accusations of an intent to create a new slavery. The Mississippi and South Carolina codes, passed first, were the harshest in these respects. They defined vagrancy in such a broad fashion as to allow magistrates to arrest almost any black man whom they defined as unemployed, fine him for vagrancy, and hire him out to a planter to pay off the fine. Both states required blacks to obtain special licenses for any occupation other than agriculture. Mississippi prohibited freedmen from renting or leasing land outside cities. South Carolina defined white employers as "masters" and black employees as "servants." Several states stipulated that freedmen under eighteen without adequate parental support (the courts to define "adequate") could be bound out as apprentices, with their former owner given preference as the master. Some states forbade employers to "entice" laborers away from their jobs by offering higher wages.

The army and the Freedmen's Bureau suspended the enforcement of those parts of the black codes that discriminated between the races. The most important impact of the codes, therefore, was not in their operation but rather in the impression they made on the North. Whatever the shortcomings of their own racial attitudes, many Northerners were incensed by the South's apparent attempt to overturn one of the main results of the war. "We tell the white men of Mississippi," thundered the *Chicago Tribune*, "that the men of the North will convert the State of Mississippi into a frog pond before they will allow such laws to disgrace one foot of the soil in which the bones of our soldiers sleep and over which the flag of freedom waves."[33] The black codes strengthened the resolve of Republican congressmen to keep the South on probation until they could work out means to protect the freedmen and to guarantee the fruits of victory. In this mood, the members of the Thirty-ninth Congress gathered in Washington in December 1865.

Twenty-seven

The Origins
of "Radical" Reconstruction

THE SCHISM BETWEEN PRESIDENT AND CONGRESS

Although Republicans enjoyed a three-to-one majority in the Thirty-ninth Congress, the old divisions between radicals, moderates, and conservatives hindered unity on reconstruction. Conservatives were generally satisfied with Andrew Johnson's policy, though some of them wished to pass additional legislation to protect the freedmen from violence and discrimination. Moderates agreed with radicals that the President's policy did not go far enough to safeguard the fruits of Northern victory. But they believed that Northern voters would not support the radical policy of black suffrage. They also wanted to prevent a break with Johnson, for they feared that such a break could benefit only the Democrats.

All Republicans, however, were united in a determination not to admit Southern representatives to Congress in December 1865. By prearrangement, the clerk of the House omitted the names of Southern representatives from the roll at the opening session, and both houses immediately voted to create a joint committee of fifteen (nine representatives, six senators) to formulate a reconstruction policy. Republicans did not construe this action as a defiance of Johnson, for in his message to Congress the President, while asserting that the Southern states had fulfilled his requirements for restoration, conceded the right of Congress to judge the qualifications of its own members. Johnson also affirmed that "good faith requires the security of the freedmen in their liberty and their property, their right to labor, and their right to claim the just return of their labor."[1]

This seemed to provide a basis for accommodation between the President and the moderate majority of Republicans. The composition of the congressional joint committee reflected a desire for accommodation. Although Thaddeus Stevens was a member, moderates dominated the committee. Senator William Pitt Fessenden of Maine became chairman, to the chagrin of Charles Sumner, who had hoped to be chairman but was not even placed on the committee. The joint committee held extensive hearings, at which army officers, Freedmen's Bureau agents, Southern Unionists, and freedmen testified to a rising wave of neo-Confederate hostility and violence. This testimony convinced Republicans of the need for a new constitutional amendment plus additional legislation to guarantee loyalty and to protect blacks. Although Northern Democrats predicted that the President would oppose any such measures, Fessenden maintained cordial relations with Johnson and expressed confidence that the President would cooperate with Congress.

Meanwhile Lyman Trumbull of Illinois, chairman of the Senate Judiciary Committee and one of the most influential Republican moderates, drafted two bills to protect the freedmen. The first extended the life of the Freedmen's Bureau, expanded its legal powers, and authorized it to build and support schools. Trumbull's second bill defined the freedmen's civil rights and gave federal courts appellate jurisdiction in cases concerning these rights. Trumbull conferred with Johnson several times about this legislation and believed that he had the President's approval. The Freedmen's Bureau bill sped through both houses with virtually unanimous Republican support.

But on February 19, 1866, Johnson dismayed his Republican supporters by vetoing the bill. The Constitution, declared the veto message, never contemplated a "system for the support of indigent persons." The jurisdiction of military courts over civil matters in time of peace was unconstitutional. Finally, said Johnson in a passage that rang ominously in Republican ears, the bill defied the Constitution because at the time of its passage "there was no Senator or Representative in Congress from the eleven States which are to be mainly affected by its provisions." The authority of Congress to judge the qualifications of its members "cannot be construed as including the right to shut out, in time of peace, any State from the representation to which it is entitled by the Constitution."[2] If this interpretation stood up, *any* legislation passed by Congress in the absence of Southern representation would be unconstitutional.

Moderates found the veto a bitter pill to swallow. An unhappy Lyman Trumbull told the Senate: "I thought in advocating [the bill], that I was acting in harmony with the views of the President. I regret exceedingly the antagonism his message presents to the expressed views of Congress. . . . He believes that the freedman will be protected without it; I believe he will be tyrannized over, abused, and virtually reenslaved without some legislation by the nation for his protection."[3] Trumbull introduced a motion to pass the measure over the President's veto. But five conservative Republicans who had previously voted for the bill now voted against it, and the motion fell just short of the required two-thirds majority.

Johnson knew that his veto would move him toward an alliance with Democrats. The latter organized mass meetings to celebrate and endorse the veto. After one of these meetings in Washington on February 22, the celebrants trooped to the White House to serenade Johnson, who favored them with one of the most remarkable presidential speeches ever delivered. Acting as though he were back on the stump in Tennessee, Johnson denounced the radicals as traitors who did not want to restore the Union. Charging that they were plotting to assassinate him, the President compared the radicals to Judas and himself to Christ.

> If my blood is to be shed because I vindicate the Union and the preservation of this government in its original purity and character, let it be shed; let an altar to the Union be erected, and then, if it is necessary, take me and lay me upon it, and the blood that now warms and animates my existence shall be poured out as a fit libation to the Union.[4]

Many Americans were mortified by the President's behavior. "Was he drunk?" they wondered. Radicals who had long since turned against Johnson said to their moderate colleagues, "I told you so!" Senator Fessenden conceded privately that "the President's recent exhibitions of folly and wickedness" had disillusioned him. "He has broken the faith, betrayed his trust, and must sink from detestation to contempt."[5]

But despite Johnston's virtual declaration of war against congressional Republicans, most moderates still wished to avoid an irrevocable break. Their hopes centered on a modified Freedmen's Bureau bill and on Trumbull's civil rights bill. Congress passed the latter with nearly unanimous Republican support on March 13, 1866.* Designed to nullify the Dred Scott decision and the black codes, the bill defined blacks as United States citizens and guaranteed their rights to own or rent property, to make and enforce contracts, and to have access to the courts as parties and witnesses. In general, it affirmed the right of blacks to enjoy "full and equal benefit of all laws and proceedings for the security of person and property as is enjoyed by white citizens." Although the civil rights bill mandated the transfer of legal proceedings from state to federal courts if the former discriminated by race, it would not revolutionize the traditional federal system, said Trumbull, for it would "have no operation in any State where the laws are equal."[6] Nor would the bill enfranchise blacks, authorize them to sit on juries, or require desegregated schools and public accommodations. Republicans therefore expected Johnson to sign this moderate bill despite his states' rights convictions. Every cabinet member except Secretary of the Navy Gideon Welles urged the President to sign.

But on March 27 Johnson sent in a veto message that once again asserted the illegality of legislation passed in the absence of Southern congressmen. The bill was unconstitutional, said the President, because it invaded the exclusive jurisdiction of state courts. It discriminated against whites by "establish[ing] for the security of the colored race safeguards which go infinitely beyond any that the General Government has ever provided for the white race" and by granting newly freed slaves the privilege of citizenship while immigrants had to wait five years for this boon.[7]

*The House passed the bill by a vote of 111 to 38; the Senate passed it by a vote of 33 to 12.

Like the first veto, this one provoked Democratic elation and Republican gloom. A Democratic editor gave thanks that Johnson did not believe "in compounding our race with niggers, gipsies, and baboons." If Congress could declare blacks citizens, said another party newspaper, "how long will it be . . . before it will say the negro shall vote, sit in the jury box, and intermarry with your families? Such are the questions put by the President." For most Republicans, this veto was the last straw. Johnson had deprived "every friend he has of the least ground upon which to stand and defend him," said a moderate congressman. From Ohio, a Republican leader reported that "those who formerly defended [the President] are now readiest in his condemnation."[8]

If Johnson's goal had been to isolate the radicals and to create a broad conservative/moderate coalition in support of his policy, he had badly miscalculated. "Instead of driving off from him a small minority of the Republican party, or even half of it," observed a leading moderate newspaper, he "drives off substantially the whole of it." A Philadelphia editor commented astutely: "The demand of the President is that the Republican party shall, to suit him, stultify itself and its whole past career and principles. By this simple process he has managed to make the term radical synonymous with the entire mass of the dominant party."[9]

THE FOURTEENTH AMENDMENT

Although Johnson had indeed driven moderates closer to the radical position, they were not yet prepared to go the whole way to reducing the Southern states to territories and enacting black suffrage therein. Instead, they concentrated on passing the civil rights bill and a revised Freedmen's Bureau bill over the President's vetoes—which they accomplished April 9 and July 16, 1866—and on drafting a constitutional amendment as the basis for readmission of the Southern senators and representatives to Congress. All through the winter and spring of 1866, the Joint Committee on Reconstruction labored to fashion an amendment acceptable to a broad spectrum of Northern opinion. Such an amendment must: (1) provide a constitutional (as opposed to merely legislative) guarantee of the rights and security of freedmen; (2) insure against a revival of neo-Confederate political power; and (3) enshrine in the Constitution the sanctity of the national debt and the repudiation of the Confederate debt. Radicals on the joint committee also pushed for an amendment to enfranchise blacks or disfranchise ex-Confederates, or both; moderates, believing that these proposals went too far, softened them to temporary disfranchisement of Confederates and an indirect inducement for the states themselves to enfranchise blacks.

On April 30, the joint committee finally submitted to Congress a five-part constitutional amendment. After lengthy debate, the revised Fourteenth Amendment emerged from both houses with the necessary two-thirds majority on June 13. Section 1 defined all native-born or naturalized persons, including blacks, as citizens (thus nullifying the Dred Scott decision) and prohibited the states from abridging the "privileges and immunities" of citizens, from depriving "any person of life, liberty, or property" without due process of law, and from denying to any person "the equal protection of the laws."* Section 2 provided for the proportional reduction of the congressional representation of any state that withheld suffrage from a portion of its adult male citizens. Section 3 disqualified from holding office any person who as a member of the federal or state governments had taken an oath to support the Constitution and afterward had broken that oath by engaging in rebellion. Congress could remove this disability by a two-thirds vote. (This section replaced a harsher committee recommendation to disfranchise until 1870 all persons who had voluntarily participated in the rebellion.) Section 4 guaranteed the national debt and repudiated the Confederate debt; Section 5 gave Congress the power to enforce the amendment by "appropriate legislation."

This complex amendment has been the basis of more litigation than all the rest of the Constitution combined. Nearly all of this litigation has concerned Section 1, and much of it has been occasioned by the ambiguity of the phrases "privileges and immunities," "due process of law," and "equal protection of the laws." This ambiguity was intentional. Its purpose was to leave the greatest possible scope for a future broadening of the meaning of these phrases. One unintended consequence of this section was an interpretation of the clause prohibiting states from depriving persons of property without due process as a limitation of the states' power to regulate corporations (legal "persons"). But since the 1930s, Section 1 has been used mainly to protect and expand the civil rights of black citizens. Whether the "equal protection" clause was meant to outlaw racial segregation in schools and public accommodations has been the subject of a prolific juridical literature. The framers probably did not so intend it, but in recent decades the courts have interpreted this clause to strike down segregation and to uphold affirmative action by government agencies to redress past injustices.

In 1866, Section 1 of the amendment was less controversial than Sections 2 and 3. Southerners and Democrats denounced Section 3 as a vindictive punishment of men who had already suffered enough for their sins. Radicals, on the other hand, believed that it did not go far enough to penalize traitors and to protect the country against their political resurgence. Abolitionists and radicals also denounced Section 2 as a cowardly evasion of Congress's duty to enfranchise the freedmen. This section was indeed an ingenious contrivance worthy of a better cause. By reducing Southern representation in the House and the electoral college in proportion to the unenfranchised black population, it protected the North,

*Although the Civil Rights Act of 1866 had defined blacks as citizens, the incorporation of this provision into a constitutional amendment would insure against any future Dred Scott–type denial of their citizenship. But the wording of the Fourteenth Amendment did leave a loophole. It states that all persons born or naturalized in the United States are "citizens of the United States and of the State wherein they reside. No State shall make or enforce any law which shall abridge the privileges or immunities of citizens *of the United States*" (italics added). The failure to add "or of the State wherein they reside" to this last sentence created an opening for the Supreme Court to distinguish between the rights of state and national citizenship, which it did in the *Slaughterhouse* decision of 1873. Since the Court in this case defined the rights of state and national citizenship narrowly, *Slaughterhouse* reduced the potential jurisdiction of the federal government over state abridgments of the rights of *state* citizenship. In recent decades, however, the courts have used the equal protection of the laws clause of the Fourteenth Amendment to broaden vastly the powers of the federal government for enforcement of civil rights.

against an increase of Southern white political power. It penalized Southern states for withholding suffrage from blacks but allowed Northern states to do so with impunity, since their black population was too small to make a difference in the basis of representation. Abolitionists considered Section 2 a "swindle," a "wanton betrayal of justice and humanity." It "is only fitted to protect the North and the white race, while it leaves the Negro to his fate," declared the American Anti-Slavery Society. "It is the blighted harvest of the bloodiest sowing the fields of the world ever saw."[10]

Radicals nevertheless had to accept the Fourteenth Amendment as the best they could get and to hope that future events would move the country toward black suffrage. The amendment became the Republican platform for the 1866 congressional elections, which were shaping up as a Northern referendum on reconstruction. Implicit in the process by which Congress passed the amendment was a commitment to readmit Southern states when they ratified it, though the lawmakers did not make this commitment explicit. When Tennessee, controlled by ex-Whig enemies of Andrew Johnson, ratified the amendment in July 1866, Congress promptly admitted its senators and representatives despite radical lamentations that this action would establish a precedent for admission of other states without black suffrage.

THE ELECTION OF 1866

After Congress passed the Fourteenth Amendment, some moderates hoped that Andrew Johnson would recognize defeat, cease his opposition, and cooperate to make reconstruction work. But they reckoned without his stubbornness. The President's fighting blood was up. He issued a statement implying that the amendment was illegal because it had been passed by a Congress from which Southern states were absent. Johnson prepared to fight the 1866 congressional elections on this issue. By the logic of the two-party system, this would push him into the Democratic camp. But a few conservative Republicans, led by the old New York Whig leaders William H. Seward, Thurlow Weed, and Henry J. Raymond (editor of the *New York Times*), still remained with the President. They hoped to build a Johnson coalition of conservatives from both old parties into the nucleus of a new party.

The first step in building this coalition had been the formation of the National Union Executive Committee in April 1866. Two months later, this committee issued a call for a National Union convention to meet at Philadelphia in August. Johnson played an active role in preparations for the convention. He expected it to mobilize a majority of Northerners in favor of his policy. The conservative Republican leaders of the movement tried to keep Democrats inconspicuous in the preconvention maneuvering, in order not to alienate Republicans who might be scared off by a copper tinge. But this proved to be difficult. Johnson's partisans had overestimated the potential Republican support for their movement. The President's actions had united nearly the whole of the party against him. Inevitably, therefore, most of the pro-Johnson congressional candidates in the North were

Democrats. The Democratic tail soon began to wag the National Union dog. Hopes for a third force in American politics succumbed to the realities of the two-party system.

On August 14, delegates from both North and South met in the National Union convention at Philadelphia. The platform called for the immediate readmission of Southern states. To symbolize the theme of unity, delegates from Massachusetts and South Carolina marched into the hall in pairs, each delegate from one state locked arm in arm with a delegate from the other. When President Johnson learned of this dramatic gesture, he was overcome with emotion and pronounced the convention more important than any that had met since 1787.

In the end, however, the National Union movement failed. It suffered from three fatal weaknesses. The first, as noted, was the fact that it was dominated by the Democrats. War memories were too fresh for most Northern voters to trust a party they still regarded as tainted by treason. Governor Oliver Morton of Indiana expressed this distrust in an 1866 speech that became a classic example of what was later known as "waving the bloody shirt." "Every unregenerate rebel," said Morton, "calls himself a Democrat."

> Every bounty jumper, every deserter, every sneak who ran away from the draft calls himself a Democrat. . . . Every man who labored for the rebellion in the field, who murdered Union prisoners by cruelty and starvation, who conspired to bring about civil war in the loyal states . . . calls himself a Democrat. Every New York rioter in 1863 who burned up little children in colored asylums, who robbed, ravished and murdered indiscriminately . . . called himself a Democrat. In short, the Democratic party may be described as a common sewer and loathsome receptacle, into which is emptied every element of treason North and South, every element of inhumanity and barbarism which has dishonored the age.[11]

A second weakness of the National Union movement was the hyperbole of its platform declaration that "there is no section of the country where the Constitution and the laws of the United States find more prompt and entire obedience than in [the Southern] states." The rising tide of violence against freedmen and Unionists, said Republicans, disproved this. Although Republicans exaggerated and exploited Southern violence for partisan purposes, the large degree of truth underlying this propaganda made it effective. The worst clashes occurred at Memphis in May 1866 and at New Orleans two months later. The affray in Memphis began with a quarrel between local whites and demobilized black soldiers; by the time it was over, white mobs—which included many policemen—had rampaged through the black sections of town and killed at least forty-six people. With Memphis as an example, commented the *New York Tribune* sarcastically, "who doubts that the Freedmen's Bureau ought to be abolished forthwith, and the blacks remitted to the paternal care of their old masters, who 'understand the nigger, you know, a great deal better than the Yankees can.' "[12]

On July 30 in New Orleans, a mob—again aided by police—assaulted the delegates to a black suffrage convention. This assemblage was a reconvened remnant of the 1864 Louisiana constitutional convention. The delegates had gathered to consider the enfranchisement of blacks as a counterweight to the control of the state government by ex-Confederates. The mayor of New Orleans, who had received a special pardon from Johnson in order to assume office, obtained the President's approval of an order to prevent the convention from assembling. But the commander of the occupation forces refused to sanction this suppression and sent troops to protect the delegates. The troops arrived late, however, and by the time they got there the mob had killed thirty-seven blacks and three of their white allies. Republicans pointed to this as yet another example of what could be expected from Johnson's policy. The President did not help his cause by a speech in St. Louis on September 8 in which he blamed Republicans for provoking the mob and expressed no regret for the victims.

The third weakness of the National Union movement was Andrew Johnson himself. Back in Tennessee, Johnson had been an effective stump speaker. He believed that he could repeat his success on the national scene by taking the case for his policy directly to the people. Against the advice of friends, he broke precedent and went on the campaign trail in a "swing around the circle" from Washington to Chicago and St. Louis and back to Washington (August 28–September 15). For Johnson, this whistle-stop tour was a disaster. He allowed himself to be drawn into shouting contests with hecklers. He bandied insults with hostile crowds. The content of his speeches seldom varied: the South was loyal; the real traitors were radicals who refused to readmit Southern representatives; and he, Andrew Johnson, was willing to give his life if necessary for the salvation of the Union and the Constitution. "He who is opposed to the restoration of this Government and the reunion of the States is as great a traitor as Jeff Davis or Wendell Phillips," he shouted at Cleveland. "Why not hang Thad. Stevens and Wendell Phillips?" Just as he had done in Washington during the preceding winter, the President reminded those who condemned his generous pardoning policy that Jesus had come to earth to forgive men rather than to condemn them. "He died and shed His own blood that the world might live. . . . If more blood is needed, erect an altar, and upon it your humble speaker will pour out the last drop of his blood as a libation for his country's salvation."[13]

Johnson had lost control of himself. And the elections showed that he had also lost control of the country. Even the confident Republicans were astonished by the one-sided nature of their victory. The party retained its three-to-one majority in both houses of Congress and gained ascendancy in every Northern state as well as in West Virginia, Missouri, and Tennessee.

THE RECONSTRUCTION ACTS OF 1867

If ever a party won a mandate, the Republicans did so in the congressional elections in the fall of 1866. But a mandate for what? Insofar as the elections had turned on a specific issue, that issue was the Fourteenth Amendment. Yet the adoption of the amendment required ratification by at least four of the unreconstructed states plus all the states the Republicans had carried. Some far-sighted Southerners read the Northern election returns correctly. They recognized that if the South did not "take the present terms, harder ones will be proposed." But most Southern whites refused to cooperate with their conquerors. Typical of their attitude was the reason offered by the governors of North and South Carolina for refusing to ratify the amendment: "If we are to be degraded we will retain some self-esteem by not making it self-abasement. . . . Worse terms may be imposed by Congress, but they will be *imposed* and not *voluntarily accepted.*"[14]

Andrew Johnson also stood fast. Although "we are beaten for the present," explained one of the President's allies, "our cause will live. If all the states not represented refuse to ratify the amendment . . . the extreme Rads will go . . . for reorganizing the southern states on negro suffrage. . . . That will present the issue squarely . . . and on that we can beat them at the next Presidential election."[15] When the legislatures of Virginia and Alabama showed signs of willingness to ratify the amendment, Johnson dissuaded them. One after another the Southern legislatures rejected the Fourteenth Amendment, in many cases unanimously. Having spurned the easiest terms they could have hoped for, they sat back to watch Congress try to decide what to do next.

This Southern attitude exasperated moderate Republicans. "They would not cooperate in rebuilding what they destroyed," said one moderate, so "we must remove the rubbish and rebuild from the bottom. Whether they are willing or not, we must compel obedience to the Union, and demand protection for its humblest citizen."[16] Southern and presidential intransigence accomplished what the radicals alone could not have accomplished: the conversion of moderates to black suffrage as the cornerstone of reconstruction.

During the three-months session of Congress following the congressional elections of 1866,* Republicans debated and passed a Reconstruction Act whose final terms represented a compromise between moderates and radicals—a compromise hammered out in an exhausting sequence of committee wrangles, caucus decisions, floor debates, parliamentary maneuvers, all-night sessions, and frayed tempers. During this process, the Democrats tried to play the role of spoiler, voting first with the radicals on amendments to make the law stronger and then with the moderates to defeat the amended measures.

Three of the radicals' objectives went beyond what moderate Republicans were willing to accept: (1) long-term disfranchisement of ex-Confederates, to give blacks and Unionists a chance to put the new state governments on a solid footing before a counterrevolution of Southern Democrats could destroy them; (2) confis-

---

*This was still the 39th Congress, elected in 1864. Under the Constitution as it then existed, Congress met on the first Monday in December of the year *after* it was elected. This meant that thirteen months elapsed between the election of most congressmen and the date of their first meeting, unless the president called them into special session or Congress itself provided by law for a different meeting date. The second regular session of any given Congress, meeting in December of the second year after its election, expired on the following March 4. This second session was therefore known as the "short" session, since it lasted only three months—from early December to March 4. The second session of the Congress elected in 1864, therefore, met in December 1866. This situation was changed by the Twentieth Amendment to the Constitution, adopted in 1933, which stipulated that a Congress would meet on January 3 of the year following the year of its election, and would not expire until January 3 two years later.

cation and redistribution of land, to give the freedmen an economic basis for their new political power; and (3) federally supported schools, to enable Southern blacks to acquire the literacy, skills, and self-confidence to protect their freedom and rights. Recognizing that they had no chance to achieve these aims in the final short session of this Congress, radicals supported a bill simply to nullify the existing Southern governments and to place the territorialized states under military rule—in the hope that the new Congress, elected in 1866 and somewhat more radical than its predecessor, would enact more thorough measures.

Radicals believed that this reduction of ex-Confederate states to the status of territories would have positive benefits in and of itself. During territorial probation, they hoped, the Freedmen's Bureau, freedmen's aid societies, Northern soldiers, Northern settlers, and Northern capital could educate the freedmen up to the level of their new responsibilities, protect them with military force, make Southern whites feel the heavy hand of national power until they gave up hope of defying it, and rebuild the South in the Northern self-image of "small farms, thrifty tillage, free schools, closely-associated communities, social independence, respect for honest labor, and equality of political rights."[17]

But this idealized vision of a free-labor South was not to be fulfilled, at least not by the legislation of the Thirty-ninth Congress. Although the House passed a bill for territorialization and military government on February 13, 1867, Senate moderates believed that Congress must enact a comprehensive law setting forth the conditions of restoration. Otherwise, the divisive issue of reconstruction would drag on indefinitely and Northern voters might lose patience with the Republican failure to come up with a "policy." Therefore the Senate passed a measure that, like the House bill, divided the ten unreconstructed states* into five military districts and declared the existing civil governments in these states to be provisional only, subject to the overriding authority of the occupation forces. But in addition, the Senate bill provided that after any of the states had called a new constitutional convention elected by manhood suffrage, had adopted a new constitution that included black suffrage, and had ratified this constitution and the Fourteenth Amendment to the federal Constitution, the state's representatives would be readmitted to Congress. Those persons disqualified by the Fourteenth Amendment from holding office were barred from voting for convention delegates and from voting on the ratification of the new constitution. But the bill did not require the states to keep them disfranchised thereafter. The House concurred with the Senate bill, and after Johnson vetoed this Reconstruction Act on March 2, both houses passed it over his veto the same day.

Although the radicals accepted this measure as the best they could get for the time being, Indiana Congressman George W. Julian expressed their misgivings about it in a speech to the House. Southern states, he warned,

---

*Including all of the states that had seceded except Tennessee, which had been readmitted after ratifying the Fourteenth Amendment in 1866.

are not ready for reconstruction as independent States. . . . If these districts were to-day admitted as States, with the precise political and social elements which we know to exist in them, even with their rebel population disfranchised and the ballot placed in the hands of radical Union men only, irrespective of color, the experiment would be ruinous. . . . The power of the great landed aristocracy in these regions, if unrestrained by power from without, would inevitably assert itself. . . . What these regions need, above all things, is not an easy and quick return to their forfeited rights in the Union, but *government*, the strong arm of power, outstretched from the central authority here in Washington, making it safe for the freedmen . . . safe for northern capital and labor, northern energy and enterprise, and northern ideas. . . . To talk about suddenly building up independent States where the material for such structures is fatally wanting is nonsense. States must *grow*, and to that end their growth must be fostered and protected.[18]

Although future events would confirm Julian's forebodings, the Reconstruction Act seemed radical, even revolutionary, in 1867. That was how Johnson described it in his veto message. With their huge majority, congressional Republicans no longer worried about the President's capacity to prevent the enactment of reconstruction laws. But as Commander in Chief of the army and as head of the branch of government charged with executing the laws, Johnson still possessed great power to frustrate the enforcement of congressional legislation. And the President made clear his intention to use this power. Therefore, while it worked out the terms of the Reconstruction Act, Congress also passed a series of measures to limit the President's authority.

Limitations on Presidential Power

The first was a bill enacted on January 22, 1867, calling the Fortieth Congress into special session immediately after the expiration of the Thirty-ninth on March 4. This ensured that the legislators could maintain oversight of their reconstruction program during the interval before the first regularly scheduled session of the Fortieth Congress met in December. Second, Congress on March 2 passed, over Johnson's veto, the Tenure of Office Act, which required the consent of the Senate for the removal of any government official whose appointment had required Senate approval. This was designed to stop Johnson's dismissal of Republican officeholders who supported the congressional reconstruction policy. In its final form, the Tenure of Office Act also required Senate consent for the dismissal of cabinet officers. This was intended to protect Secretary of War Stanton, who now supported the congressional policy and was in a crucial position to influence its enforcement. The third measure to curb Johnson's powers was a rider to an army appropriations bill (passed on March 2) providing that all presidential orders to the army must be issued through the general of the army (Grant), who could not be removed without the Senate's consent. Grant had earlier favored a mild reconstruction policy similar to Johnson's, but Southern violence toward freedmen and Unionists had convinced him of the need for a stronger policy. The appropriations rider was designed to prevent Johnson from nullifying the military enforcement of reconstruction by orders issued independently of Grant.

The Second Reconstruction Act

The Reconstruction Act of March 2 had spelled out the process by which Southerners could take the initiative to restore their states to congressional representation, but it had created no machinery to compel them to act. This soon proved
to have been a mistake. Southern whites expressed a preference to remain in limbo
under military rule, rather than to cooperate in the establishment of new constitutions with black suffrage. But most Republicans wanted to get on with the task
of political reconstruction. On March 23, therefore, the special session of the new
Congress passed a supplementary Reconstruction Act that required the generals
in command of Southern military districts to register eligible voters and to set the
machinery in motion for the election of delegates to constitutional conventions.
With the passage of this act, black leaders and Unionist whites (soon to be called
"scalawags") along with Northern settlers in the South (soon to be called "carpetbaggers") began in earnest to organize a Republican party in the Southern states.
The army undertook the task of registering voters, including freed slaves. The
nation had completed another stage in the revolution that had begun with emancipation—"the maddest, most infamous revolution in history," according to a
hostile South Carolinian.[19]

Twenty-eight

Reconstruction and the Crisis of Impeachment

JOHNSON'S CONTINUED DEFIANCE OF CONGRESS

Andrew Johnson also considered reconstruction a mad, infamous revolution. The President retained considerable capacity to weaken the enforcement of reconstruction, despite Congress's efforts to tie his hands in this regard. He could appoint conservative generals to administer Southern military districts. He could interpret the Reconstruction Acts narrowly in order to give the existing civilian governments maximum control over the registration of voters and the election of convention delegates. He could use his executive powers in a dozen ways to obstruct or delay the Southern political revolution. For these reasons, a growing number of radicals concluded that reconstruction could never work so long as Johnson remained in office. They launched a drive to impeach the President and replace him with Benjamin Wade, who as president pro tem of the Senate was next in line for the presidency.

The First Impeachment Effort

Impeachment was an extreme step. The Constitution empowered the House to impeach and the Senate to convict, by a two-thirds vote in each house, any federal official for "Treason, Bribery, or other high Crimes and Misdemeanors" (Article II, Section 4). The House had used this power only five times in the past, and the Senate had voted conviction only twice. Both cases concerned district judges. Never, before 1867, had Congress seriously contemplated using the impeachment weapon against a president.

Moderate Republicans shrank from such a prospect. They maintained that an official could be impeached only for conduct that, if he were a private citizen, would be indictable as a crime. Much as they deplored Johnson's political perversity, they did not believe that he had committed any crimes. Radicals, however, contended that impeachment was not a criminal proceeding but rather a means of punishing a public official for "grave misuse of his powers, or any mischievous nonuse of them—for any conduct which harms the public or perils its welfare."[1] Johnson deserved such punishment, they insisted, for his wholesale pardons of ex-Rebels, his defiance of Congress, his intimation that Congress was an illegal body, his disgraceful public speeches, his complicity by inaction in the New Orleans massacre, and his general obstruction of the will of the Northern people.

On January 7, 1867, radicals managed to get the House to pass a resolution calling for an impeachment investigation. But the Judiciary Committee, designated to conduct the investigation, was dominated by moderates. Although the committee held extensive hearings, these only demonstrated that without further and greater provocation by Johnson, impeachment would come to nothing. Nevertheless, in February 1867 a moderate warned: "If [Johnson] fails to execute the laws, in their spirit as well as in their letter . . . if, holding the South in his hand, either by direct advice or personal example he shall encourage them to such resistance to progress as may tend to defeat the public will . . . the President may, after all, come to be regarded as an 'obstacle' which must be 'deposed.' "[2]

For a time Johnson seemed to heed such warnings. He let it be known that he intended to carry out the reconstruction laws. He appointed generals recommended by Stanton and Grant to command the five Southern military districts. These generals supported the congressional policy.

The Southern Response to the Reconstruction Acts

In the South, too, prominent ex-Confederates advised their people to accept the inevitable and to comply with the laws. By cooperating with the reconstruction process, some Southern whites hoped to influence it in a moderate direction. Members of the upper class, in their professed role as paternal protectors and best friends of the freedmen, even hoped to control a substantial portion of the black vote. They organized interracial political meetings and barbecues at which they urged the freedmen to vote with their fellow Southerners rather than with alien Yankees. This was part of a persistent effort in postwar Southern politics, led mainly by former Whigs, to create a moderate third force independent of both Democrats and Republicans. Enfranchisement of the freedmen seemed to offer the proponents of this effort an opportunity they were quick to grasp.

But the imperatives of the two-party system doomed this endeavor, just as they had doomed the National Union movement in the North the previous year. Moreover, the Republicans soon demonstrated their ability to mobilize black voters *en masse* under their banner. The party of Lincoln and emancipation had an unbeatable advantage in this respect.

The nucleus of a Southern Republican party had existed for two years in the form of unconditional Unionists and postwar settlers from the North. So long as the franchise was confined to whites, however, this nucleus was a small minority of Southern voters except in a few staunchly Unionist areas such as east Tennessee. With passage of the Reconstruction Acts the Republicans would become a potential majority party in at least half of the Southern states if they could win the allegiance of the freedmen. This they did easily. The principal agency for recruiting blacks into the Republican party was the Union League. Founded in the North during the war as an anti-Copperhead organization, the Union League moved into the South after Appomattox. During the spring of 1867, branches of the Union League mushroomed in the South to organize and instruct the freedmen in their new political duties.

In many districts the Freedmen's Bureau aided the League in this task. Indeed, some Bureau agents served simultaneously as Union League officials and, in their military capacity, as supervisors of voter registration under the Reconstruction Acts. These partisan activities gave white Southerners another reason to condemn the Bureau—not only did it intervene in their economic relations with black laborers, but now it was helping to mobilize these laborers into an alien political party.

As Republican success in winning black voters became clear, many Southern whites who had initially urged cooperation with reconstruction changed their tune. They hoped that, somehow or other, President Johnson or the Northern Democrats could yet reverse the process and overthrow the radicals.

Their faith in Johnson was not entirely misplaced. Although the President had promised to carry out the Reconstruction Acts, he believed them unconstitutional and planned to weaken their impact by executive interpretation. An opportunity to do so arose from several actions by the army as it began to enforce the acts. The voter registration boards in many Southern districts construed the disfranchisement provisions broadly to apply to men who had held any office, down to cemetery sexton, before the war and had thereafter supported the rebellion. Some generals removed state and local officials from office for alleged obstruction and for other causes. Johnson rebuked General Philip Sheridan, commander of the Louisiana-Texas district, who had evicted several high officials. The President asked Attorney General Henry Stanbery to rule on the legality of Sheridan's action and on the disfranchisement criteria of the registration boards. Stanbery's opinion, issued in June 1867, interpreted the Reconstruction Acts in the narrowest possible fashion. He ruled that the army's supremacy over civil governments was confined to police duties; that commanders could not remove civilian officials; that only those antebellum officeholders who had taken an oath before the war to support the United States Constitution could be disfranchised for rebellion; and that registrars must accept without question a prospective voter's oath that he had not participated in rebellion.

Military commanders expressed dismay at this ruling, especially its final provision, which Sheridan described as opening "a broad macadamized road for perjury and fraud to travel on." If sustained, Stanbery's opinion would go a long way toward nullifying the intent of the Reconstruction Acts because former Confederates would dominate the voting for new constitutional conventions. Stanton and

Grant protested against the opinion; Grant informed military commanders that
it did not have the force of an order and told them to continue enforcing their
own construction of the law.

Congress reassembled in July to plug the loopholes opened by Stanbery's ruling.
On July 19 the Republicans passed, over Johnson's veto, a third Reconstruction
Act, which declared Southern provisional governments subordinate in all respects
to military rule, confirmed the power of commanders. to remove officials from
office, authorized registration boards to reject a voter's oath if they believed it
falsely sworn, and defined the categories of prewar officeholders who were liable
to disfranchisement more broadly than Stanbery had done.

The Second Impeachment Effort

This accomplished, congressional radicals wanted to revive impeachment. The
President, they asserted, had demonstrated that he had no intention of enforcing
the law in good faith. But moderates still feared that impeachment might make
a martyr of Johnson. They managed to head off the radical effort. Among themselves, however, they complained that "the President . . . *does* continue to do the
most provoking things. If he isn't impeached it won't be his fault."[3]

As if to thumb his nose at the moderates who were trying to save him, Johnson
again took the offensive as soon as Congress adjourned. Democrats had long been
imploring him to dismiss Secretary of War Stanton, the only cabinet member who
supported the congressional reconstruction program. But for reasons never made
clear, the President had not previously done so, and the Tenure of Office Act now
seemed to make it impossible for him to remove Stanton without Senate approval.
By waiting until Congress adjourned, however, Johnson could suspend Stanton
until the Senate reconvened several months later. This was what he did on August
12, 1867.

The President persuaded Grant to become interim secretary of war. This sent
shock waves through the Republican party. Grant was the most popular man in
the country. Despite his well-known aversion to politics, he seemed almost certain
to be drafted as a presidential candidate in 1868. Did Grant's acceptance of office
under Johnson mean that he agreed with the President's actions? Republicans
soon breathed easier as it became clear that he did not. Grant had strongly urged
Johnson not to suspend Stanton. He accepted the interim appointment only to
serve as a buffer between the President and the army, in order to prevent Johnson
from doing more mischief. When Johnson informed Grant on August 17 of his
intention to replace Sheridan with a more conservative general as commander of
the Louisiana-Texas district, Grant penned an earnest letter, which he leaked to
the press, imploring him not to do so. Sheridan was a great general and a good
administrator who had done as much as any man to overcome the Rebels in war
and peace, said Grant. "His removal will only be regarded as an effort to defeat
the laws of Congress. It will be interpreted by the unreconstructed element in the
South . . . as a triumph. It will embolden them to renewed opposition to the will
of the loyal masses, believing that they have the Executive with them."[4]

Johnson disregarded this advice. For good measure, he also removed General Daniel Sickles, commander of the Carolinas district, who had offended Southern whites with his aggressive enforcement of the Reconstruction Acts. Grant did his best to cushion the impact of these changes by ordering the new commanders not to restore civilian officials deposed by their predecessors—which in Sheridan's district included the governors of both Louisiana and Texas.

But the President had once again demonstrated his ability to contravene the spirit if not the letter of the reconstruction laws, and this gave the impeachment movement another shot in the arm. "What does Johnson mean to do?" worried a former attorney general. "Does he mean to have another rebellion on the question of Executive powers & duties?" The publisher of a moderate Republican newspaper asked a friend in Washington: "Is the President crazy, or only drunk? I am afraid his doings will make us all favor impeachment."[5] Several Republican editors who had previously opposed impeachment changed their minds and came out in its favor during the fall of 1867. One moderate Republican on the House Judiciary Committee switched his previously negative vote to affirmative, enabling the committee to recommend by a five-to-four vote the President's impeachment on general grounds of "usurpation of power." Before the House could vote on this resolution, however, the off-year state elections in the North produced Democratic gains that seemed to portend a conservative shift in public opinion.

Once again circumstances made state elections into a quasi-referendum on reconstruction and especially on black suffrage. Having enfranchised Southern blacks, Republicans felt compelled by reproaches of hypocrisy to try their best to enfranchise blacks in the Northern states that still denied them the ballot. Unless they did so, conceded one abolitionist, "our whole demeanor toward the southern states" would be "like that of the Pharisee toward the Publican."[6] All but two state Republican platforms in 1867 endorsed the principle of equal suffrage in Northern states. Republican legislatures in five states placed constitutional amendments for this purpose on the ballot, three of them to be voted on in 1867.

But voters in Ohio, Minnesota, and Kansas rejected black suffrage. At least 80 percent of the Republican voters in Ohio and Minnesota favored the proposal, but solid Democratic opposition caused it to lose narrowly in both states. The issue helped Democrats win control of the Ohio legislature. The party also made major gains in other Northern states, where black suffrage as well as impeachment and radical reconstruction in general were important issues. As usual, Democrats went all out to exploit racism in the campaign. "Any Democrat," observed a French newspaper correspondent, "who did not manage to hint in his speech that the negro is a degenerate gorilla, would be considered lacking in enthusiasm."[7]

Democrats magnified their gains in the 1867 elections into a "Great Reaction" against Republicans, *a revulsion of popular feeling in the North. . . .* Judging from the history of Counter Revolutions . . . the days of Radical domination are numbered." Andrew Johnson made a "victory speech" to a group of serenaders at the White House. One of the President's aides chortled: "I almost pity the

Radicals. After giving ten states to the negroes, to keep the Democrats from getting them, they will have lost the rest. . . . Any party with an abolition head and a nigger tail will soon find itself with nothing left but the head and the tail."[8]

These predictions of Republican demise proved premature. But the elections did strengthen moderates in the party at the expense of radicals. Party leaders became chary of the suffrage issue in the North. In Horace Greeley's words, "the Negro question lies at the bottom of our reverses. . . . We have lost votes in the Free States by daring to be just to the Negro." The elections also blunted the impeachment drive. "We shall have burdens enough to carry in the next campaign," said Greeley, "without making Mr. Johnson a martyr and carrying him also." A Washington correspondent reported the impeachment movement "dead, unless the President, by fresh outrages, gives it a new impetus."[9] The House confirmed this observation on December 7 by voting down the Judiciary Committee's impeachment recommendation, 108 to 57.

THE IMPEACHMENT AND ACQUITTAL OF JOHNSON

But Johnson's subsequent actions once more raised the issue from the dead. General Winfield Scott Hancock, a Democrat and Johnson's choice to replace Sheridan as commander of the Louisiana-Texas district, reversed many of Sheridan's policies and thereby handicapped Republican efforts. Johnson publicly commended Hancock. Then on December 28, the President replaced two radical-leaning generals in the Georgia-Alabama-Florida district with conservatives who were expected to follow Hancock's example. These moves encouraged the growing Southern resistance to reconstruction. Having failed to elect a majority of delegates to any of the ten constitutional conventions that met during the winter of 1867–1868, Southern Democrats organized to defeat or delay ratification of the new constitutions long enough for the much-heralded Northern ground swell to overturn reconstruction by a Democratic victory in the 1868 presidential election. "Will the white men of the North and the Great West fail to come to the rescue?" asked an Atlanta newspaper rhetorically. "We answer for them—THEY WILL NOT FAIL."[10]

Southern Republicans* expressed dismay at this newly demonstrated power of the President to strengthen their enemies. "Unfriendly military management has killed us," wrote Alabama Republican leaders. "The removal of Genls. Pope and Swayne has taken from the work of Reconstruction two able and experienced leaders. . . . Their removal is followed by such an outburst of rebel hostility that . . . no man to-day can enter the canvass without taking his life in his hands. . . . The rebels have had all their own ways in many counties. . . . What next can we do?"[11]

While these events were taking place in the South, a singular drama was unfolding in Washington. General Grant was still serving as interim secretary of

*For analyses of the Southern Republicans, see pp. 535–536 and 555–560.

war while the Senate decided whether to concur in the President's suspension of Stanton. If the Senate refused to concur, Johnson hoped to challenge the constitutionality of the Tenure of Office Act in the courts. But to do this, he needed Grant's cooperation. Johnson thought he had obtained the general's promise not to turn the War Department back to Stanton if the Senate overruled the secretary's suspension. But when Grant learned on January 14 that the Senate had done so, he vacated the office and Stanton moved back in. Johnson charged Grant with bad faith. The astonished and angry general replied that, on the contrary, he had made clear his intention not to violate the Tenure of Office Act. A bitter exchange of letters between the two men made front page copy. Johnson may have gotten the better of this verbal contest, but in making an enemy of Grant the President further eroded his own political support and boosted the general's prestige among Republicans.

Foiled in his attempt to use Grant to gain control of the War Department, Johnson decided to challenge Congress directly. He issued an order on February 21 removing Stanton and nominating Adjutant General Lorenzo Thomas as interim secretary of war. When this news reached Congress, uproar ensued. Republican senators urged Stanton to disobey the order. The dour war secretary barricaded himself in his office and refused to yield the keys when the hapless Thomas showed up the next morning with a hangover after a Washington's Birthday ball at which he had drunk too much in celebration of his new job.

The House Votes Impeachment

Johnson's apparent violation of the Tenure of Office Act changed the minds of many Republican moderates who had previously opposed impeachment. "He has thrown down the gauntlet," wrote one moderate, "and says to us as plainly as words can speak it: 'Try this issue now betwixt me and you; either you go to the wall or I do.' "[12] On February 24, 1868, the House impeached the President by a party-line vote of 126 to 47. Befitting the Republicans' angry mood, the House named a committee to draw up charges against Johnson whose members included some of the most radical men in Congress: Thaddeus Stevens, George Julian, Benjamin Butler, John Logan, and George Boutwell. In the manner of a grand jury indictment, the charges contained eleven counts framed in prolix legal language designed to cover every conceivable "high crime or misdemeanor" allegedly committed by the President. The first eight counts dealt in one way or another with his attempt to remove Stanton and to appoint a successor without the Senate's consent. The ninth article charged Johnson with trying to persuade the army commander in the District of Columbia to violate the Command of the Army Act by accepting orders directly from the President. The tenth article, written by Butler, accused the President of trying to "excite the odium and resentment of all the good people of the United States against Congress and the laws by it duly and constitutionally enacted." The final "omnibus" article in effect drew together all the charges in the previous ten.

On Trial Before the Senate

The Constitution designates the Senate to function as a court to try charges of impeachment, with the chief justice of the Supreme Court as presiding judge. The House appointed seven "managers" (in effect prosecuting attorneys), including Stevens, Butler, Boutwell, and Logan, to present the case to the Senate. The trial began March 4 and continued, with interruptions, for eleven weeks. This protracted process worked in the President's favor by cooling the passions that had come to a climax with his attempted removal of Stanton.

Johnson's defense counsel included some of the leading lawyers in the country: Henry Stanbery, the attorney general; William M. Evarts, a future secretary of state; and Benjamin R. Curtis, a former justice of the Supreme Court who had written the principal dissenting opinion in the Dred Scott case. During the trial, these men demonstrated a good deal more legal acumen than did the impeachment managers. The case for the defense rested on three arguments: a government official can be impeached only for criminal offenses that would be indictable in ordinary courts; Johnson had committed no crime by seeking to test the constitutionality of the Tenure of Office Act; and in any case, because this law applied only to cabinet officers "during the term of the president by whom they may have been appointed," it did not apply to Stanton, who had been appointed by Lincoln.

To these arguments the impeachment managers replied: Johnson was serving out Lincoln's term and therefore the Tenure of Office Act did cover Stanton; to allow a president to disobey a law in order to test it in court would set a dangerous precedent; and regardless of whether Johnson was guilty of any crime, impeachment was a political rather than a criminal process. On this last point Benjamin Butler maintained that an impeachable offense was "one in its nature or consequences subversive of some fundamental or essential principle of government, or highly prejudicial to the public interest, and this may consist of a violation of the Constitution, of law, of an official oath, or of duty . . . or, without violating a positive law, by the abuse of discretionary powers."[13]

Butler's statement got to the heart of the case for impeachment. Johnson was really on trial for two years of relentless opposition to the Republican reconstruction program. His crime, in the words of a congressman, was "the one great overshadowing purpose of reconstructing the rebel States in accordance with his own will, in the interests of the great criminals who carried them into the rebellion." Impeachment was also the culmination of a long power struggle between Congress and the executive that went back to the Lincoln administration. "The great question to be decided," wrote one partisan of impeachment, was whether "the National Legislature [is] to be as omnipotent in American politics as the English is in English politics. . . . May we not anticipate a time when the President will no more think of vetoing a bill passed by Congress than the British crown thinks of doing?"[14]

But some moderates feared the creation of a precedent by which a two-thirds majority of Congress could remove any president who happened to disagree with them. This might destroy the constitutional balance of powers in the American political system. Despite their disgust with Johnson, these moderates did not want to cripple the Presidency. "Whether Andrew Johnson should be removed from office, justly or unjustly, [is] comparatively of little consequence," wrote a conservative senator, "but whether our government should be Mexicanized and an example set which would surely, in the end, utterly overthrow our institutions, [is] a matter of vast consequence."[15] Several moderates also distrusted the radical Benjamin Wade, who would become president if the Senate convicted Johnson.

These concerns enabled troubled Republican senators to seize upon the legal uncertainties of the case to justify their doubts about impeachment. Moderate senators who abhorred Johnson's reconstruction policies but wished to vote against impeachment sought through intermediaries to reach an understanding with the President. For the first time, Johnson responded to such overtures. He conducted himself with dignity and restraint during the trial. He gave no more speeches or interviews denouncing Congress. He promised to enforce the Reconstruction Acts, and he did so. After discreet negotiations with moderate senators, Johnson appointed as secretary of war General John M. Schofield, whose efficiency and impartiality as commander of the Virginia military district commended him to all factions.

These actions strengthened the President's prospects for acquittal. But intense pressure from Republican constituencies kept the issue in doubt until the end. Every Republican state convention endorsed conviction. Southern Republicans continued to predict Rebel resurgence if Johnson remained in office. Rumors of bribes and other sinister machinations floated through Washington. When the Senate on May 16 finally voted on the eleventh article of impeachment (the omnibus article), the roll call took on the dimensions of high drama. Not until West Virginia's Republican Senator Peter G. Van Winkle, near the end of the alphabet, voted nay did it become clear that Johnson was acquitted. The vote was 35 to 19; the nay votes of seven Republicans and twelve Democrats had caused the total for conviction to fall one vote short of the necessary two-thirds. Identical votes on articles 2 and 3 on May 26 came as an anticlimax. The impeachment managers conceded defeat. Although the seven "recusant" Republican senators endured bitter denunciations for a time, the impeachment passions soon died down as the party closed ranks for the presidential election. Johnson remained on his good behavior for the rest of his term; reconstruction in the South proceeded without further presidential hindrance. A crisis that had shaken the constitutional system to its foundations ended without fundamentally altering the system.

THE SUPREME COURT AND RECONSTRUCTION

During the impeachment controversy, Congress and the Supreme Court also confronted each other in a power contest from which the Court backed away before a final showdown. The Court's ruling in the *Milligan* case (1866)—that military trials of civilians in nonwar zones were unconstitutional—seemed to invalidate military courts and martial law in the South.* Congressional Republicans denounced the *Milligan* decision as a "piece of judicial impertinence which we are not bound to respect."[16] They introduced a rash of bills and constitutional amendments to curb the Court's power by requiring at least a two-thirds majority of justices to declare an act of Congress unconstitutional, to restrict the Court's appellate jurisdiction, to enable a two-thirds majority of Congress to override a Court ruling, and even to abolish the Court. The House did pass a bill making a two-thirds Court majority necessary to declare legislation unconstitutional, but the Senate failed to act on the measure. With one exception, noted below, Congress failed to enact any proposals to curb the Court's power.

Republican attacks on the Court may have convinced some justices that discretion was the better part of valor. In 1867, the Court dismissed suits by state officials in Mississippi and Georgia for an injunction to prevent federal officials from enforcing the Reconstruction Acts. But early in 1868 the case of *ex parte McCardle* threatened a collision between Court and Congress. This case arose from the military arrest in November 1867 of a Mississippi editor named William McCardle for publishing inflammatory articles against reconstruction. After a federal circuit court had denied his petition for a writ of *habeas corpus*, McCardle appealed to the Supreme Court under the Habeas Corpus Act of 1867, which, ironically, Congress had passed to protect freedmen against imprisonment under state black codes. While McCardle's appeal was pending, Congress on March 27, 1868, repealed the statute on which it was based, thus depriving the Supreme Court of appellate jurisdiction. The Court acquiesced, despite the wish of conservative justices to accept the case on other grounds in order to rule on the constitutionality of the Reconstruction Acts.

This was not quite the craven surrender by the Court that some historians have said it was. Article III, Section 2, of the Constitution empowers Congress to regulate the Supreme Court's appellate jurisdiction. By refusing jurisdiction in this and in the earlier Mississippi and Georgia cases, the Court in effect declared that the reconstruction of ex-Confederate states was a political rather than a constitutional problem—a position explicitly affirmed in *Texas* v. *White* (1869), a decision concerning the illegality of secession. Because secession was impossible *de jure*, the restoration of states that had gone out of the Union *de facto* was an extraconstitutional and therefore essentially a political process legitimated by the constitutional duty of the national government to guarantee each state a republican form of government.

Congressional reconstruction demonstrated the resilience of the Constitution. Despite the shock of secession and civil war, reconstruction proceeded in a fashion that left the country's basic institutions intact. The Presidency survived the

---

*Justice David Davis, who wrote the *Milligan* decision, said in February 1867 that he did not mean it to apply to "insurrectionary" states, which could be regarded as still in a state of war until Congress declared otherwise. But Republicans feared that a majority of the Court might well declare the Reconstruction Acts unconstitutional if a case arising from military rule came before it. For an earlier reference to the Milligan case, see p. 510n.

gravest threat it has ever experienced. Although the Supreme Court backed down from a potential confrontation with Congress in 1868, the Court retained its stature as a coordinate branch of government with sufficient power to strike down vital reconstruction legislation in the 1870s (see p. 595). For better or worse, Thaddeus Stevens's attempt to substitute revolutionary legitimacy for constitutional legitimacy failed. The crisis of war and reconstruction temporarily altered but did not destroy the balance of powers among the three branches of the federal government.

READMISSION OF SOUTHERN STATES

While great political and constitutional issues were being decided in Washington, the reconstruction of Southern states moved forward. When the registration of voters was completed in September 1867, approximately 735,000 blacks and 635,000 whites were enrolled in the ten unreconstructed states. Blacks constituted a majority of voters in five states: South Carolina, Mississippi, Louisiana, Florida, and Alabama. An estimated 10 to 15 percent of the potential white electorate was disfranchised by the Reconstruction Acts; another 25 to 30 percent failed to register because of apathy or of opposition to the whole process.

Having failed to attract black voters, Democrats searched for other ways to control or defeat reconstruction. The presence of twenty thousand federal troops discouraged open violence. But some white landowners and employers used economic threats to keep their black employees home on election day. Some Democratic leaders urged their followers to abstain from voting in the hope that the ballots in favor of holding a constitutional convention would fall short of the required majority of registered voters. Even if this tactic failed, they said, a large white abstention would discredit the elections in the eyes of Northern moderates. "A change at the North is our only hope for civil liberty in this country," wrote a North Carolinian, "and I am quite willing the Radicals should make themselves blacker and blacker, until they become in the sight of all men—especially, all good men—*black and all black!*"[17]

Fewer than half of the registered white voters (compared with four-fifths of the blacks) voted in the elections for conventions, held during the fall of 1867, and only half of the voting whites cast ballots in favor of holding a convention. Nevertheless, in every state the proconvention vote exceeded the requisite majority of registered voters. About three-quarters of the delegates elected to these conventions were Republicans; most of the remainder called themselves Conservatives—out of deference to the former Whigs among them who could not yet accept the label Democrat. Of the Republican delegates, about 45 percent were Southern whites, 30 percent were blacks, and 25 percent were Northern men who had settled in the South since the war. Blacks were a majority of delegates in the South Carolina and Louisiana conventions; Northern whites were a majority in none.

Southern white Republican delegates were mostly wartime Unionists who represented upcountry districts; they were particularly numerous in the conventions of Virginia, North Carolina, Georgia, and Arkansas. Most of the Northern-born delegates were former Union army officers or Freedmen's Bureau agents who had decided to make their future in the new South. They possessed, on the average, more education than the other classes of delegates and more wealth than the other classes of Republican delegates. They exercised leadership in the conventions out of proportion to their numbers, serving as presidents of four of the conventions and as chairmen of nearly half of the committees. The black delegates constituted the elite of their race. At least half of them had been free before the war, and most of those who had been slaves belonged to the upper strata of slave society. About four-fifths of the black delegates were literate. Their predominant occupations were clergyman, teacher, artisan, and landowning farmer; very few were field hands or unskilled laborers.

The Constitutional Conventions

Hostile Southern whites ridiculed the "Black and Tan" conventions which met during the winter of 1867–1868. They described the delegates as "ragamuffins and jailbirds . . . baboons, monkeys, mules." In typical phrases, Louisiana conservatives branded the new constitution written by the state convention as a "base conspiracy against human nature . . . the work of ignorant Negroes co-operating with a gang of white adventurers."[18]

Such caricatures long dominated the historical image of these conventions. The reality, however, was quite different. The delegates generally conducted themselves with order and decorum. Although a certain amount of wrangling took place among different factions of the Republican majority, this was normal in American politics. But the momentous character of these conventions was far from normal: for the first time blacks and whites were working and voting together to write the fundamental law of their states.

The constitutions they produced were among the most progressive in the nation. Many of their provisions were modeled on the most advanced features of Northern state constitutions. In their enactment of universal manhood suffrage, they were ahead of most Northern states. All of the new constitutions mandated statewide systems of public schools for both races. Most of the constitutions increased the state's responsibility for social welfare beyond anything previously known in the South. Some constitutions established state boards of public charities. Several of them enacted prison reforms and reduced the number of capital crimes. These new public services made necessary a large increase in the property tax. But most states provided homestead exemptions that aided the small landowner by exempting real and personal property up to $2,000 or $3,000 from attachment for debts. This feature was popular with Southern white delegates representing constituents whose small holdings were threatened by the shaky postwar Southern economy. The increased taxes on real property were popular with black delegates and some Northerners, who hoped they might force the sale of excess land at a price affordable to black farmers. Although some radical delegates urged the confiscation of land, no convention took such action. The only gesture in this direction was the authorization by the South Carolina convention of a state land commission to buy property at market value and resell it in small tracts on liberal terms.

These measures won more or less solid support from the majority Republican coalition. Other issues, however, divided this coalition, with most Northern whites and the black delegates on one side and many Southern white Republicans joining their Conservative colleagues on the other. One such issue was public school segregation. Heated debates on this question occurred in nearly every convention. Most conventions resolved it by tabling motions either to mandate segregated schools or to prohibit them. No state constitution required the schools to be segregated, and only two—those of South Carolina and Louisiana—forbade racial segregation in public schools. In practice, however, desegregation prevailed only at the University of South Carolina and in several Louisiana elementary schools, mostly in New Orleans.

Another divisive issue was disfranchisement of ex-Confederates. North and South Carolina, Georgia, Florida, Louisiana, and Texas finally adopted constitutions that disfranchised no one for participation in the rebellion, though Louisiana required former Confederates to sign a statement confessing the error of their ways before gaining the right to vote. Arkansas, Alabama, Virginia, and Mississippi disfranchised certain categories of ex-Confederate leaders (ranging from 10 to 20 per cent of the potential white voters).* The unpopularity of these disfranchisement provisions with white voters and even with some black voters helped bring about the initial defeat of the Virginia and Mississippi constitutions, which did not go into effect until the disfranchisement clauses were removed. Alabama repealed disfranchisement soon after returning to full statehood. Arkansas, which disfranchised a larger class of former Rebels than any other ex-Confederate state, did not remove these disabilities until 1872—the last Southern state to do so.

Readmission to Congressional Representation

Once the constitutions were written, the next step was to submit them to the voters. Still hoping to thwart reconstruction by delaying it beyond the presidential election, Conservatives mounted a well-organized effort to defeat ratification. Most Southern whites could not believe that a majority of Northern voters would sustain the "infamous" Republican attempt to impose "Negro rule" on the South. If ratification of the new Southern state constitutions could be defeated, the hoped-for Democratic victory in the presidential election of 1868 would reverse the process of reconstruction and restore Southern states to self-government without black suffrage. To accomplish the defeat of ratification, many Southern whites resorted to violence to intimidate or eliminate black voters. A secret organization of night-riding terrorists with the ominous name of Ku Klux Klan made its first serious forays in these elections.

But the main Conservative tactic was to boycott the polls. If enough whites

---

*At this time (1868) ex-Confederates were still disfranchised in Missouri, Tennessee, and West Virginia.

could be persuaded or coerced to stay home, the vote in favor of the constitution might fall short of a majority of registered voters. This tactic worked in the first state to hold its ratification election, Alabama, on February 4, 1868. Although the vote in favor of the constitution was 70,812 to 1,005, this was only 43 percent of the 168,813 registered voters. Perplexed and angry congressional Republicans passed on March 11 a fourth Reconstruction Act that required for ratification of a constitution only a majority of those actually voting. During the next two months six states ratified their constitutions by voting majorities ranging from 51 percent (Arkansas) to 72 percent (South Carolina).* Republicans won control of the state offices and legislatures at the same elections. The legislatures promptly assembled and ratified the Fourteenth Amendment, thus completing the requirements for readmission.

Despite the apparent success of reconstruction, many congressional Republicans felt reluctant to take the final step of readmission. Once these states were restored to self-government, the presence of federal troops would have to be reduced. The Conservative/Democratic party had already demonstrated its potential for winning power in several states, especially after disfranchised whites regained the ballot. The Republican coalition had demonstrated its fragility and the vulnerability of its black constituency to intimidation. What was to prevent Southern Democrats from dismantling a new constitution, black suffrage and all, if they recovered control of a state? Beware of "hastening back States where rebelism is pervading them from end to end," warned a radical Senator. "There are not ten men . . . who believe it is a safe thing to do at this time," said another.[19]

But political necessities dictated readmission. Northern voters would rap Republican knuckles in the 1868 election if uncertainty and "bayonet rule" still prevailed in the South. "Things cannot drift along in this way forever," declared a House Republican leader. "Those States must be admitted some time. There must be an end of the confusion, the anarchy now prevailing. We must have civil law and civil order. We cannot always control those States by the bayonet."[20] Swallowing their doubts, Republicans in June 1868 readmitted seven states (including Alabama) to representation in Congress. The enabling acts included a "fundamental condition" that the constitutions of these states must never be amended to deprive blacks of the right to vote. Such a condition was of dubious constitutionality and enforceability (the Constitution granted Congress no power to impose or enforce such conditions), but it may have assuaged the qualms of some congressmen.

The restoration of Texas, Virginia, and Mississippi was delayed until 1869: the vast expanse of Texas and the disarray of the Republican party there slowed the completion of the state's constitution; in Virginia, Republican factionalism and the unpopularity of stringent disfranchisement provisions in the new constitution prevented the scheduling of a ratification election; and in Mississippi, a disfranchisement clause provoked Conservatives to organize an aggressive campaign that

*In Arkansas and Georgia, the proratification total was only 36 percent and 46 percent, respectively, of those states' registered voters.

defeated ratification on June 22, 1868, by a majority of 7,600 votes. Violence and intimidation had kept an estimated 20,000 Republican voters from the Mississippi polls despite the presence of 2,000 soldiers in the state.

In 1869, Texas finally completed its constitution and was readmitted. In that same year the disfranchisement clauses in Virginia and Mississippi were voted on separately and defeated, and these states were then admitted with their purged and ratified constitutions. "Reconstruction" appeared to be completed. But events were soon to demonstrate that it had barely begun.

Twenty-nine

The First Grant Administration

THE ELECTION OF 1868

Just as the 1864 presidential election had been a referendum on Republican war policies, so the 1868 contest shaped up as yet another plebiscite on reconstruction.

The Financial Question

For a time, however, it appeared that the "financial question" might rival reconstruction as a campaign issue. The origins of this question lay in the wartime legislation that established the greenbacks and the national banks. War-caused inflation and the dual currency (paper and specie) created a gold premium that made gold dollars more valuable than paper dollars. After the war, Secretary of the Treasury Hugh McCulloch, a hard-money man, set out to return the monetary system to the gold standard by bringing the greenbacks to par with gold through a gradual retirement from circulation of a portion of the $415 million in greenbacks. Congress initially endorsed this policy. By 1867, McCulloch had reduced the greenbacks to $319 million and the gold premium stood at 140 ($140 of greenbacks were required to buy $100 of gold). Meanwhile the economy had experienced a postwar recession and a deflation of about 12 percent in two years. Sectors of the economy hurt by these developments blamed the contraction of greenbacks for their plight. Alarmed, Congress in January 1868 forbade further greenback reduction.

Something of a sectional alignment on the currency question was beginning to emerge—not North against South this time, but East against West. Western congressmen, Republicans as well as Democrats, opposed contraction because the fixed limitation on national banknotes and their regional maldistribution hit the economy of this region harder than that of the Northeast. A significant minority of Eastern Republicans, however, especially Thaddeus Stevens and Benjamin Butler, also spoke out against contraction.

Divisions within each party on this question reduced the possibility of making it an issue between the parties. But Midwestern Democrats tried to make political capital from the related issue of whether the principal of the five-twenty war bonds should be repaid in gold or greenbacks. The law under which these bonds had been sold specified only that the interest must be paid in gold. By 1867 many Democrats were asking why bondholders, who had purchased these securities with depreciated paper currency, should be rewarded by redemption in gold when everyone else must accept greenbacks as legal tender. Here was an issue on which most Republicans could unite, for despite the absence of a legal requirement for redemption in gold, the Treasury had assured investors that the principal as well as interest would be paid in gold. Any deviation from that promise, said Republicans, would constitute repudiation. And since it was the old peace wing of the Democratic party that urged payment in greenbacks, the Republicans revived the charge of Copperheadism as well.

Nevertheless, the idea of redeeming the national debt in greenbacks caught on among Democrats in the Midwest, where it became associated with the name of Ohio party leader George H. Pendleton, a leading candidate for the 1868 presidential nomination. The Pendleton Plan found its way into the Democratic platform. But when the party turned to Horatio Seymour of New York as its presidential nominee, this plank became a virtual dead letter. Like most Eastern Democrats, Seymour opposed the Pendleton Plan. Because of this internal party division, the issue assumed secondary importance in a campaign that soon focused on the reconstruction issue and on the candidates' war records.

The Republican Convention

For almost a year before the Republican convention met in May 1868, Ulysses S. Grant seemed sure to become the party's nominee. Grant's only serious rival was Salmon P. Chase, a perennial candidate, whose ambitions were not satisfied by the chief justiceship of the Supreme Court. Most radicals favored Chase in 1867 and distrusted Grant because of the general's antebellum Democratic leanings and his early postwar identification with Johnson's reconstruction policy. But several developments muted these reservations about Grant: his endorsement of the congressional program in 1867; the Democratic gains in the off-year 1867 elections, which convinced many radicals that they needed to nominate a war hero rather than one of their own in 1868; and Grant's bitter break with Johnson in January 1868. Moreover, Chase's conduct of the impeachment trial, in which he had made clear his sympathy for the President's acquittal, caused the chief justice virtually to be read out of the Republican party. The Republican convention unanimously nominated Grant on a platform that pointed with pride to "the assured success of the reconstruction policy of Congress."

One nagging problem marred the self-congratulatory mood of the convention

—the problem of black suffrage in Northern states. Radicals insisted that the party must come out unequivocally for equal suffrage everywhere: "To dodge the issue, or to cover it out of sight under some meaningless generality, would be moral depravity and political folly."[1] But moderates believed that equivocation was political wisdom, not folly. Republican campaigns for Northern suffrage had hurt the party in the 1867 elections. In April 1868, Michigan voters defeated a new constitution that included black suffrage by a margin of 61 to 39 percent—which meant that at least 20 percent of the Republicans had voted against it. "Discreditable as the fact may be, it is pretty evident that the enfranchisement of the colored race in the Northern States will have to wait," declared a moderate newspaper. "The more immediate interests of reconstruction might be jeopardized by forcing the issue at this juncture."[2]

The platform committee at the national convention was the scene of a sharp struggle on this issue between radicals and moderates. Victory finally went to the moderates. The convention adopted the committee's plank, which stated that while black suffrage in the ex-Confederate states "was demanded by every consideration of public safety, of gratitude, and of justice," the "question of suffrage in all the loyal States properly belongs to the people of those States." Abolitionists and radicals denounced this "mean-spirited . . . foolish and contemptible" plank. Charles Sumner predicted accurately that "the Democrats will have a great opportunity in exposing its Janus-faced character."[3]

The Democratic Convention

In contrast to the Republicans, Democrats had a plethora of candidates for the presidential nomination. Four leaders emerged from the pack by the eve of the party's July convention: Pendleton of Ohio; Senator Thomas Hendricks of Indiana; General Winfield Scott Hancock, whose outstanding war record might neutralize part of Grant's advantage in that respect; and Andrew Johnson. Although the President evoked sympathy in the party for his battles against the radicals, he carried too many liabilities; he dropped out of contention by the third ballot. Pendleton, Hancock, and Hendricks each in turn came close to winning a majority on the eighth, eighteenth, and twenty-second ballots, respectively, but each fell far short of the necessary two-thirds. At the end of the twenty-second ballot a few states changed their votes to Horatio Seymour. The effect on the exhausted convention was electric. State after state jumped on the bandwagon. Seymour had repeatedly refused to be a candidate, and now his friends had to hustle him out of the hall to prevent him from declining the nomination on the spot. In the end the suave, frail ex-governor of New York bowed to necessity and accepted the dubious honor of running against Grant.

The Democratic platform branded the Reconstruction Acts "a flagrant usurpation of power . . . unconstitutional, revolutionary, and void," and demanded "the abolition of the Freedmen's Bureau, and all political instrumentalities designed to secure negro supremacy." This became the party's battle cry. Vice-presidential candidate Frank Blair of Missouri set the tone for the campaign with a public letter that became famous as the Brodhead letter. A wartime Republican with a fine military record, Blair had reverted to his family's ancestral Democratic allegiance after the war. In the Brodhead letter he asserted: "There is but one way to restore the Government and the Constitution, and that is for the President-elect to declare these acts null and void, compel the army to undo its usurpations at the South, disperse the carpet-bag State Governments, [and] allow the white people to reorganize their own governments."[4]

The Race Issue and the Ku Klux Klan

Unabashed by Republican outcries against such statements, Blair repeated them throughout the campaign. The Republican state governments in the South were "bastard and spurious" governments, he said. "The white race is the only race in the world that has shown itself capable of maintaining free institutions of a free government," but Southern white men were being "trodden under foot by an inferior and barbarous race." The Democrats would restore to Southern whites their "birthright." In this effort "we shall have the sympathy of every man who is worthy to belong to the white race." Other Democrats, especially in the Midwest and South, took their cue from Blair. If the Democrats won a majority of white voters in November, said a Wisconsin editor, they should "march to Washington . . . and take their seats, and reinaugurate the white man's government."[5]

Republicans replied in kind. They waved the bloody shirt. They reminded voters of Seymour's "My Friends" speech to the New York draft rioters in 1863. They contrasted the final sentence of Grant's letter accepting the nomination— "Let us have peace"—with Blair's call for a bloody counterrevolution. In an electorate weary from four years of war and nearly four years of political warfare over reconstruction, Grant's statement struck a responsive chord. Republicans made the most of it. Grant in the White House would bring a surcease of conflict; a Democratic victory would inaugurate "government by assassination and violence, instead of government by law."[6]

Some Southern Democrats seemed determined to prove the Republicans right. In several states, the Ku Klux Klan and similar organizations launched a reign of terror. Federal troops were handicapped in efforts to prevent this violence by their inability to impose martial law now that the states were "reconstructed." The hastily organized state militias could do no better.

The Klan had been founded two years earlier in Pulaski, Tennessee. Like the Confederate army, in whose ranks many Klansmen had served, this secret order recruited members from all classes of Southern white society. Among its leaders were two dozen or more Confederate generals and colonels headed by Nathan Bedford Forrest, the Klan's "Grand Wizard." By 1868, the Klan had evolved from a harmless fraternal order into a hooded terrorist organization dedicated to the preservation of white supremacy. It punished freedmen who left their employers or complained of low wages or acted in an "insolent" manner toward whites. It whipped teachers of freedmen's schools and burned down their schoolhouses. But above all, Klansmen terrorized and murdered Republican leaders and voters. The Klan and similar groups, such as the Knights of the White Camelia, became in effect armed auxiliaries of the Democratic party.

The Klan professed to act in the name of law and order. "It is, indeed, unfortunate that [our people] should be compelled to have recourse to measures of violence and blood to do away with lawless tyrants and wrong-doers," declared a Louisiana newspaper. "But who is to blame? . . . Assuredly not we people of the South, who have suffered wrongs beyond endurance. Radicalism and negroism . . . are alone to blame. . . . These northern emissaries of advanced political ideas, and of progressive social reforms . . . have met the fate they deserved." In August 1868, General Forrest publicly warned Republican leaders that they would suffer dire consequences if they dared to use the militia against the Klan: "I have no powder to burn killing negroes. I intend to kill radicals. . . . There is not a radical leader in this town [Memphis] but is a marked man, and if trouble should break out, none of them would be left alive."[7]

During the 1868 campaign, the Klan and similar organizations were most active in Louisiana, Georgia, Arkansas, and Tennessee. Although Republicans managed to carry the last two states, they did so at a great cost. More than two hundred political murders were reported in Arkansas, including the ambush killing of a Republican congressman on October 22. The death toll in Georgia was lower, but the incidence of threats and beatings higher. These tactics kept thousands of Republicans from the polls. In twenty-two Georgia counties with a total registration of more than 9,300 black voters, Grant tallied only 87 votes. The Republicans received no votes at all in eleven Georgia counties. In this manner, a Republican majority of 7,000 in the April state election became a Democratic majority of 45,000 in the presidential election.

Even worse was Louisiana, where according to the subsequent report of a congressional committee, more than a thousand persons, mostly blacks, were killed between April and November 1868. Two riots near Shreveport left more than one hundred dead, and a major outbreak at Opelousas, in St. Landry Parish, produced an estimated death toll of two hundred. A Democratic leader in St. Landry believed that this affair had taught blacks a "wholesome lesson." He was evidently right, for on election day not a single Republican voted in the parish. Indeed, seven parishes that had cast a total of 4,707 Republican ballots in April recorded none in November. Twenty-one parishes with a previous Republican vote of 26,814 reported only 501 ballots for Grant. In the state as a whole, a Republican majority of 58 percent in April was transformed into a Democratic majority of 71 percent in November.

Although by these means the Democrats managed to carry Louisiana and Georgia and to cut down the Republican majority elsewhere in the South, this probably hurt the party in the North more than it helped in the South. It lent substance to Republican charges that Rebels and Copperheads were trying to achieve by terrorism what they had failed to achieve by war. The similarity of Northern voting patterns in 1868 to those of 1864 was remarkable. Grant received virtually the same proportion of the Northern vote (55 percent) as Lincoln had received in 1864. In scarcely any state did the vote change by more than one or two percentage points. Only 7 percent of the counties in the North switched from Democratic to Republican or vice versa. Seymour carried only three Northern states: Oregon, New Jersey, and New York, the last by one percentage point— as a result, probably, of Tammany frauds in New York City. Seymour won three of the five border states (Delaware, Maryland, and Kentucky) and two of the eight reconstructed Confederate states, giving him 80 electoral votes to Grant's 214. The Democrats made a slight net gain of congressional seats, but the Republicans retained majorities of two-thirds in the House and four-fifths in the Senate.

THE FIFTEENTH AMENDMENT

During the year after Grant's election, Congress remained preoccupied with the unfinished tasks of reconstruction. The most important of these was a constitutional amendment to enfranchise black men in every state. Without such an amendment, the future of black suffrage might be doubtful in Southern states where Democrats managed to regain control. Moreover, the inequity of requiring black suffrage in the South (by the Reconstruction Acts) but not in the North bothered many Republicans. "We have no moral right to impose an obligation on one part of the land which the rest will not accept," wrote a radical. "We can have no peace until this right is made national."[8]

Although Iowa and Minnesota finally adopted black suffrage by referendums in 1868, black men still lacked the right to vote in eleven of the twenty-one Northern states and all five of the border states. One-sixth of the country's black people lived in these states. Most of them would vote Republican if enfranchised. Therefore, as a Republican congressman pointed out, "party expediency and exact justice coincide for once."[9] Since Republicans controlled twenty-five of the thirty-three state legislatures (not including the unreconstructed states of Texas, Mississippi, Virginia, and Georgia*), they could secure ratification of a national constitutional amendment without having to face the obstacle of referendums, which had so often defeated state suffrage amendments.

The drafting of the Fifteenth Amendment consumed the short session of Congress that met between Grant's election and his inauguration on March 4, 1869. Three versions of the amendment emerged from a variety of proposals: the first version would forbid states to deny citizens the right to vote on grounds of race, color, or previous condition of servitude; the second would in addition forbid states to impose literacy, property, or nativity qualifications for suffrage; the third would affirm simply that all male citizens aged twenty-one years or older had the right to vote. Whereas the first two versions would merely impose restrictions on state power, the third envisaged a radical enlargement of national power.

After much tugging and hauling, Congress passed the first and most conservative version of the amendment. Many radicals feared that this version would not prevent Southern states from disfranchising most blacks by means of literacy or

*For the special case of Georgia, see p. 546.

property qualifications. "Let it remain possible," warned one congressman, "to still disfranchise the body of the colored race in the late rebel States and I tell you it will be done."[10] But moderates believed that anything stronger than a limited prohibition of discrimination on grounds of race might defeat ratification in the necessary three-fourths of the states: legislatures might balk at giving up most of their control over voting regulations; a good many Northerners as well as Southerners doubted the wisdom of a perpetual guarantee of the right to vote to illiterate men; and a ban on nativity restrictions might prevent ratification by the three far-West states, where anti-Chinese sentiment was rising. Thus the final form of the Fifteenth Amendment, which forbade states to deny the right to vote only on grounds of race, color, or previous condition, left loopholes that enabled Southern states a generation later to disfranchise the majority of their black voters. They accomplished this by subterfuges that were clearly contrary to the purpose of the Fifteenth Amendment, however, and could not have done so if the will to enforce the amendment that existed in 1869 had still existed in 1899.

Congress passed the Fifteenth Amendment on February 26, 1869. Within four months, the seventeen Republican legislatures then in session had ratified it and the four Democratic legislatures in session had rejected it. Whether the necessary ratification by eleven more states could be obtained when the rest of the legislatures met in the fall was uncertain. But the delay of reconstruction in Virginia, Mississippi, and Texas gave Congress an opportunity to strengthen the chances of ratification. The lawmakers required these three states to ratify the Fifteenth as well as the Fourteenth Amendment as a prerequisite for readmission. They did so, and all three states were restored in early 1870.

This left only Georgia in the limbo of nonstatehood. That state's congressmen had initially resumed their places in June 1868, but an egregious violation of the spirit of reconstruction had caused Congress to remand Georgia to military rule. The Georgia legislature in 1868 was evenly divided between Republicans and Conservatives. Some of the Southern white Republicans, however, soon defected to the Conservatives. These new allies expelled twenty-eight black legislators on the grounds that the state constitution did not specifically declare blacks eligible for office. Twenty-four of the legislators who voted for expulsion were later proved to be ineligible for office themselves under the disqualifying clause of the Fourteenth Amendment! Outraged congressional Republicans rescinded Georgia's readmission. The black members returned to the legislature, the ineligible whites departed, the legislature ratified the Fifteenth Amendment, and Georgia's representatives returned to Congress in 1870.

With Georgia's ratification, the Fifteenth Amendment became part of the Constitution on March 30, 1870. Many Republicans shared the conviction that this achievement was "the last great point that remained to be settled of the issues of the war." Now it was time to turn to other problems long neglected because of preoccupation with sectional strife. Ever since the annexation of Texas a quarter-century earlier, the nation had known scarcely a moment's respite from this strife. "Let us have done with Reconstruction," pleaded the *New York Tribune* in April 1870. "The country is tired and sick of it. . . . LET US HAVE PEACE."[11]

GRANT IN THE WHITE HOUSE

Few Presidents have carried more prestige and good will into the office than
Ulysses S. Grant. His supporters were eager to address the problems of currency
and finance, civil service reform, foreign policy, and other "new issues" demanding attention now that reconstruction was "settled." But Grant's own inexperi-
ence and errors of judgment, the venality of some of his associates, and above all
the persistent and apparently insolvable problems of reconstruction dashed the
hopes with which many Americans had viewed his inauguration.

Several of the new President's appointments to government positions gave rise
to complaints about nepotism and cronyism. Grant named some of his wife's
numerous relatives to office. Other posts, including several places on the White
House staff, went to former army colleagues. Two of the latter—General Orville
Babcock, Grant's private secretary, and General William Belknap, who became
secretary of war—were later charged with accepting bribes and left the government in disgrace. The President gave the impression of a lack of discernment in
his choice of associates. He seemed to admire aggressive rich men, and naively
accepted gifts or favors from them without realizing the potential implications of
doing so. At the same time, Grant was sometimes awkward and taciturn to the
point of brusqueness in the presence of the cultured men who were soon to form
the vanguard of reform movements to make government honest and efficient.

Some of these problems came to light in connection with the bizarre effort of
two Wall Street buccaneers to corner the gold market in 1869. During Grant's
first days in office, Congress passed a Public Credit Act promising redemption of
all government bonds in gold or its equivalent and pledging to bring greenbacks
to par with gold "at the earliest practicable period." But for the time being gold
dollars still enjoyed a premium of about 130. Fluctuations in this premium attracted speculators. Two notorious characters engaged in such speculation were
Jay Gould and Jim Fisk. The previous year these *enfants terribles* of Wall Street
had won control of the Erie Railroad after a spectacular financial battle with
Cornelius Vanderbilt that had featured, among other things, the bribery of legislators, the suborning of a judge, and the illegal issue of hundreds of thousands of
shares of Erie stock. With their profits from this exploit, Gould and Fisk hoped
to corner the gold market and make a killing from the Wall Street bears who had
sold short.

But the U.S. Treasury's policy of selling specified amounts of gold monthly
stood in their way. To remove this obstacle, Gould planned to use a fellow Wall
Street speculator and brother-in-law of the President, Abel R. Corbin, to persuade
the government to suspend gold sales. Corbin introduced Grant to Gould and
Fisk, who entertained the President on their yacht and at a New York theatre
owned partly by Fisk. Gould outlined for Grant an elaborate theory whereby a rise
in the price of gold would help American farmers by lowering the dollar price of
wheat in European markets—thereby increasing exports. The President was non-
committal, but Corbin assured Gould that the government would suspend gold
sales.

Gould and Fisk thereupon began to buy gold with abandon, driving the premium up to 144 by September 23. On Black Friday, September 24, panic reigned at the New York gold exchange, where the price of gold had risen to 162. Meanwhile Grant had become suspicious. He ordered Secretary of the Treasury George Boutwell to sell $4 million of gold. This broke the market. The price quickly tumbled to 133, leaving several brokers and speculators ruined in its wake. Gould avoided disaster by selling at the top of the market, and Fisk by repudiating several of his contracts. The whole affair left a bad smell in Washington and New York. By acting promptly when they learned the truth of Gould's schemes, Grant and Boutwell escaped taint. But though the President was not implicated, his unwise fraternization with Gould and Fisk and the discreditable role played by brother-in-law Corbin tarnished the administration's image.

POSTWAR DIPLOMACY

The Alabama Claims

In foreign policy, the Grant administration achieved one great success and one fiasco. The success was the settlement of damage claims against Britain for the wartime destruction caused by the *Alabama* and other British-built Confederate cruisers. The United States accused Britain of negligence and violation of neutral obligations in allowing these ships to be built. Damage claims by American owners of destroyed ships and cargoes amounted to more than $15 million. But the British government refused to admit responsibility. For several years, strained relations existed between the two countries. Newspapers on both sides of the Atlantic traded bellicose threats.

During the final months of Andrew Johnson's administration, the United States and Britain negotiated a treaty for adjudication of these *"Alabama* claims." But the terms of the treaty leaned toward the British interpretation, so the United States Senate rejected it in April 1869 by a vote of fifty-four to one. Charles Sumner, chairman of the Senate Foreign Relations Committee, used this occasion to make a belligerent speech in which he demanded reparation not only for direct damages but also for "indirect damages," including prolongation of the war by British actions and by Southern expectations of British intervention. Sumner hinted that the cession of Canada would be a fair indemnity for these indirect damages. Although no precedent for indirect damages existed in diplomacy or international law, Sumner's extreme demands evoked a sympathetic response from many Americans who still resented Britain's role in the Civil War.

Sumner's speech upped the ante to a point that appeared to doom hopes for a negotiation of the *Alabama* claims. For more than a year no apparent progress took place on this matter. But behind the scenes Secretary of State Hamilton Fish, scion of a prominent New York family who was Grant's best cabinet appointee, worked quietly to reopen negotiations. The outbreak of the Franco-Prussian War in July 1870 forced the precedent-conscious British to think about the consequences for their merchant marine if Britain should be drawn into a war and a neutral United States should build commerce raiders for an enemy power. Meanwhile, Sumner had broken with the administration over the annexation of Santo Domingo (which is discussed later in this section). To punish the senator for this and to neutralize his power to block a compromise on the *Alabama* claims, Republican senators who supported the administration deposed Sumner from his chairmanship of the Foreign Relations Committee in March 1871. Fish worked out the creation of a Joint High Commission to negotiate terms for settlement of the *Alabama* claims and of other differences between the two countries. In May 1871 the commission completed the Treaty of Washington, which established an international tribunal to arbitrate American claims. The British made several concessions in this treaty, including an expression of regret for the depredations of the *Alabama* and other ships built in Britain.

The U.S. Senate promptly ratified the Treaty of Washington. The tribunal that met at Geneva in December 1871 consisted of arbitrators from the United States (Charles Francis Adams), Britain, Switzerland, Italy, and Brazil. The Americans pressed extravagant claims before this body. They maintained that indirect damages should include the entire cost of the war after July 4, 1863, on the grounds that only British support enabled the South to go on fighting after Gettysburg and Vicksburg. The outraged British threatened to withdraw from arbitration altogether if the Americans persisted with this "preposterous" argument. Fish and Adams quietly let it be known that the United States would not insist on indirect damages. With American acquiescence, the neutral members of the tribunal ruled out indirect claims. By a four-to-one vote (Britain dissenting) the arbitrators in September 1872 finally declared that the British government had failed to exercise "due diligence" to prevent the building and arming of the *Alabama, Florida,* and *Shenandoah,* and awarded the United States $15.5 million for the damage done by these ships. It was a victory for American diplomacy, for the peaceful settlement of international disputes, and for an improvement in Anglo-American relations.

The Santo Domingo Affair

Grant's foreign policy fiasco was the attempt to annex Santo Domingo (today the Dominican Republic). This project grew out of a revival of Manifest Destiny following the triumph of American nationalism in the Civil War. Many Republicans now shared what had once been primarily a Democratic sentiment. Secretary of State Seward's purchase of Alaska from Russia in 1867 set a precedent for the acquisition of noncontiguous territory. The Civil War had demonstrated the need for an American naval base in the Caribbean, so Seward also negotiated a treaty with Denmark for the purchase of the Virgin Islands. The Senate killed this treaty, but the idea of expansion into the Caribbean did not die.

The characters involved in the scheme to annex Santo Domingo seemed to step out of the pages of Mark Twain and Charles Dudley Warner's satirical novel *The Gilded Age.* Land speculators, commercial developers, promoters of fabulous gold and silver mines, and naval officers who wanted a Caribbean base and dreamed of an Isthmian canal formed a Dominican lobby in Washington. The wily Dominican dictator, Bonaventura Baez, favored American annexation to bolster his power against revolutionary elements. Less self-interested supporters of annexation in the United States, including Grant himself, believed that American ownership would bring peace and stability to a country of chronic revolutions, develop its rich resources, open the gateway for the extension of beneficent American influence throughout the Caribbean, and get the Isthmian canal project started.

The more Grant thought about it, the more desirable annexation became. He hoped to make it the showpiece foreign policy achievement of his administration. But his lack of political experience betrayed him. He acted as if he were still a general who needed only to give orders, instead of a president who must line up political support for an objective. Without consulting congressional leaders or the cabinet, Grant in July 1869 sent his private secretary, Orville Babcock, to Santo Domingo to investigate the possibilities. The enthusiastic Babcock exceeded his instructions and brought back a treaty of annexation. Ignoring the irregularities of this procedure, Grant presented the treaty to his astonished cabinet. Secretary of State Fish, who was cool to the whole idea, said nothing. Other members of the cabinet did the same. Finally, Secretary of the Interior Jacob Cox broke the embarrassed silence. "But, Mr. President, has it been settled, then, that we *want* to annex Santo Domingo?"[12]

It was settled in Grant's mind. He sent Babcock back to Santo Domingo with State Department authorization to renegotiate the treaty in a proper fashion. Babcock did so, returning a second time with a treaty that made Santo Domingo a U.S. territory and declared her 120,000 people to be American citizens, all at a bargain price of $1.5 million. A plebiscite of Santo Domingans approved annexation. In January 1870 Grant proudly submitted the treaty to the Senate—where the trouble began.

Charles Sumner's Foreign Relations Committee reported the treaty adversely. Sumner and Carl Schurz, now a senator from Missouri, led the antiannexation forces on the Senate floor. They castigated the corrupt promoters who had bought up land in the expectation of windfall profits from annexation. They invoked the traditional Whig/Republican hostility to expansion. Schurz questioned the wisdom of incorporating a new mixed-blood Catholic population into a polity that already had more than enough trouble with racial problems. Sumner feared that the acquisition of Santo Domingo would threaten the independence of neighboring Haiti, which except for Liberia was the only self-governing black republic in the world. "These islands by climate, occupation, and destiny . . . belong to the colored people," said Sumner. "We should not take them away. No greed of land should prevail against the rights of this race."[13]

Angered by this opposition, Grant lobbied personally with senators in behalf of the treaty. He insisted that annexation would benefit the poverty-stricken black people of both Santo Domingo and Haiti by bringing American capital, enterprise, and political institutions to the island. Grant privately denounced Sumner in harsh terms. This unhappy breach between President and senator was exacerbated by a heavy-handed administration effort to obtain protreaty votes from Southern Republican senators, who might otherwise have been inclined to follow

Sumner's lead. Attorney General E. Rockwood Hoar, a Massachusetts friend and ally of Sumner, had offended Southern Republicans with some of his appointments of federal attorneys and marshals. Hoar was also at odds with Benjamin Butler, an administration ally and emerging factional leader in the Massachusetts Republican party. To gratify Butler and secure Southern votes for the treaty, Grant dismissed Hoar on June 15, 1870, and replaced him with an obscure Georgian, Amos Akerman. The President also obliged Senator Roscoe Conkling, a treaty supporter, by appointing one of Conkling's political lieutenants to the patronage-rich collectorship of the New York port—an appointment that later bore rotten fruit in a corruption scandal. These maneuvers availed little except to alienate a growing number of Republicans from the administration. On June 30, 1870, the Senate defeated the treaty by a tie vote of 28–28, with 19 Republicans joining the 9 Democrats in opposition.

A bitter President took revenge on Sumner by dismissing the senator's protégé John Lothrop Motley from his post as minister to Britain. The administration justified this action on the grounds that Motley, like Sumner, was hindering a settlement of the *Alabama* claims by his extreme position. But Sumner's friends interpreted it—correctly—as an attempt to punish the senator. The open warfare between Grant and Sumner became more savage during the winter of 1870–1871. Grant stubbornly reopened the question of annexing Santo Domingo, even though his Senate supporters conceded that the project was dead. Seizing the opportunity, Sumner excoriated the President in a Senate speech that accused Grant of following in the footsteps of Franklin Pierce, James Buchanan, and Andrew Johnson. This was too much. Soon after Sumner's speech, proadministration senators deposed him as chairman of the Foreign Relations Committee.

These events seriously divided the Republican party. Both sides in the squabble over Santo Domingo had demonstrated traits of petty vindictiveness. Sumner's vain ego and righteous moralism seemed to grow more excessive with age. But to many of the senator's friends among the old Free Soilers and Conscience Whigs, Grant's vendetta seemed to be an attack on the idealism that had made the Republican party great. They feared that the party was falling into the hands of spoilsmen and opportunists such as Conkling and Butler who had no roots in the antislavery movement and no commitment to moral ideals. This breach between "old" and "new" Republicans (to oversimplify a complex reality) was widened by the movement for civil service reform that gained momentum during Grant's first administration.

CIVIL SERVICE REFORM

The "spoils system"—by which the victors in an election rewarded party workers with appointments to public office—was one of the most venerable institutions in American politics. The hope of office was the glue that kept the party faithful together when the party was out of power. An assessment of 2 or 3 percent on government salaries kept party coffers filled when in power. But in the 1860s, a growing number of reformers attacked this system as wasteful and corrupt. They urged that government officials be appointed on the basis of merit rather than party fidelity. To accomplish this goal, Representative Thomas Jenckes of Rhode Island introduced at every session of Congress from 1865 to 1871 a bill to create a civil service commission to administer competitive examinations for appointment to office. Although Jenckes's bill never got out of committee, support for some kind of action continued to grow, until civil service reform became one of the most powerful reform movements of the 1870s.

Its proponents were mainly well-educated men in professional occupations who resided in the Northeast. Most of them were Republicans, identified with the old Conscience Whig element of the party. They admired the incorruptible efficiency of the British civil service and wanted to emulate it. Professional politicians looked askance at such notions. To them, patronage was the lifeblood of democracy. They accused the reformers of elitism, and ridiculed them as dilettantes trying to play at the serious business of politics.

At the beginning of Grant's administration, reformers had high hopes for this nonpolitical President. Grant seemed to share their reform sentiments. Like all new occupants of the White House, he suffered the unwanted entreaties of swarms of office seekers. "Patronage is the bane of the Presidential office," Grant told a friend. "There is no man in the country so anxious for civil service reform as the President. . . . He is necessarily a civil service reformer because he wants peace of mind."[14]

But Grant's record on this issue was, at best, mixed. On the positive side, Secretary of the Treasury Boutwell, Secretary of the Interior Cox, and Attorney General Hoar instituted impartial examinations for certain kinds of promotions and appointments in their departments. Grant's annual message to Congress in December 1870 urged reform legislation. Although the lawmakers balked at this, they did pass a joint resolution authorizing the President to appoint a commission to prescribe new rules for civil service appointments. To head the commission, Grant named George William Curtis, editor of *Harper's Weekly* and a leading reformer. The commission recommended competitive examinations for various grades of civil service positions. It also urged the abolition of party assessments on salaries. Grant promulgated the regulations by executive order to go into effect on January 1, 1872. But Congress refused to appropriate sufficient funds to enable the Civil Service Commission to enforce the new rules effectively. Although some government departments implemented part of the regulations, a thoroughgoing reform of the spoils system was not achieved in the 1870s.

Those Republicans in Congress who had been most closely identified with Grant in the Santo Domingo affair also played a prominent role in crippling the Civil Service Commission. This raised doubts among reformers about the President's sincerity on the issue. Several of Grant's appointments to the customs service and to the internal revenue service disappointed reformers. And the naked use of patronage and the sacrifice of Attorney General Hoar in the Santo Domingo treaty fight appalled them. In October 1870 came another shock: the conscientious Secretary of the Interior Jacob Cox resigned after a bitter fight with spoilsmen who were trying to subvert his appointments policy. Congressman James

Garfield said of this development: "It is a clear case of surrender on the part of the President to the political vermin which infest the government and keep it in a state of perpetual lousiness."[15]

The Roots of Liberal Republicanism

Cox, Hoar, Sumner, Motley—to reformers it looked as if the President was sacrificing the best elements of the party to its worst elements. By 1871 a new noun, "Grantism," had entered the language. It stood for all the things that reformers thought were wrong with postwar America: spoilsmanship and corruption in government; crude taste and anti-intellectualism in culture; dishonesty in business; and a boundless materialism, a get-rich-quick acquisitiveness of the sort satirized by Mark Twain and Charles Dudley Warner in their 1873 novel, whose title—*The Gilded Age*—gave a name to the era.

It was, of course, unfair to saddle Grant with responsibility for these things. He was personally honest; he genuinely desired reform; and his administration deserved credit for several important achievements. Moreover, the corruption in the federal government paled in comparison with knavery elsewhere. The pilfering in the New York customs house was not in the same league with the massive depredations of the Tweed Ring in the same city. The New York legislature was a notorious marketplace for the buying and selling of politicians. It was said of the Pennsylvania legislature that the Standard Oil Company could do anything with it except to refine it. The postwar relaxation of tensions and the explosive economic growth following the 1867 recession heightened speculative fever and loosened standards in the whole society. The wartime expansion of the government bureaucracy and of government contracts had opened new vistas for the unscrupulous. At the same time, the emergence of a strong postwar reform movement focused a harsh light on dark corners of corruption hitherto unillumined because of preoccupation with the sectional problem. During the Grant administration, many government agencies actually made progress toward eliminating abuses that had flourished in the Johnson and even in the Lincoln administrations.

Whether unfair or not, however, Grant became the scapegoat for many of the perceived ills of the country—an experience not unfamiliar to more recent presidents. His association with Jay Gould and Jim Fisk and with some of the unsavory promoters of Santo Domingo's annexation, his vendetta against Sumner, and the apparently growing influence of such men as Conkling and Butler in his administration sparked a revolt by reform Republicans. They hoped at first to win control of the party, purge the spoilsmen, and replace Grant with a reform nominee for president in 1872. But this proved impossible, so the reformers bolted the party and organized their own "Liberal Republican" party. Their goal, as Carl Schurz phrased it in his keynote address to the Liberal Republican convention in 1872, was to create a government "which the best people of this country will be proud of."[16] (For more on the Liberal Republicans, see pp. 567ff.)

When Liberals looked to the South, they discovered that some of the "best people" there were former Confederates, many of them disqualified from holding office or otherwise denied power by Republican regimes. From the Liberal viewpoint, Grantism in the South was as bad as Grantism in Washington. "Carpetbag-Negro government" and "bayonet rule" became the foremost issues in the 1872 presidential election.

Thirty

The Southern Question, 1869-1872

SOUTHERN REPUBLICANS: BLACKS, CARPETBAGGERS, AND SCALAWAGS

The Southern Republican party during Reconstruction was unique in the history of American politics. The party had no indigenous roots in the region. Most whites perceived it as an alien instrument of hateful change. In the North the Republican party represented the most prosperous, educated, and influential elements of the population; in the South most of its adherents were poor, illiterate, powerless—and black. The wonder is not that the Southern Republicans were ousted from power after only a few years, but that they ever held power at all.

About 80 percent of the Southern Republican voters were black men. Although most of them were landless ex-slaves, their leaders came primarily from the elite strata of the black community. Of the black men elected to state or federal office, at least four-fifths were literate and more than one-quarter had been free before the war. Several had been born and educated in the North. About two-fifths practiced professional occupations, with clergymen forming the largest single category; nearly a third were farmers, most of them owning the land they farmed; more than a quarter were artisans or small businessmen (carpenters, tailors, etc.). Although less is known about the blacks who held local office, the proportion of professionals and antebellum free men appears to have been lower and the proportion of farmers, artisans, and illiterate men higher than among those who filled state and federal positions.

Of the fourteen black congressmen and two black senators elected in the South from 1868 through 1876, all but three had obtained some secondary school education. Four had attended college. Several black state officeholders had also enjoyed exceptional educational opportunities. Jonathan Gibbs, secretary of state in Florida from 1868 to 1872 and state superintendent of education from 1872 to 1874, was a prewar graduate of Dartmouth College and of Princeton Theological Seminary. Francis L. Cardozo, who served as South Carolina's secretary of state for four years and as state treasurer for another four, had attended the University of Glasgow and theological schools in Edinburgh and London.

Neither the black leaders nor their constituents were so ignorant or incompetent as the traditional image of Reconstruction has portrayed them. It is true that four-fifths of the black voters and perhaps one-quarter of the black officeholders could not read and write. The fault for this, however, lay not with Reconstruction but with the old regime that had denied them education. Although contemporary accounts cited examples of black men who went to the polls with a basket to carry home the promised "vote," and of county treasurers who could neither read nor count, such stories provide a distorted picture of reality. The abilities of most black officials equaled the responsibilities of their offices. And most black voters understood what they were doing. Illiteracy did not preclude such an understanding for blacks, any more than it did for Irish immigrants in the North. Participation in Union League meetings and the experience of voting were themselves a form of education. "We are not prepared for this suffrage," conceded William Beverly Nash, an untutored ex-slave delegate to the South Carolina constitutional convention in 1868. "But we can learn. Give a man tools and let him commence to use them, and in time he will learn a trade. So it is with voting. We may not understand it at the start, but in time we shall learn to do our duty."[1] Whatever the shortcomings of black politicians and voters during Reconstruction, these men could hardly be said to have served their states worse than did their white predecessors who led the South into disaster in 1861.

Linked to the myth of black incompetence was the legend of the "Africanization" of Southern governments during Reconstruction. A Northern journalist, James Shepherd Pike, presented a classic indictment of "Negro rule" in his 1873 book about South Carolina entitled *The Prostrate State*. Describing the state house of representatives, Pike wrote:

> The Speaker is black, the Clerk is black, the door-keepers are black, the little pages are black, the chairman of the Ways and Means is black, and the chaplain is coal-black. At some of the desks sit colored men whose types it would be hard to find outside of Congo. . . . It is the dregs of the population habilitated in the robes of their intelligent predecessors, and asserting over them the rule of ignorance and coruption. . . . It is barbarism overwhelming civilization by . . . the rude form of the most ignorant democracy the world ever saw.[2]

This theme of "Negro supremacy," by which the "barbarous African" exercised "uncontrolled power" in ten Southern states, was a staple of Democratic propaganda. It became enshrined in many textbooks and in the popular memory of Reconstruction.

In sober truth, however, blacks held no more than 15 or 20 percent of the offices even at the height of Reconstruction in the early 1870s. Only 6 percent of the Southern congressmen from 1868 to 1877 were black. Although several black men served as lieutenant governors, secretaries of state, and state treasurers, none was ever nominated or elected governor. Only one black man, Jonathan J. Wright of South Carolina, became a justice of a state supreme court. And only in South Carolina did blacks hold office in numbers approaching their proportion of the population. In the state legislature, 61 percent of the representatives and 42 percent of the senators from 1868 through 1876 were black. Blacks held 52 percent of all state and federal elective offices in South Carolina during those years. In no other state legislature did blacks ever have a majority in either house. Such was the reality of "Negro rule."

Although whites cast only about 20 percent of the Southern Republican votes, they dominated the party's leadership. Settlers from the North provided about 30 percent of the Republican officeholders while contributing at most 2 or 3 percent of the Republican votes. These carpetbaggers did even better in the higher offices: more than half the Republican governors and nearly half the Republican congressmen and U.S. senators were migrants from the North.

"Carpetbagger" and "scalawag" are among the most pejorative words in the American political lexicon. This book will use these terms, without their pejorative connotations, because they have become part of the language of history. The term scalawag supposedly came from Scalloway, a tiny Scottish island noted for its scrubby cattle and horses. To Southern Democrats, "scalawag" seemed an eminently suitable word to describe Southern whites who joined the Republicans, for such men were "vile, blatant, vindictive, unprincipled . . . the mean, lousy and filthy kind that are not fit for butchers or dogs." Democrats professed to prefer "the blackest man that can be found to the vilest renegades of the South . . . those who have dishonored the dignity of the white blood, and are traitors alike to principle and race." Carpetbaggers acquired their cognomen from the carpetbags containing their worldly goods that they allegedly carried southward on their way to plunder a helpless people. "Gangs of itinerant adventurers, vagrant interlopers," as Southerners described them, they were "too depraved, dissolute, dishonest and degraded to get the lowest of places in the states they had just left."[3]

Although some scalawags and carpetbaggers fitted these stereotypes, most did not. On the average, Southern Republican leaders were neither more nor less honest and able than their counterparts in the other party or in other regions. If anything, they possessed more courage and—particularly in the case of the carpetbaggers—more idealism than the average politician, for they served in the front lines of progressive and unpopular change.

Most of the carpetbaggers were Union army officers who had stayed on in the South after the war. Some served as Freedmen's Bureau agents; some were teachers or superintendents of freedmen's schools; others liked the climate or the economic opportunities in the new frontier of the postwar South and decided to settle there. Nearly two-thirds of the carpetbag congressmen and senators practiced a profession—law, medicine, engineering, or teaching. Half of the senators were college graduates. Indeed, the carpetbaggers may have been the best-educated group of Americans in politics, North or South. Many of them brought not skimpy carpetbags but rather considerable capital, which they invested in the

South. They also invested human capital—themselves—in a drive to modernize the region's social structure, revive its crippled economy, and democratize its politics. If this crusade provoked Southern hostility, carpetbaggers knew that as members of an invading army they had not been exactly welcomed to the region in the first place.

Many scalawags shared the carpetbaggers' vision of a new South. The Republicans, said a North Carolina scalawag, were the "party of progress, of education, of development. . . . Yankees and Yankee notions are just what we want in this country. We want their capital to build factories and work shops, and railroads. . . . We want their energy and enterprise to operate these factories, and to teach us how to do it." An Arkansas scalawag asked voters: "Do you want good roads throughout your state? Do you want free bridges? Do you want free schools and the advantages of education for your children?" If you do, he concluded, vote Republican.[4]

Scalawags were recruited largely from the Unionists of 1860–1861. Most of them lived in the upland counties of eastern Tennessee, western North Carolina and Virginia, and northern Georgia, Alabama, and Arkansas. They had never liked the plantation regime and were as likely to have fought against the Confederacy as for it. They became Republicans because the party promised to overthrow the power of the planter class. A Republican handbill of 1868 addressed to the "Poor White Men of Georgia" expressed this sentiment: "Let the slave-holding aristocracy no longer rule you. Vote for a constitution which educates your children free of charge; relieves the poor debtor from his rich creditor; allows a liberal homestead for your families; and more than all, places you on a level with those who used to boast that for every slave they were entitled to three-fifths of a vote in congressional representation."[5]

Republicans also drew some support from former Whigs in the black belt and in the cities. Reluctant secessionists in 1861, many of these men were loath to join the Democrats after the war. Heirs of the futile antebellum attempts to foster Southern commercial and industrial development, these erstwhile Whigs turned to the Republicans as the party of modernization. Eight of the ten white Republican counties in Mississippi adjoined two new railroad lines built to open up a lumbering industry. Whiggish scalawag leaders in Alabama expected Republicans to promote "the revival of industry and prosperity" by mobilizing private and public capital. "Unite north and south Alabama by railroads," wrote a scalawag editor, "and do it by state aid, as a great State necessity."[6]

Thus the Southern Republican party in 1870 was a fragile coalition of blacks and whites, natives of the South and the North, hill-country yeomen and low-country entrepreneurs, illiterates and college graduates. The party was weakest along the seams where these disparate elements joined. Scalawags were particularly prone to defection because of their vulnerability to the charge of racial treason. For a Southern white man to defy the mores of his society required courage and conviction. An old friend of one scalawag refused to speak to him because "any white man who will go around with nigger clubs is too low to speak to a gentleman." A Mississippi Republican wrote sadly in 1872: "Even my own kinspeople have turned the cold shoulder to me because I hold office under a Republican administration."[7]

Democrats did their best to rip the Republicans apart along the racial seam. "THE GREAT and paramount issue is: SHALL NEGROES or WHITE MEN RULE NORTH CAROLINA?" proclaimed the state's leading Conservative newspaper. "All other issues are . . . subordinate and should be kept so." Such tactics whittled away scalawag strength. "It is hard . . . to carry the eternal nigger," confessed one white Republican. Black candidates for office hurt the Republicans' chances with white voters. "Should the negroes insist on having a negro on the ticket," said a North Carolina scalawag in 1868, "it will kill it dead."[8]

Sensitive to this problem, many black leaders initially maintained a low profile. But as time passed, they began to insist on a role more commensurate with their voting strength. "Are not in all States, and in all parties, the classes who have the largest majorities first considered?" asked a black South Carolinian in 1870. "No people have become a great people who had not their own leaders."[9]

This drive for black power produced an increasing number of black officeholders for a few years after 1870. But it also eroded white Republican strength, especially in states and counties with black majorities, where scalawags soon began to defect to the Conservatives.* The whites who tended to stay with the Republican party the longest were those in the upland regions where there were fewer blacks, and the carpetbaggers. As outsiders, carpetbaggers were less susceptible to local pressures; with antebellum roots in the Republican party, they would not easily turn their coats. Since many of them had worked for black education and equal rights, they were not likely to be shocked by the sight of black men in office. "The radicals of northern birth," noted a Tennessee Republican, "having naturally more anti-slavery feeling . . . [than] native Tennessee loyalists are more ready to sustain new rights or claim new privileges for the blacks than the other section of the radical party and as a result . . . have a larger share of the confidence of the colored population."[10]

This did not mean that harmony and sweetness prevailed between carpetbaggers and blacks. On the contrary, tensions among them often erupted into verbal conflict. Black leaders accused carpetbaggers of paternalism for wishing to limit blacks to minor offices. For their part, some carpetbaggers predicted disaster if black Republicans tried to break away from white tutelage too soon. "There is not," wrote a South Carolina carpetbagger in 1871, "enough virtue and intelligence among the Blacks to conduct the government in such a way as will promote peace and prosperity."[11]

But the frictions between carpetbaggers and blacks paled in comparison with those between carpetbaggers and scalawags. More radical than native white Republicans on racial issues, the Northerners sometimes voted with blacks on such sensitive matters as the desegregation of public accommodations and schools. Other, less ideological, frictions grew out of internal party battles for power and

---

*Most Democratic organizations in the South continued for several years to call themselves "Conservative" or "Democratic and Conservative" to ease the transition for erstwhile Whigs.

patronage. "Our Federal office Holders [are] composed almost entirely of the
Carpet Bag class," complained a North Carolina scalawag. "Deserving men
. . . and first rate politicians of our own people are thrust aside to keep these men
in power." A prominent white Republican in Alabama echoed this lament. "What
can a native Union man do, expect, or calculate on in the future? The Carpetbaggers have already landed everything that is Republican in Hell. . . . The political
offices, University, Schools, all carpetbagged!"[12]

Another weak seam in the Republican fabric joined the predominantly mulatto
antebellum free Negroes and the largely black ex-slaves. In Louisiana and South
Carolina, the early monopolization of black leadership by the mulatto class
aroused the color and class tensions never far from the surface in the black
community. Mulatto-black frictions sometimes became more serious than black-
white divisions in the party. A mulatto candidate for the 1868 constitutional
convention in South Carolina reportedly said: "If ever there is a nigger government—an unmixed nigger government—established in South Carolina, I shall
move." On the other side, a black leader said of the mulattoes: "To what race do
they belong? . . . I know that my ancestors trod the burning sands of Africa, but
why should men in whose veins run a great preponderance of white blood seek
to specially ally themselves with the black man, prate of 'our race,' when they are
simply mongrels."[13]

In contrast with these internal Republican divisions, Southern Democrats became increasingly united during the early 1870s. As "outs" pursuing the single
goal of expelling the hated black/carpetbag governments, they achieved a concord
that eluded the unstable Republican coalition. A study of the relative cohesion*
of each party in the South Carolina legislature found that from 1868 to 1876, the
Democrats maintained an average score of 75 percent compared with the Republicans' 45 percent.[14]

In nearly every state, a significant number of Republicans went over to the
Democrats/Conservatives in at least one important election. This paved the way
for the "redemption" (a Democratic term) of one state after another by conservative coalitions. The redemption process began with Virginia in 1869;
Tennessee followed later in the same year, North Carolina and Alabama in 1870
(though Republicans regained control of the latter in 1872, only to lose it again
in 1874), Georgia in 1871, Texas in 1873, and Arkansas in 1874. Although the
Republicans' national victory in the 1872 election temporarily interrupted this
process, the party's strength in the South ebbed from the outset of radical
Reconstruction.

SOUTHERN REPUBLICANS IN POWER

During their brief tenure in office, however, Southern Republicans did score some
modernizing advances. They established statewide public school systems for both

*A political science concept that measures the degree to which members of the same party vote alike on
legislative roll calls.

races, and provided state aid to railroad construction.* They continued the work of rebuilding levees, bridges, roads, public buildings, and other facilities destroyed by the war. They created industrial commissions to attract investment in Southern enterprises. They reorganized and modernized the judicial system. In some states they passed civil rights and antidiscrimination laws that, though seldom enforced, nevertheless evinced at least a theoretical commitment to racial equality.

Many of these achievements cost money—more money than Southern states had ever spent in peacetime. Emancipation nearly doubled the number of citizens requiring state services. A public school system had to be built almost from scratch, and though the Freedmen's Bureau and Northern freedmen's aid societies provided financial help in the initial stages, the schools still absorbed large amounts of state funds. The rehabilitation of war-ravaged properties and loans to railroads soaked up much more. As a consequence, state and county expenditures, taxes, and debts mushroomed during the early years of Republican rule. Tax rates in 1870 were three or four times as high as in 1860. Although Southern taxes in the 1870s were no higher on the average than those in rural Midwestern states, the war had destroyed wealth and slashed property values and thereby reduced the Southern tax base. Emancipation had further reduced it, for a significant source of revenue under the old regime had been a tax on slaves. Thus the small white landowner paid a larger share of a larger taxation than he had done under slavery. This alone soured many whites on the Republicans. Property owners formed taxpayers associations in nearly every Southern state to demand retrenchment. Their inability or refusal to pay taxes crippled schools and social services, and the ensuing fiscal chaos discredited Republican state governments in the eyes of many Northerners as well as Southerners.

The Corruption Issue

The much-advertised corruption of Reconstruction regimes also discredited the Republicans. "Such a Saturnalia of robbery and jobbery has seldom been seen in any civilized country," wrote a contemporary observer soon after the end of Reconstruction. "As voting power lay with those who were wholly unfit for citizenship, and had no interest, as taxpayers, in good government . . . greed was unchecked and roguery unabashed." This interpretation became engraved as historical truth. "Saddled with an irresponsible officialdom," wrote one scholar in a passage typical of most historical analyses until the 1950s, "the South was now plunged into debauchery, corruption, and private plundering unbelievable—suggesting that government had been transformed into an engine of destruction."[15]†

Seldom has the truth been so distorted. To be sure, many of the Reconstruction governments were scarcely models of efficiency or honesty. Railroad promoters bribed legislators and governors for favored treatment. Officials awarded inflated

*These two activities are discussed in the next chapter.
†For a perceptive review of the traditional historical scholarship on this question, see Kenneth M. Stampp, *The Era of Reconstruction 1865–1877* (New York, 1965), chap. 1.

contracts to friends and accepted kickbacks as their reward. Some of the funds for schools and public services stuck to the fingers of administrators. The state lottery in Louisiana seemed to corrupt everyone it touched. State printing contracts became a lucrative business: in South Carolina the printing costs for the eight-year period 1868–1876 exceeded total printing expenditures for the preceding eighty years. The South Carolina legislature voted a bonus of $1,000 to the Speaker of the House after he had reportedly lost that amount at a horse race. South Carolina's governors Robert Scott (1868–1872) and Franklin Moses (1872–1874) probably deserved much of the calumny heaped on their heads.

But Louisiana's carpetbag governor Henry Clay Warmoth (1868–1872), perhaps the most calumniated of all, may have been more sinned against than sinning. Corruption certainly flourished in Louisiana during his administration. But so had it flourished earlier, and so would it continue to flourish long afterward. Warmoth probably did as much or more to stem corruption as to participate in it. In 1870 he told a delegation from New Orleans that had petitioned for good government:

> You charge the Legislature with passing, corruptly, many bills looking to the personal aggrandizement of individuals and corporations. Let me suggest to you that these individuals and corporations are your very best people. For instance, this bank bill that is being lobbied through the Legislature now by the hardest kind of work. We have been able to defeat this bill twice in the House, and now it is up again. Who are doing it? Your bank presidents . . . whispering bribes into these men's ears to pass this measure. How are we to defend the State against the interposition of these people who are potent in their influence?

On another occasion, Warmoth told a congressional committee: "These much-abused members of the Louisiana legislature are at all events as good as the people they represent. Why, damn it, everybody is demoralizing down here. Corruption is the fashion."[16]

As Warmoth suggested, Republican corruption must be put in perspective. For one thing, many Democrats participated in and profited from it. A Democratic editor in Georgia confessed: "It is a mortifying fact that the extravagance of [Governor Rufus] Bullock's administration—we say nothing as to the corruption —benefitted about as many Democrats as Republicans."[17] For another, much that was accounted corruption could better be described as the inefficiency of inexperienced governments trying to deal with unprecedented problems amid the chaos of the postwar South. Moreover, some of the "extravagance" of Reconstruction governments was a fiction. The state debts provide an illustration. Contemporary writers and historians alike have wrung their hands in despair at the apparently huge increases in these debts. In 1867, at the beginning of Republican Reconstruction, the total indebtedness of the eleven Southern states was about $175 million. During the next four years it rose to $305 million. But when this increase of $130 million is analyzed, nearly $100 million turns out to have consisted of state endorsements of railroad bonds. For the states, these were contingent debts secured by liens on railroad property. If the railroads defaulted, as some did, their assets became the property of the state to be applied against the indebtedness. State endorsement of railroad bonds had long been a common practice in both North and South. During Reconstruction the Southern states experienced little real increase in their indebtedness from these ventures, while they ultimately benefited from the railroad expansion that resulted.

Finally, the graft that took place in the South must be set in a national context. All the Southern governments combined probably stole less from the taxpayers than did the Tweed Ring in New York. The South Carolina and Louisiana legislatures were more exotic but perhaps no more corrupt than those of New York and Pennsylvania. Southern railroad "rings" could not hold a candle to the operations of Jim Fisk and Jay Gould with the Erie Railroad. The postwar era of relaxed standards and entrepreneurial aggressiveness affected the South as it affected the rest of the country.

The Amnesty Question

In truth, Southern Democrats abhorred *corrupt* government less than *Republican* government. An honest Republican regime was in some respects more alarming than a dishonest one, for it belied their accusations of black incompetence and carpetbag roguery. The charges of corruption were part of a Democratic campaign to discredit Southern Republicans. The campaign succeeded because a good many Northerners were prepared to believe black people incapable of responsible participation in government. Some Yankees also began to feel a sense of guilt for the sufferings of white Southerners. As the decade of the 1870s began, a movement in behalf of forgiveness and reconciliation gathered momentum in the North.

Carl Schurz and Horace Greeley emerged as the most prominent leaders of this movement. Schurz headed a drive to end the disfranchisement of former Confederates in Missouri. This issue split the state's Republican party, which had controlled Missouri since the war. In 1870 the "Liberal" Republicans bolted the party and, with Democratic support, carried the state. Meanwhile Horace Greeley's *New York Tribune* orchestrated a campaign for reconciliation with the South and total amnesty for ex-Rebels. Greeley insisted that Reconstruction could never work without the cooperation of the "better class" of Southern whites. To continue a policy of force and proscription, he warned, would only drive all whites into the Democratic party and intensify Ku Klux terrorism. But restraint and amnesty would encourage the growth of a moderate Southern Republican party dominated by the region's "natural leaders," especially those who like Greeley had once been Whigs. In the spring of 1871, Greeley carried this message to the South in a well-publicized lecture tour. Some Republicans who had grown disillusioned with Grant began to mention Greeley as a possible presidential candidate in 1872.

But most Republicans denounced Greeley's suggestions as a formula for disaster. Many of them no longer opposed amnesty in the narrow sense of removing the remaining political disqualifications of ex-Confederates. But in the lexicon of the Liberal movement, amnesty meant more than that. It connoted total forgiveness of Rebels and a willingness to entrust to their stewardship the results of

Northern victory. The time for this had not yet come, according to *Harper's Weekly,* because the majority of Southern whites still consisted of those "who hate the government, who hold to paramount allegiance to the State, who hunt and harass the colored race, who compose the Ku-Klux."[18]

THE KLAN ISSUE

Terrorism persisted in many parts of the South after the 1868 elections. The Klan's excesses reputedly caused Grand Wizard Forrest to disband the order in 1869. But Forrest's ability to enforce any such directive was limited. The Klan had never been centrally controlled. Local bands, whether they called themselves Ku Klux Klans or something else, had operated on their own before 1869 and continued to do so after that date. Legend has it that the Klan now became dominated by irresponsible lower-class elements and that the South's Democratic leaders turned against it. The most scholarly history of the order, however, finds little evidence for this. Various kinds of information on Klan members—arrests by state militia or federal troops, grand jury indictments, convictions, and confessions—indicate that while in some areas poor whites did predominate, Klansmen came from all social classes and the leaders were often prominent men or the sons of prominent men.[19] Most Klansmen were in their twenties and early thirties, and most were probably Confederate veterans. Their hit-and-run guerrilla tactics made them, in effect, a paramilitary arm of the Southern Democratic party's effort to overthrow Republican rule in the South.

One purpose of Klan violence was the social and economic control of the black population. Black schools, perceived as a threat to white supremacy, received special attention. Scores of black schoolhouses went up in flames. Democratic newspapers sometimes made fun of such occurrences. In 1869 an Alabama newspaper facetiously reported the appearance of a comet whose tail had dropped to the ground and burned several schools. "The antics of the tail of this wonderful comet have completely demoralized free-nigger education in these counties; for negroes are so superstitious that they believe it to be a warning for them to stick, hereafter to 'de shovel and de hoe,' and let their dirty-backed primers go."[20]

But the Klan's principal purpose remained political. The level of violence rose during the months before an election. Alleged Republican misrule served as the main justification for Klan activities. As the *Yorkville* (S.C.) *Enquirer* phrased it in 1871: "The intelligent, honest white people (the tax-payers) of this county shall rule it! We can no longer put up with negro rule, black bayonets [i.e., Negro militia], and a miserably degraded and thievish set of lawmakers. . . . We are pledged to stop it; we are determined to end it, even if we are 'forced, by force, to use force.' " Once this force had overthrown Republican rule, Democratic leaders counseled peace and order. In February 1871, editor Henry W. Grady of the *Rome* (Ga.) *Commercial,* who may have been a Klan member himself, advised all members of "secret organizations" to "*remain perfectly quiet and orderly, for the present.* . . . The exciting elections have all passed; the good cause has triumphed; the enemies of Georgia are beat to the dust. . . . Let the harsh asperities that were necessary during the 'reign of terror' pass away like a dream."[21]

Northern leaders wondered aloud why Southern Republicans could not defend themselves and maintain order. It was not for lack of trying. Republican sheriffs formed posses to go after the Klan. Governors organized militia companies and sent them to trouble spots. But the sheriff of Fayette County, Alabama, explained why such efforts often failed:

> When I gather my posse . . . I could depend on them; but as soon as I get home, I meet my wife crying, saying that they have been there shooting into the house. When we scatter to our houses, we do not know at what time we are to be shot down; and living with our lives in our hands in this way, we have become disheartened, and do not know what to do.[22]

The militia accomplished little more. If the troops were whites, their commander might doubt their reliability because the Klan was known to have infiltrated some militia companies. Several governors, particularly in South Carolina, organized black militia units. But the occasional use of these troops inflamed white fury to a fever pitch and tended to exacerbate rather than to subdue violence. Governors became reluctant to employ black militia for fear of starting an all-out race war. Even federal troops seemed ineffective against the Klan before 1871. For one thing, few cavalry units were stationed in the South (except on the Texas frontier), and infantry could not cope with the hit-and-run tactics of the mounted Klan. For another, the army in Southern states operated under the constraints of civil law.

If law enforcement officers did manage to apprehend Klansmen, what then? Even in Republican counties it proved difficult to empanel a jury that would convict, no matter what the evidence. Although federal troops might be able to protect witnesses and jurors during a trial, they could not prevent retaliation on a dark night months later. And sometimes the intimidation occurred during the trial itself. To cite just one example, the district attorney in northern Mississippi saw a case fall apart when five key witnesses were murdered. The example was not lost on witnesses and jurors elsewhere.

Martial law and the large-scale use of troops seemed to be the only answer to Klan violence. But state legislatures were reluctant to give their governors authority for these actions. Only in Arkansas and Tennessee did state forces carry out successful campaigns against the Klan. In 1868–1869 Arkansas' carpetbag governor, Powell Clayton, a tough Union army veteran with anti-guerrilla experience in Missouri, organized reliable white and black militia companies, put them under the command of former Union officers, and sent undercover agents to infiltrate the Klan. He proclaimed martial law in ten counties, attacked and scattered the Klan, arrested and tried numerous Klansmen in military courts, and executed several of them by firing squad. This broke the back of the Klan in Arkansas. Governor William G. Brownlow of Tennessee mobilized a similar militia effort in 1869. The legislature gave him authority to declare martial law, which he did in nine counties. All of these counties were in middle and western Tennessee, while the militia came from solidly Republican eastern Tennessee. Little actual fighting occurred, for the Klan leaders decided to disband their forces before the militia arrived. Few arrests and no convictions took place. Although this campaign appeared to have achieved success, other forms of intimidation persisted, and the Republicans lost control of Tennessee in the fall of 1869.

North Carolina's Governor William W. Holden came to grief because of his attempt to stamp out the Klan. County sheriffs and civil courts proved helpless to contain a rising wave of terror that swept over the state in early 1870. The legislature authorized Holden to proclaim a state of insurrection but refused him the power to declare martial law or to suspend the writ of *habeas corpus.* Knowing that nothing short of these actions would do the job, Holden in effect declared martial law by executive order. The militia arrested scores of Klansmen, while dozens of others turned state's evidence in hope of a light sentence. In response to mounting pressures, Holden dropped his plan to try the offenders in military courts. As usual, none of those arrested could be convicted in civil courts. After the Democrats won control of the legislature in 1870, they impeached and convicted Holden in March 1871 for having illegally declared martial law. He was the first governor in American history to be removed from office by impeachment.

Congressional Legislation Against the Klan

In several states, the Klan and Klan-like organizations grew bolder during 1870. The death toll mounted into the hundreds. Southern Republicans desperately petitioned the national government for help. Tough legislation to enforce the Fourteenth and Fifteenth Amendments became major items of congressional business. A stumbling block to such legislation was the traditional federal system, under which the states possessed jurisdiction over the crimes of murder, assault, arson, and the like. In the view of many moderate Republicans, the prosecution of such crimes by federal officials would stretch the Constitution to the breaking point. Nevertheless, the clauses of the Fourteenth and Fifteenth Amendments giving Congress the power to enforce their provisions by appropriate legislation seemed to provide constitutional sanction for a departure from tradition. On May 31, 1870, Congress passed an enforcement act that made interference with voting rights a federal offense punishable in federal courts. The key section of this law defined as a felony any attempt by one or more persons to deprive another person of his civil or political rights.

This section became the basis for subsequent prosecutions and convictions of Klansmen. But during the first year of the law's existence, President Grant and Attorney General Hoar did little to enforce it. Their Southern policy relied more on the velvet glove than on the iron fist. By 1871, however, it was clear that the government's soft tactics were failing; Klan violence was on the rise. Grant and his new attorney general, Amos Akerman, readied the iron fist. On February 28, 1871, Congress passed a second enforcement act, which established machinery for the federal supervision of registration and voting. But the most important law was the enforcement act passed by a special session on April 20, 1871, popularly known as the Ku Klux Act. This law strengthened the felony and conspiracy provisions of the 1870 law, authorized the president to use the army to enforce it, and empowered him to suspend the writ of *habeas corpus* in areas that he declared to be in a state of insurrection. Although this last provision fell short of true martial law (indicted persons would still be tried in civil courts), it was a significant step in that direction. The Ku Klux Act also gave the courts power to purge suspected Klansmen from juries by an oath backed with stiff penalties for perjury.

Under these laws, the Grant administration cracked down on the Klan. Government detectives infiltrated the order and gathered evidence of its activities. In 1871 a congressional committee also conducted an investigation of the Klan that produced twelve volumes of testimony documenting its outrages. The President sent to the most violent Southern districts several companies of cavalry to cope with the fast-riding Klansmen. Because Grant was sensitive to Democratic charges of "military despotism," however, he used his powers sparingly. He suspended the writ of *habeas corpus* in only nine counties of South Carolina. There and elsewhere, especially in North Carolina and Mississippi, federal marshals aided by soldiers arrested thousands of Klansmen. Hundreds of others fled their homes to escape arrest. Federal grand juries handed down more than three thousand indictments. Several hundred defendants pleaded guilty in return for suspended sentences. The Justice Department dropped charges against nearly two thousand others in order to clear clogged court dockets for trials of major offenders. About 600 of the latter were convicted and 250 acquitted. Of those convicted, most received fines or light jail sentences, but sixty-five were imprisoned for sentences up to five years in the federal penitentiary at Albany, New York.

Most arrests of Klansmen took place in 1871–1872, though their trials dragged on until 1875.* The government's main purpose was to destroy the Klan and to restore law and order in the South, rather than to secure mass convictions. Thus the courts granted clemency to many convicted defendants, and Grant used his pardoning powers liberally. By 1875 all the imprisoned men had served out their sentences or received pardons. The government's vigorous action in 1871–1872 did bring at least temporary peace and order to large parts of the former Confederacy. As a consequence, the 1872 election was the fairest and most democratic presidential election in the South until 1968.

THE ELECTION OF 1872

Despite Grant's restraint in enforcing the Ku Klux Act, bayonet rule became a central issue in the 1872 election. In the end, however, the administration's Southern policy proved to be more of a political asset than a liability.

As the probability of Grant's renomination was becoming a near certainty by early 1872, Republicans disaffected from his administration decided to form a

*Arrests and trials under the legislation of 1870 and 1871 continued for two decades after 1875, but at a much diminished rate. Supreme Court decisions in 1876 (see p. 595) struck down significant portions of the enforcement acts, and a Democratic Congress repealed most of this legislation in 1894.

third party. This movement began in Missouri, where Liberal Republicans with
Democratic support had recently wrested control of the state from the regular
Republicans. On January 24, 1872, the Missouri Liberals issued a call for a
national convention to meet at Cincinnati in May. Pursuant to this call, Republican dissidents in every state had organized themselves around the Liberal banner
and elected convention delegates.

The Liberal Republican Convention

The men who gathered at Cincinnati represented a broad range of viewpoints.
Some shared the laissez-faire ideals of nineteenth-century British liberalism: individual liberty, limited government, and free trade. They opposed the protective
tariffs favored by most Republicans; they supported civil service reform and
expressed disillusionment with Grant's failures in this area; and they urged amnesty and an end to bayonet rule in the South. Having changed parties at least
once before in their careers—from Whig or Democrat to Republican, with perhaps the Free Soil party as an intermediate step—many of them did not regard
the Republican party as a permanent institution. The party had won the war,
preserved the Union, abolished slavery, and reconstructed the South. These were
glorious achievements. But Liberals believed that unprincipled spoilsmen and
politicos had captured the party. Therefore the time had come again, as in 1848
and 1854, to form a new party to apply the old ideals to the new issues of the
1870s.

The idealistic Liberals rubbed elbows at Cincinnati with political brokers who
cared little for any of these issues. From both the North and the South arrived
delegates who had lost factional or patronage battles within the party and who
saw the Liberal movement as a means to recoup their political fortunes. This
would make them unlikely proponents of civil service reform. To complicate the
picture further, every shade of tariff opinion found expression at the convention.
Therefore the tariff plank of the platform emerged as a meaningless compromise.
(In the meantime, Congress in 1872 lowered tariff rates by an average of 10
percent and removed the duties on coffee and tea altogether, thereby robbing the
issue of some of the potential it might have had.) The platform did take a firm
stand on civil service reform. Under Grant, it declared, the bureaucracy had
"become a mere instrument of partisan tyranny and personal ambition . . . a
scandal and reproach upon free institutions . . . dangerous to the perpetuity of
republican government." Reform of these abuses, impossible under the "tyranni-
cal" Grant administration, was "one of the most pressing necessities of the
hour."[23]

Despite this emphasis on civil service reform, the Southern question became
the main issue of the Liberal Republican movement. This happened primarily for
two reasons: the party's need for a coalition with Democrats; and the personality
of the presidential nominee, Horace Greeley. In 1871, a number of dissident
Republicans had begun to urge the Democratic party to repudiate its racist past
and to accept the legitimacy of Reconstruction. This would pave the way for a

coalition between the "better class of Democrats" and the anti-Grant Republicans. Many Northern Democrats were ready to bury the "dead issues" of the past and to undertake such a "New Departure" toward future success. When the arch-Copperhead himself, Clement Vallandigham, proposed resolutions to a county Democratic convention in May 1871 accepting the Fourteenth and Fifteenth Amendments as "the natural and legitimate results of the war," the New Departure became a reality. A dozen state Democratic conventions adopted the resolutions in 1871. As a consequence, said the party's national chairman, "the game of charging us with disloyalty and Copperheadism is played out."[24]

This prediction turned out to be premature. Moreover, the Democratic endorsement of Reconstruction contained some small print. The party continued to adhere to its states' rights principles. Congressional Democrats voted against the enforcement acts of 1870–1871 and denounced the arrests of Klansmen as "tyranny" and "despotism." This created a problem for Liberal Republicans, many of whom had initially supported these laws. They tried to resolve the problem by endorsing the purpose of the laws but criticizing the use of "bayonets" to carry them out. This ambivalence found its way into the Liberal Republican platform. Two planks pledged fidelity to "the equality of all men before the law . . . equal and exact justice to all of whatever nativity, race, color, or persuasion." But two other planks demanded amnesty for all former Confederates, advocated "the supremacy of the civil over the military authority," called for "local self-government" (already a code phrase for white rule in the South), and condemned Grant's use of "arbitrary measures."[25] Since "bayonets" and "arbitrary measures" had proven to be the only way to protect equal rights in the South, these platform phrases were widely recognized as a bid for an alliance with the Democrats.

A second reason for the emergence of the Southern question as a central issue was the Liberals' surprising nomination of Horace Greeley for president.

Greeley's name was almost a household word. But some of the reasons for his fame worked against his credibility as a candidate. During his nearly forty years as a journalist, he had lent his support to a wide range of unpopular, contradictory, or just plain quackish positions. His quixotic personality and cherubic appearance made him a cartoonist's delight. His temporary acquiescence in peaceful secession in 1861, his subsequent oscillation between advocacy of total war and negotiated peace, and his postwar support of a tough reconstruction policy combined with the forgiveness of Rebels had created an image of a muddling, confused mind. Greeley's long record of partisan attacks on Democrats made him an unlikely prospect to head a coalition with that party.

Despite all this, Greeley was the most influential newspaperman in the country. By 1871 he had also made himself the leading spokesman for amnesty, reconciliation, and self-government in the South. Even so, Greeley did not figure as a probable nominee in the preconvention maneuvering. The two leading candidates were diplomat Charles Francis Adams and Supreme Court Justice David Davis. Austere and impeccably correct, Adams received the support of New Englanders and principled reformers. The professional politicians leaned toward Davis. In

Horace Greeley
*(Reproduced from the
Collections of the Library of
Congress)*

effect, the two men neutralized each other, paving the way for Greeley to pick up Davis delegates and to emerge as the victor amid pandemonium on the sixth ballot. Adams's supporters, including Carl Schurz and most other founders of the Liberal movement, were stunned by Greeley's nomination. Some of them defected from the party and either endorsed Grant or sat out the campaign. But most of them swallowed their disappointment and prepared to do their best to elect Greeley.

The Campaign

In the spirit of the slogan "Anything to beat Grant," the Democratic national convention overlooked the enmities and barbs of four decades and endorsed Greeley's nomination. Liberals and Democrats set up fusion tickets at the state level. In the early stages of the campaign, the Greeley candidacy appeared to develop a strong momentum.

But of the three issues that had initially impelled the Liberal movement—civil service reform, tariff reduction, and sectional reconciliation—Greeley was indifferent toward the first and hostile toward the second. This left amnesty and self-government as the "great watchwords" of the Liberal Republican party. In his acceptance letter, Greeley announced an intention to make Grant's "Federal subversion of the internal polity" of Southern states the main campaign issue "in the confident trust that the masses of our countrymen . . . are eager to clasp hands across the bloody chasm which has too long divided them."[26]

The Republican Congress acted to defuse the potential appeal of the Liberals' amnesty plank by removing the officeholding disqualification from all but a handful of ex-Confederates in May 1872. Apart from this, however, Greeley's stand on Southern questions turned out to be politically counterproductive. Most Northern voters did not yet trust the white South or the Democrats. *Harper's Weekly* cartoonist Thomas Nast, famous for the biting cartoons that had helped overthrow the Tweed Ring, did a similar job on Greeley. One cartoon showed the editor shaking hands "across the bloody chasm" with a Rebel who had just shot a Union soldier. Others pictured Greeley shaking hands across Andersonville prison and across a Ku-Kluxed black man. One that really hit below the belt showed him stretching a hand across Lincoln's grave to John Wilkes Booth. Nast's most famous campaign cartoon portrayed Greeley as a pirate captain bringing his craft alongside the ship of state while Confederate leaders, armed to the teeth, hid below waiting to board and destroy it.

Although several former Free Soilers became Liberal Republicans, the mainstream of antislavery and abolitionist sentiment remained with the Republicans. So did nearly all black voters. Frederick Douglass spoke for the latter when he branded the Liberal movement "mischievous and dangerous." "Whatsoever may be the faults of the Republican party," said Douglass, "it has within it the only element of friendship for the colored man's rights." The Democratic endorsement of Greeley confirmed William Lloyd Garrison's belief that the Liberal movement was "simply a stool pigeon for the Democracy to capture the Presidency." And Lydia Maria Child, who though she could not vote was one of the most astute political observers among the abolitionists, wrote that while the Liberal and Democratic platforms professed to affirm equality before the law,

> the Rebels and Democrats have taken care to put in some loopholes through which they can creep out of all they have promised. They claim "self-government for the States," which means the "State Sovereignty" for which the Rebels fought. . . . They demand that "the nation should return to methods of peace, and the supremacy of civil over military authority," which means that when the Ku Klux renew their plans to exterminate Republicans, white and black, they shall be dealt with by Southern civil authorities—that is, by judges and jurors who are themselves members of the Ku Klux associations.[27]

As the campaign proceeded, the Greeley candidacy began to wilt. The makeshift Liberal organization proved to be no match for the well-financed Republican machine. Many Democrats who could not bring themselves to vote for Greeley decided to stay home on election day. Grant's apparent success in quashing the Klan helped him more than the corruption issue hurt him. On November 5 the President scored a solid victory over his challenger. Grant won 56 percent of the popular vote, the highest proportion for any candidate between 1828 and 1904. He carried every Northern state and ten of the sixteen Southern and border states. The Republicans regained a two-thirds majority in the House and preserved a similar majority in the Senate. Worn out from the campaign, despondent at its outcome, and grieving over the recent death of his wife, Greeley died three weeks after the election.

The Liberal Republican party also died. But the issues of reform and reconciliation remained alive, despite the apparent electoral mandate for a tough Southern policy. When the nation's booming prosperity collapsed into depression after the Panic of 1873, the Republicans became vulnerable to the kind of attacks on their record that had failed in 1872.

Thirty-one

Social and Economic Reconstruction

EDUCATION IN THE SOUTH

One of Reconstruction's proudest achievements was the planting in the South of a public school system for both races. It was a tender plant, buffeted by the storms of violence, corruption, taxpayer revolts, and Democratic counterrevolution. But it survived and grew to maturity, bringing literacy to the freedmen and some semblance of a modern educational system to the South.

The work of freedmen's education societies expanded rapidly with the coming of peace. The freedmen remained eager for schooling. Next to ownership of land, blacks looked upon education as their best hope for advancement. "My Lord, ma'am, what a great thing larning is!" said a South Carolina freedman to a Northern teacher. "White folks can do what they likes, for they know so much more'na we." A black Mississippian vowed in 1869: "If I nebber does do nothing more while I live, I shall give my children a chance to go to school, for I considers education the next best ting to liberty."[1]

Many Southern whites disliked the idea of educating blacks because they feared that such education might threaten white supremacy. Other Southerners, more far-seeing, recognized that education of the freedmen was necessary to prepare them for the responsibilities of freedom. But they feared that Yankee teachers would instill "false notions of equality" in black minds. Much of the violence against freedmen's schools took the form of attacks on Northern teachers. Southern moderates who sympathized with the idea of black education urged fellow whites to support black schools in order to forestall Yankee domination of the enterprise.

But such appeals availed little. Southern whites did next to nothing for black education in the early Reconstruction years. By default, therefore, Northern missionaries, the federal government, and freedmen themselves created a network of black schools from the elementary to college level. Protestant denominations, especially Congregationalists through the American Missionary Association, took the lead in these efforts. Many nonsectarian freedmen's aid societies also sprang up in the North. Most of these merged in 1866 to form the American Freedmen's Union Commission. Black denominations, especially the African Methodist Episcopal Church, also founded schools. In 1866 the Freedmen's Bureau became involved in education on a large scale.

This was a unique experiment in joint private and public support of education. The Freedmen's Bureau owned many of the school buildings, paid transportation for teachers from the North, and maintained a general oversight of affairs. The freedmen's aid societies and mission associations recruited and paid the teachers and determined the curriculum and content of the schooling. The initial preponderance of Northern teachers fell to less than half by 1870. In that year about half of the teachers were blacks and a handful were Southern whites. From 1865 to 1870 the expenditures for freedmen's education totaled approximately $9 million, of which the Freedmen's Bureau contributed $5 million, the Northern societies more than $3 million, and the freedmen the remainder. In 1870 there were 4,000 freedmen's schools with 9,000 teachers and more than 200,000 pupils. Despite these impressive statistics, only 12 percent of the 1,700,000 black children of school age (6–17 years old) were enrolled in 1870. The proportion of Southern white children attending some kind of school, however, was not much higher.

The establishment of public schools by the reconstructed state governments gave promise of an enlarged and permanent educational system. But the promise was not entirely fulfilled. The insecure tenure of these governments, the difficulty of collecting taxes, the waste and corruption in the disbursement of some school funds, the added expense of maintaining a dual school system for the two races, the shortage of qualified teachers and administrators especially for black schools, the persistent white hostility to black education, and the low population density of rural areas slowed the development of a flourishing public school system. Most of the good schools were located in the cities and larger towns, while schools in the countryside rarely functioned for more than three months a year if they functioned at all. Nevertheless, there was some progress. By 1876, more than half of the white children and nearly two-fifths of the black children of school age in the former slave states were enrolled in school. This represented a threefold increase in only six years. Though still a tender plant, the public school system had definitely taken root in the South.

With the establishment of public schools, the nonsectarian Northern freedmen's societies turned their properties over to the states and went out of existence. The denominational societies also deeded most of their elementary schools to the states; but they continued to operate academies and "colleges," the latter at first functioning mainly as secondary schools. The main purpose of these institutions was to train black teachers, clergymen, and other professional leaders—the group that the black leader W. E. B. Du Bois later called "the talented tenth." The American Missionary Association continued to lead the way in this endeavor.

From the schools founded and sustained by this and other Northern Protestant societies evolved most of the leading black colleges: Fisk, Atlanta, and Dillard Universities; Talladega, Tougaloo, Morehouse, and Spelman Colleges; and many others. The efforts of these institutions and of the public schools slowly and painfully reduced the black illiteracy rate from more than 80 percent in 1870 to 45 percent by 1900.

The Segregation Issue

A school integration debate generated much heat but little light in the 1870s. Freedmen's aid societies confronted this question in their schools as early as 1865. Consistent with their abolitionist heritage, they welcomed both races to their schools. The American Freedmen's Union Commission declared in 1866 that although integration would "produce difficulties in the South," the policy was "inherently right" and the commission would never "shut out a child from our schools because of his color. . . . It took America three-quarters of a century of agitation and four years of war to learn the meaning of the word 'Liberty.' God grant to teach us by easier lessons the meaning of the words 'equal rights.' "[2]

In practice, however, few Southern whites chose to attend these schools. From 1867 to 1870 whites made up only 1 percent of the students enrolled in schools supervised by the Freedmen's Bureau. With the exception of one school, the few white students in the mission societies' secondary schools and colleges were mainly the children of Northern instructors who taught in these institutions. The exception was Berea College. Founded by the American Missionary Association in eastern Kentucky, Berea enrolled whites as well as blacks from 1866 on. For nearly forty years, until the Kentucky legislature banned integration in 1904, Berea's student population averaged about half black and half white, making it the most thoroughly integrated school in the United States.

Several Northern states moved toward the desegregation of public schools during Reconstruction. In 1866 and 1867 the legislatures of Rhode Island and Connecticut followed Massachusetts' earlier example and prohibited public school segregation. During the next decade Michigan, Minnesota, Iowa, and Kansas took similar action by legislative act or court decision. Although enforcement of these laws was spotty, most of the few black children in the upper North attended nonsegregated schools.

The South was another matter. White spokesmen, including scalawags, repeatedly warned that compulsory integration would destroy the fledgling public schools by driving all whites away. Only Louisiana and South Carolina mandated nonsegregated schools in their constitutions. Florida did so by statute in 1873. But implementation was nonexistent there and in most parts of Louisiana and South Carolina as well. In a few Louisiana parishes, white and black children apparently attended the same schools for a time. For several years in the 1870s about one-third of the New Orleans public schools were mixed. Carpetbagger administrators compelled the admission of black students to the University of South Carolina in 1873. But this policy achieved a dubious success. Nearly all of the whites withdrew from the university. By 1875 nine-tenths of the students were black, and the few remaining whites were mostly the sons of carpetbaggers or Northern missionaries. The achievement of integration in New Orleans resulted in part from the cosmopolitan ethnic heritage of the city, whose population contained a spectrum of colors that made it difficult to tell where "black" left off and "white" began. Even so, integration in New Orleans produced tension and violence. Several thousand white children transferred to private schools or dropped out of school altogether. The restoration of Democratic control in Louisiana and South Carolina in 1877 ended the South's first experiments in desegregated public education.

The Civil Rights Act of 1875

The federal government also got into the act of trying to legislate desegregation. In 1870, Senator Charles Sumner introduced a bill to prohibit racial discrimination in schools, juries, and all forms of transportation and public accommodations anywhere in the United States. Backed by an abolitionist campaign to mobilize public support for this effort to "remove the last lingering taint of slavery," Sumner reintroduced his bill at each subsequent session of Congress until his death in 1874. But many lawyers doubted the bill's constitutionality, for the Fourteenth Amendment seemed to ban only racial discrimination imposed by states and not that practiced by individuals or corporations. Although public schools clearly fell within the category of state agencies, doubt existed whether the equal protection clause of the amendment prohibited separate schools. The same Congress that passed the Fourteenth Amendment had also established a segregated public school system in the District of Columbia. Moreover, many radicals who sympathized with Sumner's purpose in theory expressed concern that the law might destroy Southern schools in practice. Even though segregated schools were based on an "unreasonable prejudice," wrote a radical editor, "we have lived long enough to know that this prejudice, so far as it exists, is not to be corrected by the legislative coercion of a civil rights bill. It is far better to have both [races] educated, even in 'separate' schools, than not to have them educated at all."[3]

Despite these doubts, the Senate passed Sumner's bill in May 1874—several senators probably voting aye only as a memorial gesture to Sumner, who had died two months earlier. But the House cut the school provision from the bill before passing it in February 1875. Even without the school clause, this law turned out to be far ahead of its time. Many congressmen who voted for it did not believe it would survive legal challenges or that it could be enforced if it did. The Justice Department made little effort to enforce the law. Although some railroads, streetcar lines, and even restaurants and theaters in the South as well as the North served blacks on a nonsegregated basis after passage of the law, most in the South did not. Several discrimination cases made their way on appeal through the lower courts to the United States Supreme Court. In 1883, the Court ruled the 1875 law unconstitutional (except the provision relating to juries) on the grounds that the Fourteenth Amendment gave Congress no power to legislate against discrimination by individuals, only against discrimination by states.

THE NEW ORDER IN SOUTHERN AGRICULTURE

Just as black education took a great leap forward during Reconstruction and then settled into a pattern of separate and unequal,* so the economic status of the freedmen at first improved dramatically but then settled into a pattern of exploitation and poverty.

Economic studies of emancipation have revealed an apparently large rise in the freed slaves' standard of living during the early postwar years. The reason was simple. High cotton prices continued for several years after Appomattox. At the same time, chaotic postwar conditions created a labor shortage. In these circumstances, the freedmen possessed bargaining power to bid up the price of their labor. If a planter did not offer satisfactory wages, his workers could go elsewhere. This mobility of labor was the chief economic benefit of emancipation. The efforts of Southern whites to neutralize it by antienticement laws, vagrancy laws, violence, and other means could not fully overcome economic realities. In 1865, planters offered freed workers provisions and housing plus money wages of only $5 or $6 per month or share wages of one-tenth of the crop. By 1867, the freedmen had pushed this up to an average of $10 per month for a full hand (an adult male) or as much as one-third of the crop. From Texas came a typical report: "The old-line planters, who only a few weeks before had driven off their negroes, endeavored to secure their services by offering greater inducements. They offered part of the crop—first, one-fourth, then one-third, and now one-half—rather than let their plantations remain idle."[4]

Several economic historians have attempted to calculate the income gains of blacks during the first decade of freedom. The most painstaking of these analyses[†] is based on estimates of the shares of return going to each of the three inputs in cotton growing: capital (land, seed, implements, etc.), labor, and management. Under slavery, the slaves received only 22 percent of the return—in the form of food, clothing, and shelter. With freedom, labor's share jumped to 56 percent. For two reasons, however, not all of this increase represented a clear gain in black income. First, the South suffered a general decline in per capita output from prewar levels. Blacks got a bigger slice of the pie, but it was a smaller pie. Second, the freedmen chose not to work as hard as they had been compelled to work as slaves. Some black children went to school rather than to work; some mothers stayed at home to raise their children instead of going to the cotton fields; men worked shorter hours. Their freedom to choose these options represented one of

*The expenditures per student for white schools seem to have been 30 to 40 percent greater than those for black schools during the 1870s. This disparity persisted during subsequent decades, and it widened during the early twentieth century.

†Roger L. Ransom and Richard Sutch, *One Kind of Freedom: The Economic Consequences of Emancipation* (Cambridge, 1977); Roger L. Ransom and Richard Sutch, "Growth and Welfare in the American South of the Nineteenth Century," *Explorations in Economic History*, 16 (1979), 207–36.

emancipation's benefits. It also helped to produce the labor shortage that bid up the price of labor but at the same time reduced the potential income of individual families by reducing the overall product of their labor.

After factoring all these variables into their calculations, economists Roger Ransom and Richard Sutch estimate that black per capita agricultural income in the cotton states increased by 46 percent between 1857 and 1879, with most of this increase coming in the first years of freedom. At the same time, the per capita agricultural income of whites in the cotton states declined by 35 percent. Put another way, black per capita income rose from a relative level of only 23 percent of white income under slavery to 52 percent of white income by the 1870s. While the freedmen enjoyed a standard of living only half as high as that of Southern whites, their *relative* gains since slavery represented the greatest proportionate redistribution of income in American history. Table 31.1 illustrates the changes in per capita income.[5]

Table 31.1
PER CAPITA AGRICULTURAL INCOME IN SEVEN COTTON STATES

	1857	*1879*
Black	$ 28.95	$ 42.22
White	124.79	80.57
Average	74.28	60.13

Most of this income redistribution occurred at the expense of former slaveholders, who could no longer expropriate so large a share of their laborers' output. Postwar planters complained bitterly about their straitened circumstances. "The Negro laziness, and the fall in the price of cotton made me come out a loser, that is, in debt, after surrendering everything I made," wrote a Georgia planter in January 1868. "I worked harder than any negro I employed and made less, because they got their food and clothes for their families and I got nothing." Later in the year, the same planter professed to have "nothing to say that is not gloomy and discouraging. . . . We are more despondent, more degraded, more prostrate, and poorer today than we have ever been, and with negro legislatures, juries, and executive officers, we must sink into a deeper abyss. . . . If I could sell my land or raise enough money to pay my railroad fare, I would not stay here a week."[6]

The Evolution of Tenantry

The freedmen's bargaining power plus other economic factors also forced a reorganization of the methods of plantation labor. Slaves had generally worked in gangs under the supervision of an owner, overseer, or driver. Planters tried to reimpose this system after the war, with the payment of wages as the only new feature. But the effort soon broke down. The chronic shortage of cash in the postwar South made the payment of money wages difficult or impossible for many planters. Thus the practice arose of offering a share of the crop as payment. For planters this had the advantage of giving workers a stake in successful operations. To the freedmen it provided a sense of proprietorship. They began to demand that instead of working in gangs with payment of wages in shares or money, they be allowed to work a plot of land independently and pay a share of the crop as rent. Under this plan, the freedmen became, in effect, farm operators rather than farm laborers. They enjoyed at least partial independence from the day-to-day supervision of white men.

Share tenantry did not become universal. In fact, a bewildering variety of land and labor systems had come into existence by the 1870s and persisted for the next half-century or more. In 1880, one-quarter of the blacks employed in Southern agriculture (along with some whites) worked for wages. Of the remainder, which the census defined as "farm operators," two-thirds of the whites and one-fifth of the blacks owned part or all of the land they farmed. One-tenth of the whites and one-quarter of the black operators paid a fixed rent; one-quarter of the whites and slightly more than half of the blacks rented their land for a share of the crop. Fixed rent took one of two forms: payment in cash or payment in a specified number of pounds or bushels of the crop (standing rent). Share tenantry also took one of two forms, which outside observers sometimes failed to distinguish: share renting and share cropping. In the former, the landowner provided land and housing only; the renter provided livestock, seed, and implements as well as his labor, and paid one-fourth of the crop in rent. In share *cropping*, the cropper provided only his labor and received half the crop as his payment. Share cropping became more common than share renting, for most share tenants lacked the capital to provide their own work animals, seed, and machinery.

The Ownership of Land

The various forms of land tenure ranked themselves in an ascending order of status, from sharecropping at the bottom to ownership at the top. Reconstruction brought a shift in the relative percentages of white and black farm owners. On the eve of the Civil War more than four-fifths of the white farmers and planters had owned their land. By 1880, three principal causes had reduced this proportion to two-thirds in the cotton South. The first was the movement of white upcountry farmers from marginal land to rich lowland soils in response to the demand for labor. In the process they exchanged the ownership of poor land for the promise of higher income as renters or croppers. The second reason why some white owners lost their land was lack of capital, which forced them into debts that many could ultimately pay only by yielding their land to creditors. The third reason was increased taxation during Reconstruction, which forced some white farmers into tenantry. While this was happening, many freedmen who had emerged from slavery with almost nothing managed by hard work, thrift, and luck to buy land. By 1880 about one-fifth of the black farm operators owned land. The average number of acres they owned was less than half the average owned by whites, and black-owned land was worth less per acre than white-owned land. Nevertheless, for a people who had owned nothing in 1865 to have done this well by 1880 was a significant achievement, all the more remarkable because it occurred while many white farmers were losing their land. These black gains and white losses help to explain some of the white violence against blacks during Reconstruction.

Despite the promises of 1865, the national government did little to help the freedmen obtain land (see pp. 506–509). Three agencies that did offer assistance deserve mention, however: the freedmen's aid societies; the Freedman's Bank; and the South Carolina Land Commission.

Several of the freedmen's aid societies bought land in the South and resold it in small lots to freedmen, or they served as agents for Northern philanthropists doing the same. The most ambitious effort to encourage capital accumulation among blacks was the Freedman's Savings and Trust Company, founded in 1865 by antislavery whites and commonly called the Freedman's Bank. The bank established branches in the South that solicited deposits from freed slaves. During the nine years of the bank's life, more than 100,000 depositors maintained accounts totaling $57 million. Thousands of freedmen used these savings to buy homes, farms, and businesses. But the story of the Freedman's Bank had an unhappy ending. Petty embezzlements from branch offices, speculative investments in Washington real estate, and high-risk loans to insiders diminished the bank's reserves. The Panic of 1873 finished what these actions had begun. The bank failed in 1874. The 61,000 remaining depositors lost an average of $20 each.

The South Carolina Land Commission also had a mixed record of achievement adulterated by fraud. Created by the legislature in 1869, the commission was capitalized at $500,000 with power to buy land and resell it at cost with liberal credit terms in plots ranging from twenty-five to one hundred acres. Although corrupt administrators siphoned off some of its funds, the commission did manage to sell land to about 14,000 buyers, most of them black. When Democrats regained control of South Carolina in 1877, they preserved the Land Commission but changed its purpose. The Republican practice of lax foreclosure on defaulted mortgages came to an end, and the state thus recovered much of the black-owned land and resold it in large blocks to whites. When the commission closed its books in 1890, it had conveyed 68,000 acres to white purchasers and 44,000 to blacks.

The Crop Lien System

Whether they acquired land of their own or remained renters or croppers, black as well as white farmers found themselves squeezed by an exploitative credit system that impoverished many of them and retarded the growth of Southern agriculture.

After the war, planters and factors tried to rebuild the antebellum marketing structure, whereby factors purchased supplies, arranged credit, and marketed the crop through mercantile firms in the South's cities. But as the development of sharecropping and tenantry multiplied the number of farm operators, the factors found it impossible to serve the hundreds of thousands of new smallholders and tenants. Nor could small-town banks provide farmers with credit as they did in the Midwest. The war wiped out the South's banks, which had been none too plentiful in the first place. Even if bank loans had been available, few Southern farmers owned sufficient property for collateral. Yet they desperately needed credit to purchase seed, fertilizer, and supplies to sustain themselves until they could harvest and sell the crop. Into this credit vacuum stepped the rural crossroads merchant, whose store advanced supplies to the farmer on credit secured by a lien on his crop.

A complex relationship developed between landowners, country merchants, and tenants. In the old plantation areas the landowners sometimes established their own stores. Successful merchants often became landowners themselves, either through purchase or by attachment of property for debt. Thus a black tenant could experience a double indebtedness to the same person, who might be his former master: he owed part of the crop in payment for rent, and part or all of the remainder in payment for food and supplies sold on credit. If a tenant made a good crop and got a good price for it, he might come out with a profit after paying his store bill. But if cotton prices dropped, or if drought or floods or army worms or any of a dozen other potential disasters reduced his crop, he was likely to find himself more deeply in debt at the year's end than at the beginning. Even farmers who owned their land suffered this cycle of indebtedness, which gripped the South ever more tightly as time went on.

The merchant received his goods on credit from an urban wholesaler who in turn was probably financed by a Northern bank or mercantile firm. Each middle-man in this chain extracted profit and interest charges. The country merchant charged a premium of 50 to 60 percent above the cash price for goods sold on credit. In effect, this credit markup became the interest rate for his loan. Some merchants succumbed to the temptation to cheat debtors by doctoring their accounts. Most black sharecroppers were illiterate and powerless to resist such exploitation. Nor could they easily shop around for better prices, since the number of country stores in that preautomobile age averaged only one to every seventy square miles. The forces of law and order lined up on the side of planters and merchants, especially after the overthrow of Reconstruction removed Republicans from power. Black farmers became increasingly the victims of racial and economic exploitation, which by 1880 had slammed the door to further upward mobility.

In another way also, the crop lien system imposed a vicious cycle on Southern agriculture. To repay their loans, many farmers had to plant their land up to the doorsills with the most marketable cash crop—cotton. This drove cotton prices down, intensified the South's one-crop economy, and exhausted the soil. The lower the price of cotton, the more a farmer must plant in order to meet his debts. This only drove the price down further. It also reduced the amount of land devoted to food crops. Farmers who might otherwise have produced their own cornmeal and bacon became even more dependent on merchants for these sup-plies. Before the war, the cotton states had been almost self-sufficient in food. In the postwar decades, however, they had to import nearly half their food at a price 50 percent higher than it would have cost Southern farmers to grow their own.

Everyone, from the university agronomist down to the lowliest sharecropper, understood that only diversification could break this cruel cycle. But the crop lien system locked Southern farmers into it. "We ought to plant less [cotton and tobacco] and more of grain and grasses," said a North Carolina farmer in 1887, "but how are we to do it; the man who furnishes us rations at 50 percent interest won't let us; he wants money crop planted. . . . It is cotton! cotton! cotton! Buy everything and make cotton pay for it."[7] As a result, the output of cotton more than doubled between 1869 and 1889; but the price of cotton dropped by half, while the cost of supplies to farmers decreased by only one-fifth.

The Poverty of Southern Agriculture

The drop in the price of cotton was one reason for the general postwar decline of Southern income. A second reason was emancipation, which reduced by one-third the hours worked by the black labor force. A third reason was the destruction of Southern wealth by the war. And a fourth was the reluctance of outside capital after 1870 to invest in Southern agriculture when more attractive opportunities beckoned elsewhere. Southern agriculture remained the most labor-intensive, capital-starved, and retarded sector of the American economy. Its per capita output did not reach the prewar level for more than a half-century after Appomattox. Southern per capita income, which had been two-thirds of the Northern average in 1860, declined to only two-fifths by 1880 and remained at that level for the rest of the century. The average income of blacks, which had jumped from one-quarter to one-half of the Southern white average between 1857 and 1879, leveled off at that point and did not begin again to increase relative to white income until the mid-twentieth century. The economic promise of emancipation, like the political promise of reconstruction, remained only half-fulfilled during the generation that experienced these revolutionary events.

POSTWAR COMMERCIAL AND INDUSTRIAL DEVELOPMENTS

Because the South remained primarily agricultural, retardation in that sector slowed development of the rest of the region's economy. While the per capita production of Northern agriculture and manufacturing increased by 30 and 45 percent respectively between 1860 and 1880, Southern per capita production declined by 19 and 2 percent. Whereas in 1860 the eleven Confederate states had possessed 10 percent of the country's manufacturing capital and 30 percent of its railroad mileage, these states in 1880 possessed only 5 percent of the manufacturing capital and 17 percent of the railroad mileage.

Postwar Railroad Development

The experience of railroad construction illustrated Southern handicaps. Democrats and Republicans alike recognized the crucial role of improved transportation for regional economic growth. Both parties advocated state aid to railroad construction. Reconstruction governments granted state lands to railroads and lent them a specified amount per mile of construction or backed railroad bonds with state credit. Local governments bought railroad stocks. Antebellum state and local governments had done the same. Yet Republican-sponsored state aid to railroads during Reconstruction became controversial because the corruption that accompanied it provided Democrats with a potent political issue. Republicans were vulnerable not only because of corruption but also because they seemed to accomplish so little. From 1865 through 1879, only 7,000 miles of new track were laid down in the South compared with 45,000 miles in the North. The main reason for this was neither corruption nor inefficiency, however, but rather the destruction of Southern railroads by the war. Most investment and construction during the early postwar years went into rebuilding. Not until 1870 were Southern railroads restored to their prewar condition. Only then could new construction go forward with vigor, but the depression following the Panic of 1873 slowed the pace.

In the North, railroad construction and operations formed the leading edge of economic development for two decades after the war. Railroads were the nation's largest nonagricultural employers. Forward and backward linkages continued to generate new industries and technologies. During these years the iron horse switched from wood to coal as a fuel, which helped to triple coal production between 1865 and 1880.* Railroads also replaced iron with steel rails during the postwar decades. The mass production of steel by the new Bessemer process thereupon zoomed from an insignificant 19,000 tons in 1867 to 1,247,000 tons in 1880. The development of a refrigerated railroad car in the 1870s made possible the long-distance transportation of processed meat. This in turn gave rise to a meat-packing industry centered in Chicago and spawned the classic cattle kingdom in Texas and the plains states. As the steel rails crisscrossed these states in the 1870s and 1880s, they helped to transform this kingdom from open-range grazing and the long cattle drive to tamer and more scientific methods of livestock agriculture.

Railroading also generated important technological innovations to improve the comfort, efficiency, and safety of its own operations: George Pullman developed the sleeping car in the 1860s; George Westinghouse invented the air brake in the 1870s; several men contributed to the development of the knuckle coupler to replace the dangerous link and pin method. In 1883 the railroad industry, weary of the scheduling havoc caused by a multitude of different local times, divided the country into four time zones and created the concept of standard time that exists today.

Innovations in Technology and Marketing

The fifteen years after the war brought many other inventions that changed the economy and still influence the way people live today: the typewriter, barbed-wire fencing, the telephone, the incandescent electric light, the phonograph. The two

---

*Coal-generated steam also replaced wood and water as the principal source of industrial power after the war.

last-named inventions sprang mainly from the fertile mind of Thomas A. Edison, whose laboratories in 1881 also constructed the first successful "dynamo" (generator) to generate electricity. This helped lay the groundwork for the emergence of electricity as the major source of industrial power as well as lighting in the twentieth century.

Several factors combined to make the 1860s and 1870s a key period in the evolution of new methods for marketing industrial products. Two of the most important were the railroads and the Civil War itself. For centuries, the "merchant" had dominated the exchange of goods in the market economy. As wholesalers, jobbers, commission salesmen, importers, or retailers, merchants had functioned as middlemen through whose hands products passed on their way from producer to consumer. The mid-nineteenth-century expansion of the railroad network began to erode this merchant domination in two ways. First, by enlarging the distribution network it made possible the concentration of manufacturing in fewer places and in fewer but larger firms, which could exert some influence over their markets. Second, as consumers of rails, locomotives, cars, wheels, and other products, the railroads provided the first large concentrated market to which producers could sell contracted items in volume without the need for middlemen. The Civil War created a second concentrated market: the government. The war also freed many manufacturers from their previous dependence on wholesalers and mercantile houses for short-term credit. Wartime inflation and profits enabled producers to liquidate debts and to build up cash reserves for the internal financing of future expansion.

The postwar decline of the merchant middleman occurred especially in such rapidly growing industries as iron and steel manufacturing, in which producers sold their products (in massive quantities) to other industries—railroads, stove manufacturers, wire producers, and the like—rather than to individuals. In addition, many consumer-goods industries, taking advantage of the increasing concentration of markets created by the growth of cities, established their own distribution and marketing networks, which eliminated all middlemen between manufacturer and retailer. In meatpacking, for example, Gustavus Swift set up a nationwide chain of refrigerated warehouses from which Swift beef and pork could be sold directly to retailers. In petroleum, John D. Rockefeller's Standard Oil Company began to do its own wholesaling of kerosene and lubricants in urban centers. Other consumer-goods industries followed suit, or tried to. Railroads played a vital role in this process. They shipped meat from the Chicago packing houses to company warehouses all over the country. Rockefeller was able to undersell competitors and drive them out of business not only by doing his own wholesaling but also by compelling railroads to give him volume discounts on freight rates, in the form of rebates.

Antirailroad Sentiment

While railroads contributed in crucial ways to economic growth, they gave rise to problems and criticism as well. Railroad construction proceeded at a frenetic pace from 1866 to 1873. During those years, as many miles of new rail (35,000) were laid down as in all the years from 1830 through 1865. The building of the first transcontinental line across 1,800 miles of sparsely settled plains and rugged mountains excited awe and admiration. The much-photographed driving of the golden spike that linked the Union Pacific and Central Pacific at Promontory Point, Utah, on May 10, 1869, became a symbol of the age. But the construction of these and other western lines also illustrated some of the problems associated with postwar railroads. The huge amount of risk capital necessary to build tracks across forbidding terrain in advance of settlement could be provided only by the government, in the form of land grants and loans. In a race to lay down as much trackage as possible to increase its subsidy, the Union Pacific built poorly and soon had to rebuild parts of the line. The financing of Union Pacific construction also produced one of the Gilded Age's foremost scandals—the Crédit Mobilier.

This exotic-sounding corporation was formed by the Union Pacific's stockholders as a construction company to build the railroad. In their capacity as directors of one company—the Union Pacific—they awarded contracts to another company —the Crédit Mobilier—of which they were themselves also directors. Not uncommon in that age, this practice reduced the financial risk in railroad construction. But in this case the government was assuming much of the risk. And some of the Union Pacific–Crédit Mobilier directors could not resist the temptation to enrich themselves by padding construction contracts.

To make sure that Congress did not inquire too closely into these affairs, a Massachusetts congressman named Oakes Ames—who happened to be head of a company that sold construction equipment to the Crédit Mobilier, as well as a director of the latter and a director of the Union Pacific—sold Crédit Mobilier shares at token prices to several influential congressmen in 1867 and 1868. Writing privately that "there is no difficulty in inducing men to look after their own property," Ames placed these shares "where they will do the most good to us."[8] In 1872 a New York newspaper exposed these transactions. Public outrage compelled a congressional investigation, which produced a censure of Congressman Ames and cast shadows across the future careers of several other Republican politicians. The notion of conflict of interest, previously almost nonexistent, came into its own with the adverse publicity surrounding this affair.

By this time, 1873, railroads were under fire from several directions. The building of a second transcontinental line, the Northern Pacific, precipitated a financial panic that burst the bubble of postwar prosperity. The economy plunged into a depression from which it did not begin to recover until 1878. The hero of Union Civil War finance, Jay Cooke, became the goat of the Panic of 1873. Cooke's Philadelphia banking firm had taken over financial management of the Northern Pacific in 1869. Despite a huge land grant and loans authorized by Congress, the company had not yet laid a mile of track. Under Cooke's management, the Northern Pacific began in 1870 to build westward from Duluth. Cooke pyramided every conceivable kind of equity and loan financing to keep the funds flowing to construction crews. Other banks, railroads, and industries were doing the same in a feverish cycle of expansion and speculation. In September 1873 the pyramid of paper collapsed. Badly overextended, Cooke's firm was the first to close its doors. Like dominoes, hundreds of other banks and firms succumbed to the panic. Of the country's 364 railroads, 89 went into bankruptcy. Eighteen thousand businesses failed in two years. Unemployment mounted to 14 percent by 1876, and "hard times" settled on the country like a pall.

Even before the panic, railroads in the Midwest had provoked hostility from their customers. Having initially welcomed the iron horse as a transportation link to distant markets, many farmers came to curse it for its monopoly grip on the transport lifeline. A decline in war-inflated crop prices exacerbated the situation. The price of wheat dropped by half between 1867 and 1870, and corn prices dropped by half between 1869 and 1872. Freight rates, though declining, did not go down by anything like this much. Farmers blamed the railroads for their distress. The railroads lent credence to this theory by keeping rates higher in areas of no competition (most farmers lived in districts served by only one line) than in areas with competing transport. Railroad companies also owned many of the grain elevators that came under attack for cheating farmers by classifying grain below its actual quality.

Farmers organized cooperative marketing and purchasing associations to bypass middlemen in the selling of crops and buying of supplies. The umbrella organization for many of these cooperatives was the Patrons of Husbandry, or Grange, founded in 1867. But farmers could not build their own railroads. So they did the next best thing: they went into politics, organized "antimonopoly" parties, and elected state legislators who worked with representatives of other shipping interests to enact "Granger laws" in a half-dozen states. These laws established state railroad commissions and fixed maximum freight rates and warehouse charges. Railroads challenged the laws in court. Eight of these "Granger cases" made their way to the U.S. Supreme Court, which handed down its decision in 1877 in *Munn v. Illinois.* The Court held that states could legitimately use their police powers to regulate businesses clothed with "a public interest"—common carriers, millers, innkeepers, and so on. Although thus sanctioned by the highest court, some of the Granger laws nevertheless proved difficult to enforce. The campaign for effective railroad regulation remained very much alive.

Labor Strife

Railroads also became the focal point of labor unrest and industrial violence. The railroad strikes of 1877 climaxed a decade of labor ferment and four years of depression.

The real wages of workers advanced by an average of 25 percent from 1865 to 1873—that is, actual wages rose slightly while the general price index declined 20 percent from its inflationary wartime level. Most of these gains accrued to skilled workers, while the unskilled, especially women and children, continued to labor long hours for marginal pay. And although skilled workers experienced improved living standards, the continuing mechanization of many trades eroded old craft skills and provoked anxieties about a loss of independence when craftsmen who had once controlled their own trades were forced to become employees of manufacturers who owned the new machines.

These crosscurrents of prosperity and unease produced a wave of unionization. Twenty-two new national trade unions came into existence alongside the ten that had been organized before and during the war. Many of these unions joined together to form the National Labor Union in 1866. The NLU's principal goal was the reduction of the average ten- or eleven-hour day to eight hours—with no reduction of wages. Unions tried to achieve this goal not only by collective bargaining and strikes, but also by legislation. Several labor reform parties sprang up in the more industrialized states, particularly Massachusetts, where the party's gubernatorial candidate won 13 percent of the vote in 1870. Labor's political weight secured the passage of eight-hour laws in six states. But the laws proved to be full of loopholes and lacking in enforcement machinery. In 1872, politically oriented labor spokesmen formed the National Labor Reform party. These political activities caused tensions among union leaders, many of whom feared a diversion of energies from the more practical matter of collective bargaining for better wages and working conditions. The National Labor Reform party's presidential candidate in 1872 garnered only 0.5 percent of the popular votes. In the wake of this debacle, both the Labor Reform party and the National Labor Union collapsed.

Industrial violence discredited unions in the eyes of many middle-class Americans. In 1875, headlines featured spectacular revelations about the "Molly Maguires" in the anthracite coal fields of eastern Pennsylvania. This area constituted a microcosm of ethnic and class tensions in American society. Most of the mine owners were Scots-Irish Presbyterians; many foremen and skilled miners were Welsh and English Protestants; and most of the unskilled workers were Irish Catholics. This was a volatile mixture. The skilled miners formed the Workingmen's Benevolent Association, which had won modest gains for its members by 1873. Many Irish belonged to the Ancient Order of Hibernians, whose alleged inner circle—the Molly Maguires*—planned and carried out a series of assassinations and other vendettas against owners, foremen, and workers. The trials and convictions of Molly Maguires (twenty were hanged for murder) in 1875–1877 not only discredited the order but also gave mine owners the opportunity to cripple the Workingmen's Benevolent Association by invoking a repressive campaign for law and order against all labor organizations.

The violent railroad strikes of 1877 aroused even greater fears and hatreds. During the previous three years several eastern railroads, citing declining revenues, had instituted wage cuts of as much as 35 percent (during the same period retail prices declined about 8 percent). Workers organized and tried without success to resist these cuts. But when the Baltimore and Ohio on July 16, 1877, announced its third 10 percent cut, workers at two points on the line spontaneously struck and prevented trains from moving. The strike spread to other eastern lines almost as fast as the telegraph could carry the news. Workers tied up rail traffic as far west as Chicago and St. Louis. Ten states called out the militia, which in some cases fired on the strikers but in other cases fraternized with them. In response

---

*Named after an antilandlord organization in Ireland that resisted the eviction of tenants.

to urgent requests from state governors, President Rutherford B. Hayes sent federal troops to more than a half-dozen cities. Troops, militia, and police finally brought the situation under control by the first week of August. At least a hundred strikers, troops, and innocent bystanders lost their lives, and hundreds more were injured. In the aftermath of the strikes, some railroads partially rescinded their wage cuts. But states and cities also strengthened their riot-control forces. The specter of class conflict that appeared during these strikes frightened many Americans with its desperate vision of the future.

The Money Question

These events occurred against a backdrop of increasing controversy over the nation's monetary system. Responding to cries of distress from farmers and other producers hit by declining prices following the panic, Congress in 1874 passed a bill to increase the amount of greenbacks and national banknotes by about 10 percent. But anti-inflationary advisers prevailed upon President Grant to veto the bill. Divisions within the Republican party between sound-money men and inflationists hurt the party in the 1874 congressional elections. To heal these divisions before the 1876 presidential campaign, Senator John Sherman, the party's financial expert, drafted a specie resumption bill. For sound-money men, this measure had the advantage of promising to redeem greenback dollars at par with gold by January 1, 1879. For inflationists, the bill's attraction was that it removed the limitation on national banknote circulation while fixing the greenback circulation at a minimum of $300 million. The bill accomplished its political purpose of uniting the Republican party on the financial question, and Congress passed the measure in 1875 by a party-line vote. In theory, the Specie Resumption Act allowed an increase in banknote circulation to meet the needs of the economy. But because the issue of banknotes remained tied to the banks' holding of U.S. bonds, the continuing reduction of the war-created national debt and the tendency of banks to sell their bonds and invest the proceeds elsewhere prevented an increase of banknote circulation. The Specie Resumption Act, on the other hand, did accomplish the goal of sound-money proponents—bringing greenbacks and gold dollars to par. As secretary of the treasury, Sherman himself presided over this achievement at the end of 1878. The United States joined the nations of western Europe on the gold standard.

These actions did not end the debate over monetary policy; on the contrary, they intensified it. A group of monetary theorists, labor leaders, farm spokesmen, and manufacturers insisted that the trouble with the American economy was an insufficient circulating medium. This deficiency hurt especially the South and the West, which suffered from a shortage of banks and banknotes. It hurt debtors, who found that deflation enlarged their debts by increasing the dollar's value; it hurt seekers of capital by raising interest rates and drying up the sources of credit; it hurt farmers by driving down the prices of their crops. The specie resumption policy, insisted its critics, would worsen the situation by further increasing the value of greenbacks. The greenbackers, as antiresumptionists came to be called, believed that money should be based on the productive capacity of the economy. They insisted on a single circulating medium—fiat money issued by the national government and backed only by the confidence that citizens had in their economy. In 1876 the greenbackers formed the Greenback party. Although their presidential candidate received only 1 percent of the vote, the deepening depression attracted many of the discontented to their banner in 1878, when they won 15 percent of the congressional vote and elected fourteen congressmen.

The Silver Issue

Meanwhile the monetary debate took a new turn with the emergence of the silver issue. In 1873, after several years of discussion, Congress had demonetized silver by enacting a coinage law that omitted the silver dollar as a coinage unit (the mint continued to produce fractional silver coins). This measure was intended to prepare the United States for a gold standard as part of an international movement in that direction. The law attracted little attention at the time; but as monetary arguments heated up after 1875, the antideflationists began to brand it "The Crime of 1873"—a dark international conspiracy to enrich bankers and defraud farmers and workers by abolishing the people's money, silver.

Pressures began to build for the remonetization of silver. Two principal developments fueled these pressures. Various theorists and interest groups believed that the injection of silver into the economy would cure the twin evils of deflation and depression. At the same time, U.S. silver production tripled between 1869 and 1876 while gold production declined. This reversed the trend that had prevailed since the California gold discoveries of 1848. Booming gold production then had lowered the market price of that metal relative to the price of silver, until silver commanded a higher price on the open market than the official U.S. mint ratio of sixteen ounces of silver to one ounce of gold. But with the opening of new mines during the 1860s, especially the fabulous Comstock Lode in Nevada, the rising production of silver drove its price below the sixteen-to-one ratio and added to the clamor for remonetization.

These pressures finally overwhelmed Congress, which in 1878 passed, over President Hayes's veto, the Bland-Allison Act authorizing the renewed coinage of silver dollars. This was not an unalloyed victory for the silver forces, however. They had urged unlimited coinage of all silver offered for sale to the mint at the sixteen-to-one ratio. But since this would overvalue silver and take the country off the gold standard by driving gold dollars out of circulation, the law authorized a limited coinage of $2 million to $4 million monthly. The Treasury thereafter coined the minimum amount and maintained the gold standard by offering to redeem silver as well as greenbacks in gold. The amount of silver currency in circulation increased from $60 million in 1878 to $180 million in 1884, but this did not reverse the era's deflationary trend. For the next thirty-five years, four kinds of dollars circulated in the United States: U.S. notes (greenbacks); national banknotes; silver (including silver certificates redeemable in coin); and gold (including gold certificates).

Although the Bland-Allison Act by no means ended the monetary debate, it did quiet things down for a few years. Recovery from the depression after 1878 also lowered the temperature of economic discontent. While the depression lasted, however, the preoccupation with economic issues plus the revelation of new scandals in the Grant administration weakened the Republican party and helped pave the way for a retreat from Reconstruction.

Thirty-two

The Retreat From Reconstruction

RECONSTRUCTION UNRAVELS, 1873–1876

President Grant's landslide reelection in 1872 seemed to confirm the nation's commitment to reconstruction. A majority of voters rejected the Liberal Republican appeal for "home rule" by the South's "best people." Republicans regained their two-thirds majority in Congress and retained control of seven of the eleven ex-Confederate states. The Ku Klux prosecutions proceeded apace.

But events during Grant's second term exposed the foundation of sand upon which these successes rested. A growing Northern disenchantment with Southern Republicans was the first sign of trouble. Although the Liberal and Democratic cry against bayonet rule and carpetbag corruption had left most Republican voters unmoved in 1872, the cry grew louder in subsequent years. Most of the controversy in 1873–1874 centered on Louisiana.

The Louisiana Imbroglio

A schism among Louisiana Republicans had produced two party tickets in 1872, one of them endorsed by the Democrats. The confused outcome of the election caused bitter wrangling over who had won. Each faction created its own "returning board" to canvass the returns and throw out fraudulent votes. The regular Republicans and the Liberal Republican/Democratic coalition each convened their own legislature and inaugurated their own governor. Congress refused to count Louisiana's electoral votes for either presidential candidate. Grant spoke for most Americans when he commented, with regard to Louisiana politics, that "the muddle down there is almost beyond my fathoming."[1] A federal district judge finally declared the regular Republicans to be the legitimate government. Grant ordered federal troops to enforce the ruling.

The moral force of this action was tarnished by the unsavory reputation of the regulars. Grant himself privately conceded that the carpetbag governor, William P. Kellogg, was a "first-class cuss."[2] Some staunch Republican congressmen branded the Kellogg administration a "bogus government" kept in power only by federal bayonets. Louisiana whites refused to accept its legitimacy and, in effect, formed a shadow government supported by armed paramilitary units known as White Leagues. Controlling much of the countryside, White Leaguers launched attacks on Republicans and blacks wherever the opportunity presented itself. Sheriff's posses and the state's largely black militia did little to stop such attacks, and federal troops were too few to extend their power much beyond New Orleans. The worst violence occurred at Colfax in upstate Louisiana, where on April 13, 1873, a clash between black militia and armed whites left two white men and an estimated seventy black men dead, half of the latter killed in cold blood after they had surrendered. Although the federal government arrested and indicted seventy-two white men for their part in the Colfax massacre, the United States Supreme Court eventually freed them in a ruling that declared unconstitutional those portions of the 1870 enforcement act under which they had been indicted.

Tension and violence escalated during the months preceding the 1874 elections. The worst of many rural incidents occurred at Coushatta, near Shreveport, where in late August the White League murdered six Republican officeholders. Two weeks later, on September 14, New Orleans became the scene of a battle between the police and the state militia on one side and the White League on the other. Although the casualties of thirty killed and one hundred wounded were about evenly divided, the White Leaguers routed their opponents. After this affray Grant sent in more federal troops. They put an end to large-scale violence and ensured a peaceful election, but they could do little to prevent intimidation and economic pressure against black voters on distant plantations and farms.

The election of state legislators in 1874 produced a new round of disputed results and military intervention. The Democrats appeared to have won a majority in the lower house. But the Republican returning board threw out the results of several parishes on grounds of intimidation. The board certified the election of fifty-three Republicans and fifty-three Democrats, with five cases undecided and referred to the lower house itself. When this body convened on January 4, 1875, the Democrats carried out a well-planned maneuver to name a speaker, swear him in, and pass a motion to seat the five Democratic claimants before the befuddled Republicans could organize to prevent it. In response, Governor Kellogg asked federal troops to eject the five Democrats who had no election certificates. Labeling the White Leaguers "banditti" who should be tried by military courts, General Philip Sheridan upheld the conduct of his field commander, who had marched into the capitol and expelled the five Democrats.

This affair provoked an uproar in Congress and in the country. Most radicals and some moderate Republicans endorsed the army's action. The White Leagues deserved no quarter, said more than one radical newspaper. "Crush them, utterly, remorselessly. . . . Better military rule for forty years than the South be given over to lawlessness and blood for a day."[3] But Democrats and a good many Republicans condemned the administration for sanctioning the unprecedented military invasion of a legislature. "If this can be done in Louisiana," said Carl Schurz, "how long will it be before it can be done in Massachusetts and in Ohio? . . . How long before a soldier may stalk into the national House of Representatives, and, pointing to the Speaker's mace, say, 'Take away that bauble!' "[4]

The Wavering Commitment of Northern Republicans

Congress finally imposed a compromise on Louisiana by which the Democrats gained control of the lower house in return for a promise not to disturb the remaining two years of Kellogg's term as governor. This compromise brought an uneasy peace to Louisiana. But other Southern states experienced growing disruption in 1874–1875: the Brooks-Baxter "war" between rival Republican factions in Arkansas; squabbling and schisms among Republicans in South Carolina and Florida; the formation of Democratic "rifle clubs," which attacked Republicans in Mississippi. Texas came under Democratic control in 1873, Arkansas and Alabama in 1874. A growing number of Northern Republicans were willing to concede these losses without a fight. A party leader in Maine admitted that voters were "tired and sick of carpet-bag governments." Grant's postmaster general lamented that the ranks of carpetbaggers contained "not one really first class man. . . . We have got a hard lot from the South, and the people will not submit to it any longer, nor do I blame them."[5]

The Republican commitment to black rights had never been very deep. Only the party's radical wing had supported racial equality with genuine conviction, and by 1874 the convictions of some had been shaken. The revolutionary achievements of the war and reconstruction—emancipation, civil equality, Negro suffrage, black participation in Southern governments—owed more to anti-Southern than to pro-black motivation. They sprang primarily from the military exigencies of war and the political exigencies of peace, rather than from a considered social purpose. With the emergence of new issues of vital concern to Northern voters —depression, declining farm prices, wage cuts, unemployment, monetary uncertainty—these voters lost interest in the plight of faraway blacks for whom they had never felt much sympathy in the first place. The leading Republican newspaper in Washington observed in January 1874: "People are becoming tired of . . . abstract questions, in which the overwhelming majority of them have no direct interest. The negro question, with all its complications, and the reconstruction of the Southern States, with all its interminable embroilments, have lost much of the power they once wielded." A Republican politician said the same thing more bluntly a year later: "The truth is our people are tired out with this worn out cry of 'Southern outrages'!!! Hard times & heavy taxes make them wish the 'nigger,' 'everlasting nigger,' were in ———— or Africa."[6]

Republican setbacks in the 1874 elections intensified the party's disillusionment with reconstruction. Democrats won control of the next House of Representatives for the first time in eighteen years. They scored an astonishing net gain of seventy-seven seats in the House and ten in the Senate. And these gains occurred in every region of the country. Even Massachusetts elected a Democratic governor for the first time in a generation. An important cause of this Democratic "tidal wave" was the depression. As always, voters punished the party in power during hard times. But Republican analysts attributed their losses also to voter disgust with the party's Southern policy. They began to speak of "unloading" the dead weight of carpetbag-black governments before 1876 to avoid going down to defeat in the presidential election.

The unloading policy bore its first fruit in the Mississippi state election of 1875. Democrats in the state evolved the "Mississippi Plan" for this campaign. The plan's first step was to herd all whites into the Democratic party. Democrats used social and economic pressures, ostracism, and threats to compel the 10 or 15 percent of the state's whites who still called themselves Republicans to change sides. A white Republican who succumbed to these pressures explained that the Democrats made it "too damned hot for [us] to stay out. . . . No white man can live in the South in the future and act with any other than the Democratic party unless he is willing and prepared to live a life of social isolation and remain in political oblivion."[7]

A second step in the Mississippi Plan was a relentless intimidation of black voters. Democratic newspapers adopted the slogan: "Carry the election peacefully if we can, forcibly if we must." Economic coercion proved quite effective among black laborers and sharecroppers, who were informed that if they voted Republican they could expect no further work. But this alone was not enough. Democrats organized rifle clubs and turned party headquarters into arsenals. They discovered that their best political tactic was the "riot." When Republicans gathered together—for a Fourth of July picnic, a political rally, or whatever—armed whites would provoke an incident and then open fire. One of the earliest and deadliest such affairs was the Vicksburg riot prior to a county election in December 1874, in which at least thirty-five blacks and two whites were killed. Three months later the Vicksburg Democratic newspaper declared: *"The same tactics that saved Vicksburg will surely save the State, and no other will."*[8] Democrats in other parts of the state took the advice. Several riots erupted, smaller in scale than Vicksburg's but with about the same ratio of black-to-white casualties.

In September 1875, Governor Adelbert Ames—a native of Maine, a medal of honor winner in the war, and one of the ablest carpetbag governors—appealed to Washington for troops to control the violence. Grant intended to comply, but his attorney general and a delegation of Ohio Republicans dissuaded him. The Mississippi Republicans would lose the election even if troops were sent, they said, and the bayonet rule issue would tip the narrow balance in the forthcoming Ohio elections to the Democrats. In a letter informing Ames of the rejection of his request for troops, the attorney general lectured the governor: "The whole public are tired out with these annual autumnal outbreaks in the South, and the great majority are now ready to condemn any interference on the part of the government. . . . Preserve the peace by the forces in your own state, and let the country see that the citizens of Mississippi, who are . . . largely Republican, have the courage to *fight* for their rights."[9]

Ames did try to organize a loyal state militia. But he had difficulty doing so, and in any case he was reluctant to use his black troops for fear of provoking an even greater bloodbath, in which blacks would be the main victims. Instead, he negotiated an agreement with Democratic leaders whereby the latter promised peace in return for a disbandment of the militia. "No matter if they are going to carry the State," said Ames wearily, "let them carry it, and let us be at peace and have no more killing."[10]

Violence nevertheless continued, though an unusual quiet prevailed on election day itself. Republicans were conspicuous by their absence from the polls in several counties. In five of the state's counties with heavy black majorities, the Republicans polled twelve, seven, four, two, and zero votes, respectively. The Mississippi Plan converted a Republican majority of 30,000 at the previous election into a Democratic majority of 30,000 at this one.

The Supreme Court and Reconstruction

As the presidential election of 1876 approached, Republican governments had been "unloaded" in every Southern state except South Carolina, Louisiana, and Florida. Events in Washington meanwhile crippled the government's ability to protect Southern Republicans even if the will to do so had still existed. The Democratic House cut the Justice Department's appropriation in order to compel a reduction of its enforcement apparatus in the South. Even more damaging were two rulings by the U.S. Supreme Court in the spring of 1876. The two cases, *U.S.* v. *Reese* and *U.S.* v. *Cruikshank*, had started their ways through lower courts in 1873 and 1874, respectively. *Reese* concerned an attempt by whites in Kentucky to prevent blacks from voting; *Cruikshank* grew out of the indictment of whites involved in Louisiana's Colfax massacre. Circuit court rulings in both cases called into question the constitutionality of the 1870 enforcement act on which the indictments were based. While the cases were pending before the Supreme Court, the Justice Department suspended further prosecutions under the enforcement acts. "I do not believe that any convictions can be obtained under existing circumstances," wrote the attorney general in 1875. "Criminal prosecution under these acts ought to be suspended until it is known whether the Supreme Court will hold them constitutional or otherwise."[11]

The Court's rulings, when they finally came in 1876, were less than clear-cut. The indictments in both cases were dismissed, but mainly on grounds of technical defects in certain sections of the 1870 law. Nevertheless, the thrust of Chief Justice Morrison Waite's opinions in both cases narrowed the scope of the Fourteenth and Fifteenth Amendments. These amendments, according to the Court, empowered Congress only to legislate against discrimination by states. "The power of Congress . . . to legislate for the enforcement of such a guarantee, does not extend to the passage of laws for the suppression of ordinary crime within the States. . . . That duty was originally assumed by the States; and it still remains there."[12] The effect of the *Reese* and *Cruikshank* decisions, combined with the Northern loss of will to carry out reconstruction, was to inhibit further enforcement efforts.

Government Scandals

New scandals that came to light in 1875 and 1876 also demoralized Republicans. Although these scandals did not concern the South, their spillover effect discredited Grantism everywhere and further undermined the party's willingness to uphold carpetbag government. Suspicions of malfeasance pervaded nearly every level of the federal bureaucracy. The attorney general's wife and the secretary of the interior's son were accused of accepting bribes in return for influencing the policies of these departments. Both cabinet officials resigned in 1875. In March 1876, the House impeached Secretary of War William W. Belknap for accepting bribes (transmitted through his wife) in return for appointments to army post exchanges in Western territories. President Grant, unaware of the implications of his action, accepted Belknap's resignation before his trial by the Senate, thereby allowing him to escape conviction.

The most spectacular scandal of the decade was the "Whiskey Ring." This was an intricate network of collusion among distillers and government revenue agents, centered in St. Louis, whereby the government was cheated of millions of tax dollars annually. The man chiefly responsible for exposing the ring was Secretary of the Treasury Benjamin Bristow, appointed to the office in 1874 after his predecessor had resigned under suspicion of wrongdoing. Bristow assembled a team of incorruptible agents. On May 10, 1875, Bristow's men seized distilleries and internal revenue offices in three Midwestern cities. What they found revealed a deep vein of corruption, which reached into the White House itself. Grant's private secretary Orville Babcock—who had negotiated the ill-fated annexation treaty with Santo Domingo in 1870—turned out to be a member of the ring. Shocked, Grant instructed Bristow to "let no guilty man escape." Federal grand juries brought indictments against more than 350 distillers and government officials. Bristow himself managed the cases against 176 men and obtained convictions of 110.

But Babcock was not among those convicted. As the prosecutions went forward, Bristow became the hero of reform Republicans—including many who had denounced Grant and opposed his reelection in 1872. The President grew convinced that Bristow's actions, and especially the approving chorus from reformers, were really an indictment of his administration. He also came to believe that Bristow's zeal was motivated by a desire for the Republican presidential nomination. His stubborn anger aroused, Grant in February 1876 made a deposition in favor of Babcock's good character for use in his secretary's trial. Faced with this deposition, jurors reluctant to antagonize the President of the United States voted for Babcock's acquittal. This was one of the sorriest episodes of Grant's presidency, and it marked a bad beginning for his last year in office.

That centennial year, 1876, witnessed one of the most tense presidential elections in American history—exceeded only by the election of 1860. The multiplying revelations of corruption in high places ensured that reform would emerge as one of the campaign's main issues. And disillusionment with Grantism in the

South as well as in Washington ensured that no matter who won the election, the remaining carpetbag governments were likely to be reformed out of existence.

THE ELECTION OF 1876

Democrats gave notice of their intent to capitalize on the reform issue by nominating Samuel J. Tilden of New York for president. As chairman of the state Democratic party, Tilden had earned a reform reputation for his role in overthrowing the Tweed Ring. In 1874, he won the governorship and proceeded to expose the machinations of a "Canal Ring" that had defrauded the state with padded repair contracts on the Erie Canal. Tilden ran for president in 1876 on a platform that contained the word "reform" twelve times. Only a Democratic victory, declared the platform, could save the country "from a corrupt centralism which, after inflicting upon ten States the rapacities of carpet-bag tyrannies, has honeycombed the offices of the Federal Government itself with incapacity, waste, and fraud."[13]

The Republicans did not lack for reform candidates. Chief among them was Benjamin Bristow, fresh from his triumphs over the Whiskey Ring. But the preconvention favorite was James G. Blaine of Maine, a congressman since 1862 and Speaker of the House from 1869 to 1875. Possessing a magnetic personality and political talents of a high order, Blaine nevertheless fell victim to the reform wave. While Speaker of the House he had purchased securities of the Little Rock and Fort Smith Railroad. When these securities declined in value, Blaine sold some of them to the Union Pacific for a price well above their market value. Both railroads had received land grants from the government and therefore had a keen interest in maintaining friendly relations with a man of Blaine's influence. Blaine's enemies discovered and publicized his railroad transactions. The congressman protested innocence of impropriety, but the damage was done. The prospect of running a tainted candidate in a campaign where reform and hard times would be prime issues caused many Republicans to blanch. Although the Maine congressman held his lead through six ballots at the Republican national convention, a coalition of Bristow supporters and anti-Blaine radicals joined together on the seventh to nominate Rutherford B. Hayes.

A Civil War general and three times governor of Ohio, Hayes was a good compromise candidate. His reform credentials were strong, and he had been a moderate on Southern policy. The Republican platform pledged both "permanent pacification" of the South and enforcement of "exact equality in the exercise of all civil, political, and public rights."[14] Since most white Americans had become convinced by 1876 that these two goals were contradictory, the party's future Southern policy remained a puzzle. Hayes received conflicting advice on how he should treat the Southern question in his acceptance letter, which would stand as a more important statement than the platform. Carl Schurz wanted Hayes to declare that "the Constitutional rights of local self-government must be respected." But the nominee objected to this phrasing. It seemed "to smack of the bowie knife and the revolver. 'Local self-government' has nullified the Fifteenth Amendment in several States, and is in a fair way to nullify the Fourteenth and

Thirteenth." Hayes's letter contained something for everybody. To those disillusioned with carpetbag rule it promised support for "honest and capable local government" in the South. On the other hand, it affirmed that "there can be no enduring peace if the constitutional rights of any portion of the people are permanently disregarded."[15]

This did little to clarify future Republican policy. And Hayes refused to say anything more for public consumption during the campaign. Despite his statement to Schurz, however, Hayes had for several years considered "bayonet rule" a failure. A former Whig himself, he hoped that the substitution of conciliation for coercion could win erstwhile Southern Whigs over to a Republican party purged of corrupt carpetbaggers. He believed that the good will and influence of Southern moderates would provide better protection for black rights than federal troops could provide.

But events in the South plus the Republicans' need for a campaign issue soon caused the party to take a hard line. In Hamburg, South Carolina, a minor Fourth of July incident between a company of black militia and two white men escalated four days later into a pitched battle between the militia and 200 whites. Afterward, five captured black men were shot and killed "while attempting to escape." This affair revived some of the old Republican militancy in the North and united South Carolina's whites behind a determined effort to elect a Democratic state ticket. Armed "Red Shirt" units mobilized to "bull-doze" Republican voters in South Carolina. Governor Daniel H. Chamberlain, a Massachusetts native and an alumnus of Yale College and Harvard Law School, called on the federal government for more troops. This time the Grant administration responded positively. The President personally branded the Hamburg massacre "cruel, blood-thirsty, wanton, unprovoked . . . a repetition of the course that has been pursued in other Southern States," whereby several of these states were governed "by officials chosen through fraud and violence such as would scarcely be accredited to savages."[16] The government not only sent additional troops to trouble spots, especially in South Carolina, but also placed several thousand deputy marshals and election supervisors on duty in the South. This show of force reduced violence at the polls. But it could do little to stop the threats and assaults that took place far away from the polls. Such tactics reduced the potential Republican tally in ex-Confederate states by an estimated 250,000 votes in 1876.

Southern outrages and the alleged danger of Rebels returning to power became staples of Republican campaign oratory. Even Hayes encouraged these bloody shirt tactics. "Our strong ground is the dread of a solid South, rebel rule, etc. etc.," he wrote to a fellow Republican. "I hope you will make these topics prominent in your speeches. It leads people away from 'hard times,' which is our deadliest foe." One of the most successful practitioners of this advice was Colonel Robert Ingersoll, the famous agnostic, whose speech to a GAR* convention in Indianapolis in September became a classic of the bloody shirt genre:

*Grand Army of the Republic, the organization of Union army veterans, which had become an influential political pressure group.

Every state that seceded from the United States was a Democratic State. . . . Every man that tried to destroy this nation was a Democrat. Every man that loved slavery better than liberty was a Democrat. The man that assassinated Abraham Lincoln was a Democrat. . . . Every man that raised blood-hounds to pursue human beings was a Democrat. . . . Soldiers, every scar you have got on your heroic bodies was given to you by a Democrat.[17]

But many Northern voters remained more concerned with hard times than with "the everlasting Negro question." On election eve, most Republican leaders privately expressed pessimism. If the Democrats could carry every former slave state (which they were confident of doing) they would need only 47 electoral votes from the North to win the 185 necessary for victory. New York and Indiana, or New York, New Jersey, and Connecticut, would do the trick. As it happened, Tilden won all four of these states. But on the day after the election great uncertainty prevailed about whether he had carried all the Southern states.

The Disputed Returns

From South Carolina, Louisiana, and Florida came conflicting reports of the results. On the face of the returns from Louisiana and Florida, Tilden had carried both states and the Democrats had elected the governors and a majority of both legislatures. Although South Carolina reported a narrow victory for Hayes, the Democratic gubernatorial candidate Wade Hampton had apparently won his election and carried a Democratic majority into control of the next legislature. But accusations of force and fraud raised questions about these results. In all three states the existing Republican administrations controlled the returning boards responsible for canvassing the accuracy and fairness of the returns. Louisiana Republicans had earlier shown what such boards could do by way of turning apparent Democratic victories into Republican victories. They prepared to do so again in 1876. Such a purpose was not necessarily a subversion of justice, as Democrats charged. On the contrary, it was the Democratic subversion of justice by force and intimidation that made the returning boards necessary. To cite just one example of what confronted the Louisiana board: a parish that in 1874 had recorded 1,688 Republican votes reported only one in 1876.

Several dozen "visiting statesmen"—national leaders of both parties—descended on the three states to oversee the canvasses by their returning boards. This process took place in the glare of national publicity amid rising tensions. The stakes were no less than the Presidency itself. Even without these three states, Tilden had 184 electoral votes. Hayes needed all nineteen of their electors to win; Tilden needed only one. Well-founded rumors of bribery and perjury flew about. The Louisiana returning board converted an apparent Tilden majority of 7,500 into a Hayes majority of 4,500 and certified the election of a Republican governor and legislature by throwing out or modifying the returns from several bulldozed parishes. The South Carolina board ratified the victory of the Hayes electors and also invalidated enough Democratic votes to certify Governor Chamberlain's reelection with a Republican legislative majority. In Florida, the returning board changed an apparent Tilden victory into a Hayes victory but failed to overturn the Democratic capture of the governorship and legislature.

The official returns from these states, therefore, raised Hayes's electoral vote to the 185 necessary to elect him.* Democrats cried fraud and challenged the results. In South Carolina and Florida they obtained court orders to certify the transmission to the electoral college of returns showing a Tilden victory. In Louisiana the Democratic shadow governor whom the party claimed to have elected in 1872 signed the certificate transmitting alternate returns to Washington. Democrats and Republicans in Louisiana and South Carolina each inaugurated their own governors and legislatures. Only the presence of federal troops in these states maintained the facade of Republican governments, whose real authority scarcely extended beyond the capitol buildings. From December 1876 to April 1877, whites in Louisiana and South Carolina paid taxes to the Democratic governments. While the legal controversy remained unsettled, the Democrats maintained *de facto* control of the governments of both states.

THE COMPROMISE OF 1877

This unprecedented situation presented Congress with a grave dilemma. A genuinely free and fair election would probably have produced Republican victories in South Carolina and Louisiana—and for that matter in Mississippi and North Carolina as well. Tilden's national plurality of 252,000 popular votes would have been neutralized by the estimated 250,000 Southern Republicans who had failed to vote because they were afraid to do so. On the other hand, Republican frauds may have canceled Democratic intimidation in Florida, thereby robbing Tilden of a legitimate majority in that state.

The Constitution offered no clear guidance in this crisis. The Twelfth Amendment states only that the electoral college shall transmit its votes to "the President of the Senate" (normally the vice president of the United States) "who shall, in the presence of the Senate and the House of Representatives, open all certificates and the votes shall then be counted." This was of little help. *Who* should count them? Since 1864 Congress had operated under the twenty-second joint rule, which required the concurrent vote of both houses to count the electoral votes of a state. But this rule had expired in 1875, and Congress—divided between a Republican Senate and a Democratic House—had failed to agree on anything to take its place. The constitutional provision requiring the House to choose a president (and the Senate a vice president) if no candidate had a majority of electoral votes was not applicable, for it could be invoked only after the votes had been counted. In 1876 the issue was how to count them.

While Congress grappled with this problem, passions in the country rose toward the danger level. Rumors circulated among Republicans of neo-Copperhead rifle clubs in the North as well as the South that were reported to be preparing to

*One electoral vote from Oregon was contested on a technicality that made a Republican elector ineligible. But no one doubted that Hayes had carried Oregon. The Democratic challenge there was a diversionary tactic.

inaugurate Tilden by force if necessary. Democrats held mass meetings and made angry speeches. Editor Henry Watterson of the *Louisville Courier-Journal* called for 100,000 Democrats to gather in Washington for a demonstration. Talk of a new civil war abounded. President Grant quietly strengthened the army garrison in Washington.

But little substance underlay all the rumors and rhetoric. Few Southerners had any taste for another civil conflict. Congressman James Garfield reported to Hayes that "the leading southern Democrats in Congress, especially those who were old Whigs, are saying that they have seen war enough, and don't care to follow the lead of their northern associates who . . . were 'invincible in peace and invisible in war.'" Tilden himself discouraged Democratic militancy. "It will not do to fight," he told hotheaded partisans. "We have just emerged from one civil war, and it will not do to engage in another civil war; it would end in the destruction of free government."[18]

The Electoral Commission

Many interest groups pressed Congress for a compromise solution. Business spokesmen in particular pointed out that a prolonged crisis would only plunge the economy into a deeper depression. Congress created a joint committee to work on the problem. After sifting through dozens of proposals, the committee recommended the creation of an electoral commission to arbitrate the disputed returns. The commission's decisions would be final unless overruled by both houses of Congress. The commission was to contain fifteen members: five senators (three Republicans and two Democrats); five representatives (three Democrats and two Republicans); and five Supreme Court justices. In theory the latter would be impartial; but in fact two would be Democrats, two Republicans, and the fifth was expected to be David Davis of Illinois, a one-time Lincoln associate, who had become a Liberal Republican in 1872 and was now an independent. Because Democrats expected Davis to side with them, they supported the idea of a commission with greater enthusiasm than did the Republicans. Democratic congressmen and senators voted 150 to 18 in favor of a commission, while Republicans opposed it by 84 to 57. President Grant signed the bill creating the commission on January 29, 1877.

Suddenly, however, news from Illinois sent a bolt of dismay through the Democratic camp. A coalition of Democrats and Greenbackers in the legislature elected Davis to the U.S. Senate. This action seems to have resulted from a miscalculation by certain Democratic leaders, including Tilden's nephew. They believed that such a gesture would cement Davis to the party and ensure his vote on the electoral commission. Instead, Davis accepted the senatorship (which he saw as a steppingstone to the presidency) and declined appointment to the commission. Since the Supreme Court contained no additional Democrats, the fifth Court appointee became the independent-leaning Justice Joseph Bradley.

The first case to come before the commission was Florida's. Democrats maintained that the state returning board had illegally reversed the outcome of the election there. Republicans replied that the certificate of election signed by the governor was the only valid one, and that the commission could not go behind these official returns unless it also went behind the local returns to investigate every aspect of the balloting. This could hardly be done before March 4, when the next president must be sworn in. The commission divided 7 to 7 according to party affiliation, with Justice Bradley yet to be heard from. An immense responsibility rested on his shoulders. On February 9, Bradley cast the deciding vote—to accept the official Florida returns.

Although Democrats cried foul and hinted darkly that Bradley had been bribed (no evidence supports this suspicion), the die was cast. If the commission would not go behind the returns from Florida, it would not do so for Louisiana or South Carolina. Tilden privately gave up and began to plan a European trip. On February 16 the commission endorsed the Hayes electoral votes from Louisiana, and on February 28 it did the same with respect to South Carolina. According to the legislation that established the commission, both houses of Congress would have to reject its rulings to overturn them. The Senate promptly approved them. But some House Democrats were not yet ready to give up. They conceived the idea of a filibuster to delay the formal completion of the count beyond March 4. Since neither candidate would then have a majority, the House could invoke its constitutional power to elect a president, and choose Tilden.

Negotiations Behind the Scenes

While these ominous proceedings went forward in public, informal negotiations of various sorts occurred behind the scenes. The most important of these took place between Republican associates of Hayes and some of the more moderate Southern Democrats. The latter had a weak hand, but they played it with the unblinking bluff of an expert gambler. In any real showdown the Democrats could scarcely hope to prevail. Republicans controlled the Senate, the Supreme Court, the presidency, and the army. Equally important, they still controlled the North's reservoir of patriotism. Once the electoral commission had made its decisions, Republicans could brand any resistance as revolutionary. Northern Democrats, who had barely begun to shed their wartime Copperhead image, could scarcely afford to come out on the wrong side again in a national crisis. This helps to explain the refusal of Tilden and most other Eastern Democrats to approve any scheme to resist Hayes's inauguration. Deserted by Northern allies, many Southern Democrats began to think about making the best possible bargain with the Republicans. Southerners who had once been Whigs were especially inclined toward this course. They cautiously established contacts with Hayes Republicans.

The latter were open to such contacts. Hayes had pretty much committed himself to the reform wing of the party. He intended to carry out civil service reform with vigor. He also hoped to rebuild the Southern Republican party on the foundations of Whiggery—as Lincoln had hoped to do a dozen years earlier. The interests of Northern Whiggish Republicans and Southern Whiggish Democrats intersected at several points. The latter wanted federal land grants and loans for the Texas and Pacific Railroad. They wanted federal subsidies to help rebuild the Mississippi River levees and to carry out other internal improvements. Most Northern Democrats opposed such subsidies, but the Republicans might support them in return for Southern acquiescence in Hayes's inauguration.

Southern Democrats who talked with Hayes's lieutenants also raised the possibility of a cabinet appointment and of federal patronage for themselves. Above all, they wanted to know what Hayes would do about Louisiana and South Carolina. Would he use the army to uphold the carpetbag regimes, or would he withdraw the troops and allow the Democrats who already governed these states in fact to do so in law as well? Hayes let it be known that he sympathized with all of these Southern aspirations—indeed, they coincided with his own views. In return, he asked only for promises of fair treatment of the freedmen and respect for their rights. The informal conversations also raised the possibility that enough Southern Democrats might vote with the Republicans to enable the latter to control the next House of Representatives (in which the Democrats would have a nominal majority of only ten or twelve).

Nothing as formal as a "deal" was concluded in any of these matters. But on both sides a series of unwritten "understandings" had emerged by late February. The threat of a filibuster to delay the electoral count enabled Southerners to nail down some of these understandings a little more firmly than they might otherwise have been able to do. With more than half of the Northern as well as Southern Democrats now refusing to support a prolonged filibuster, the delaying tactics collapsed, the count was completed, and Hayes was peacefully inaugurated.

So far as it was in his power to do so, Hayes carried out his part of the understandings. His cabinet choices foreshadowed the administration's new policy of reform and conciliation. They included Secretary of State William M. Evarts, who had been Andrew Johnson's defense attorney in the impeachment trial; Secretary of the Interior Carl Schurz, the leading Liberal Republican in 1872; and Postmaster General David M. Key, an ex-Confederate Tennessee Democrat, who promptly began to dispense some of the rich patronage of his office to Southern moderates. The administration lent its support to numerous internal improvements appropriations for the South. The section received more federal money in 1878 than ever before. Although the Hayes administration in the end did not sanction federal aid for construction of the Texas and Pacific Railroad, it did encourage the building, without subsidies, of the Southern Pacific, which finally linked the old South to the new Southwest in 1881. Most important, in return for pledges from the Democratic gubernatorial claimants in South Carolina and Louisiana to uphold black rights, in April 1877 Hayes ordered the federal troops withdrawn from the capitals. The Republican governments in those states immediately collapsed. Along with the other nine ex-Confederate states, South Carolina and Louisiana were now "redeemed."

Old-guard radicals, Blaine Republicans, and most abolitionists denounced Hayes's withdrawal of the troops as a betrayal of the freedmen. Benjamin Wade declared: "To have emancipated those people and then to leave them unprotected would be a crime as infamous as to have reduced them to slavery when they were free." With his old-time vehemence, William Lloyd Garrison excoriated Hayes's "policy of compromise, of credulity, of weakness, of subserviency, of surrender," a policy that sustained "might against right . . . the rich and powerful against the poor and unprotected." As for Southern promises to respect black rights, said Wendell Phillips, "the whole soil of the South is hidden by successive layers of broken promises. To trust a Southern promise would be fair evidence of insanity."[19]

But these voices could scarcely be heard above the national sigh of relief that the electoral crisis was over. Most Americans wanted no more reconstruction if it meant military intervention in state affairs. "I have no sort of faith in a local government which can only be propped up by foreign bayonets," wrote the editor of the *New York Tribune* in April 1877. "If negro suffrage means that as a permanency then negro suffrage is a failure."[20] In truth, Hayes had little choice but to remove the troops. Such action had been foreshadowed by Grant's refusal to intervene in the Mississippi election of 1875 and by the Supreme Court's rulings in the *Reese* and *Cruikshank* cases in 1876. The House of Representatives had already cut Justice Department appropriations and now threatened to withhold War Department appropriations if the army was again used in the South—at a time when Indian troubles on the frontier following Custer's disaster at Little Big Horn in 1876 and railroad strikes in the North in 1877 were making urgent demands on the army. Even prominent black leaders, most notably Frederick Douglass, endorsed Hayes's course. "What [is] called the President's policy," said Douglass in May 1877, "might rather be considered the President's necessity. . . . Statesmen often [are] compelled to act upon facts as they are, and not as they would like to have them."[21]

Although no Southern Democrats deserted their party to help the Republicans organize the House, the rest of the Compromise of 1877 seemed to be working out. Quiet descended on the region below the Potomac for the first time in a generation. In September 1877, Hayes proudly stated that "there has been no other six months since the war when there have been so few outrages committed upon the colored people." A year later, Hayes's principal political adviser still insisted that "it is only a question of time when there will arise a really Republican party in the South numbering in its ranks the intelligence, the culture, the wealth, the Protestantism of the Southern white people, who will give protection and support to the colored people."[22]

Thirty-three

The New South

THE PERSISTENCE OF THE SOUTHERN QUESTION

The 1878 congressional elections produced consternation among many supporters of Hayes's conciliatory Southern policy—including the President himself. Violence and intimidation characterized the campaigns in South Carolina and Louisiana despite their governors' pledges of fair dealing. Throughout the lower South, the Republican share of the vote in 1878 dropped sharply from the previous election. Only 62 of 294 counties with black majorities went Republican, compared with 125 two years earlier. Several black counties recorded not a single Republican ballot. Hayes's attempts to attract ex-Whig Southern Democrats into the Republican party produced no discernible results. The President expressed his disappointment in a newspaper interview. He had launched a new Southern policy, said Hayes, "with an earnest desire to conciliate the Southern leaders . . . and to soften the asperities of political strife." But now, he continued, *"I am reluctantly forced to admit that the experiment was a failure. The first election of importance held since it was attempted has proved that fair elections with free suffrage . . . in the South are an impossibility."*[1]

What could be done about this? Hayes promised "the most determined and vigorous action."[2] Federal marshals arrested twenty-two South Carolina whites for violations of existing federal election laws. Republicans called for new legislation to enforce the Fifteenth Amendment. They urged Congress to refuse to seat Southern representatives elected by violence and fraud. But all of this was futile. No Southern jury would convict whites indicted for electoral crimes. The Democrats already controlled the House, and after the 1878 elections they would control the next Senate as well. No new enforcement legislation could be passed, and Democrats made clear their intent to block any presidential initiative under the existing laws. Five times in 1879 they attached riders to vital appropriations bills repealing what was left of the 1870–1871 enforcement acts. Five times Hayes vetoed these bills, even though some governmental operations ground to a halt as funds ran out. The Democratic congressional majority finally backed down. But the enforcement acts nevertheless remained a dead letter.

By 1879, even Republican radicals had come to recognize the futility of government action in the South under existing circumstances. Their only hope was to regain control of Congress. A solid North must outvote the solid South. How would this help Southern blacks? Northern solidarity, said a Republican newspaper, would teach Southern whites that they could not control the government by "intimidation, bulldozing [and] ballot-box stuffing. . . . We are not going to let any party rule this country that will not deal justly by the political rights of the Negro."[3]

During the 1879–1880 session of Congress, Republicans unfurled the bloody shirt in preparation for the 1880 presidential election. They made much of the "Rebel Brigadiers" who now ruled Congress. In truth, Southerners once again constituted a majority of Democratic congressmen. And more than 90 percent of the Southern congressmen had served in the Confederate armed forces or government. Eighteen Confederate generals sat in Congress, a Confederate editor was secretary of the Senate, and the commander of a Confederate prisoner of war camp where, as one Republican editor put it, "many a poor boy met an inglorious death of starvation and disease," was chairman of the Senate Pensions Committee. It was enough to alarm any Union veteran who thought he had fought on the winning side. The Republican party, with the help of the Grand Army of the Republic, prepared to capitalize on this alarm in the 1880 election.

The Presidential Election of 1880

After remaining deadlocked through thirty-five ballots, the Republican national convention nominated the Ohio dark horse James Garfield for president on the thirty-sixth. A self-made man (like Lincoln, he was born in a log cabin), Garfield had risen to the rank of major general during the war and was elected in 1863 to Congress, where he had served until nominated for president in 1880. In an attempt to break the Republican monopoly on the patriotism issue, the Democrats —for the first and only time—also nominated a Union general, Winfield Scott Hancock, hero of the battle of Gettysburg.

Republicans portrayed Hancock as a figurehead candidate, a captive of the Southern Democrats with whom he had sympathized since the war. A GAR circular insisted that "a thousand Union Generals . . . could not palliate . . . the terrors and the torture, the bloodshed and massacre, with which the Democratic party has prepared, and again sets in the field, a Solid South against the Soldiers and Sailors of the patriotic North." Republicans did not hesitate to hit below the belt; a cartoon by Thomas Nast showed Hancock contemplating the graves of Rebel soldiers killed at Gettysburg, with the caption: "The 'Silent (Democratic) Majority.' General Hancock will miss them on Election Day."[4]

The Republican "solid North" strategy paid off. While Hancock carried every former slave state, Garfield carried all but three Northern states—all small ones —and thereby won a comfortable majority of electoral votes despite his razor-thin plurality of only ten thousand popular votes out of more than nine million cast. The Republicans won about 41 percent of the popular vote in the South, the same as in 1876.

But the Southern states with the largest percentages of black voters recorded sharp declines in their Republican totals. The Republican platform had pledged to protect all voters against "terrorism, violence or fraud." Such pledges were easier made than fulfilled. Although the party regained control of the House by a narrow margin, the balance of power in the Senate was held by a single independent elected from Virginia, William Mahone. This suggested a new Republican Southern strategy. President Hayes's effort to win former Whigs into the Republican party having failed, President-elect Garfield toyed with the idea of promoting coalitions between Republicans and the emerging independent parties in several Southern states. After Garfield's assassination in midsummer 1881, his successor, Chester Arthur, did his best to carry out such a coalition policy.

The Readjuster Movement in Virginia

After redeeming their states, Southern Democrats had experienced internal divisions over economic and other nonracial issues. The most spectacular schism occurred in Virginia, where the state debt became the leading political issue during the 1870s. Saddled with a large antebellum debt (twice the national per capita average in 1870) contracted at high interest rates, Virginia struggled to maintain payments despite the wartime destruction of resources and the loss of one-third of the state's white population resulting from the detachment of West Virginia. Attempts to get West Virginia to assume a share of the debt broke down. The conservative "Bourbons" who ruled Virginia during the 1870s insisted that the entire debt must be repaid in order to preserve the state's honor and credit. To do this, they imposed high taxes and slashed public services, especially schools. "Free schools are not a necessity," insisted the governor in 1878. "Our fathers did not need free schools to make them what they were. . . . [Schools] are a luxury . . . to be paid for, like any other luxury, by the people who wish their benefits."[5]

Such sentiments sparked a rebellion that split the Democrats into "Funders" and "Readjusters." Under the leadership of William Mahone, a railroad promoter and a former Confederate general, the Readjusters organized a separate party in 1879. Following the example of several other states, the Readjusters proposed to reduce the interest rate on Virginia's debt* and to repudiate that portion of it which should fairly have been borne by West Virginia. This would not only reduce

---

*The deflationary trend added one or two percentage points per year to nominal interest rates in the 1870s and 1880s. The cumulative impact of deflation could therefore add 15 or 20 percent to the nominal interest rate after ten years. This burden produced widespread movements, especially during the 1873–1878 depression, to renegotiate interest rates downward on state debts.

ruinous taxes, said Readjusters, but would liberate the state's resources and energy for productive enterprises. It would increase the state's human capital—both black and white—by restoring the public schools. With support from black as well as white voters, the Readjusters in 1879 won control of the Virginia legislature. In 1881 they elected the governor and sent Mahone to the United States Senate.

The Readjusters fulfilled their promises. They scaled down the debt by one-third and reduced the interest rate from 6 to 3 percent. And they tripled the number of schools, teachers, and pupils. Black Virginians were prominent participants and beneficiaries in these actions. Readjuster/Republican coalitions elected several blacks to the legislature. One-third of the delegates to the 1881 Readjuster convention were blacks. The Readjuster government abolished the whipping post as a punishment for crime (a legacy of slavery), enrolled blacks as jurors, and repealed the poll tax, which had kept many poor men of both races from voting. Mahone also moved to consummate a formal merger with Virginia's Republican party.

This development projected Virginia's politics onto the national scene. Although some Northern Republicans expressed concern about the fiscal ethics of debt readjustment, most welcomed an alliance with a movement that shared progressive Republican values and promised to break the solid South. The debt question, said a Massachusetts radical, "has assumed in this movement a position of secondary importance; the real principles on which the party plumes itself are equal rights, a fair ballot, an honest count, and a thorough system of public education." Republicans liked the sound of Readjuster assertions that Virginia must abandon the "dead customs and effete traditions" of the old South and align itself with the "great and growing States of the North" to develop the industrial and human resources of the new South. An Indiana Republican praised Mahone as "the one *statesman*" the South had produced since the war. "He seems to have grasped the great fact that the South, with her great natural wealth, can be and ought to be made as rich, as powerful, and as prosperous as the most favored part of the country."[6] Senator Mahone voted with the Republicans to enable them to organize the Senate in 1881. In return, President Arthur gave Mahone control of the federal patronage in Virginia and sanctioned the creation of a Republican/Readjuster coalition there.

Readjuster success in Virginia inspired a proliferation of independent movements in other Southern states. Arthur used patronage to encourage these movements also. But none of them matched the Readjuster achievements. Moreover, while these movements paid lip service to black political rights, their voting constituencies consisted mainly of poor white farmers, who were not noted for sympathy with blacks. Even in Virginia, the race issue brought down the Republican/Readjuster coalition in 1883. Appealing to the traditions of white supremacy and white unity, Democrats denounced Readjusters as latter-day scalawags and exploited an election-eve race riot in Danville to sweep the legislative elections on the color-line issue. Mahone thereafter became leader of the Virginia Republican party, which came close to carrying the state in 1888. But independent parties elsewhere died out, and the South remained solid for the Democrats.

IDEOLOGY AND REALITY IN THE NEW SOUTH

With recovery from the depression after 1878, the American economy leaped forward. Steel production quadrupled during the 1880s. Railroad construction crews laid down 75,000 miles of new track during the decade, nearly doubling the 86,000 miles in existence at its beginning. Rapid industrial growth called forth a similar growth in the membership of labor unions. The Knights of Labor enrolled an estimated 700,000 members in 1886. The American Federation of Labor was founded the same year. Several major strikes and the Haymarket Square bombing in Chicago produced in 1886 the highest level of labor violence since the railroad strikes of 1877. Despite this, the economic mood of the 1880s remained optimistic.

The Ideology of the "New South"

The South shared this expansive mood. According to legend, the Democratic loss of the 1880 presidential election convinced forward-looking Southerners that they could not achieve salvation through politics. Therefore they rolled up their sleeves and went to work to build a "New South" of commerce, cotton mills, and foundries. Like all legends, this one embodied some truth. A new spirit of enterprise quickened Southern life in the 1880s. Prominent journalists and industrial promoters emerged as spokesmen for an ideology of economic modernization modeled on the Yankee example.

The New South creed was not entirely new in the 1880s. Several antebellum Southerners had futilely urged economic diversification and industrialization. After the war, many of the South's leading thinkers attributed the Confederacy's defeat to its lack of a modernized economy. Having lost the war, the South must imitate the victors. *"We have got to go to manufacturing to save ourselves,"* declared *De Bow's Review* in 1867.[7] Economic depression and a preoccupation with reconstruction politics delayed the emergence of a full-blown Southern ideology of modernization. But in the 1880s that ideology came into its own.

Henry Grady, editor of the *Atlanta Constitution,* became the foremost proponent of the New South ideology. What the region needed, said Grady in 1880, was "fewer stump-speakers and more stump-pullers. . . . The defeat of Hancock will be a blessing in disguise if it only tends to turn our people from politics to work." This emphasis on the "gospel of work as the South's great need" became the litany of New South prophets. By 1886 Grady could say, in a speech to Northern businessmen which achieved instant fame, that the New South creed had already paid off: "We have sown towns and cities in the place of theories, and put business above politics. We have challenged your spinners in Massachusetts and your ironmakers in Pennsylvania. . . . We have established thrift in city and country. We have fallen in love with work."[8]

The Industries of the New South

Some real achievements lay behind Grady's rhetoric. Under the slogan "Bring the Cotton Mills to the Cotton," the Southern textile industry expanded rapidly during the 1880s. Along the piedmont from Virginia to Alabama, new cotton mills and company towns to house their workers sprang up. The labor force—40 percent women, 25 percent children, and almost entirely white—worked for wages about half as high as those in New England. The number of Southern cotton spindles increased ninefold between 1880 and 1900. In 1880 the South possessed only 5 percent of the country's textile-producing capacity; by 1900 the section possessed 23 percent, and it was well on the way to surpassing New England by 1930. Most of the initial capital for the Southern textile industry came from the South itself. But after 1893 an increasing amount came from the North, as New England mill owners began to see the advantages of relocating in the low-wage, nonunion Southern climate.

Another Southern industry developed from a regional agricultural crop—tobacco. Southerners provided most of the capital for this industry also. The reigning genius was James B. Duke of Durham, North Carolina. Duke's entrepreneurial talents and tactics rivaled those of John D. Rockefeller. In 1890 Duke incorporated the American Tobacco Company, which for a time achieved a virtual monopoly of tobacco manufacturing until broken up by Supreme Court decree in 1911. Unlike textile mills, tobacco factories employed substantial numbers of blacks.

Two New South industries dependent on Northern capital were railroads and iron. During the 1880s the pace of railroad construction in the South exceeded the national average. In 1886, Southern railroads shifted from their traditional 5-foot gauge to the national standard of 4 feet 8½ inches. This change integrated the Southern lines into the national network. It also served as a symbol of increasing Northern domination of Southern railroads. By 1890, Yankees constituted a majority of directors in companies that controlled two-thirds of Southern mileage. Northern control increased still more when the depression of 1893–1897 compelled the reorganization and consolidation of many Southern lines by Northern banking firms.

The Southern iron industry experienced spectacular growth in the 1880s. Most of the expansion was concentrated in northern Alabama, where the proximity of coal, limestone, and ore made the new city of Birmingham "the Pittsburgh of the South." In 1880, the former slave states had produced only 9 percent of the nation's pig iron; by 1890 that proportion had more than doubled. Northern capital figured prominently in this growth: during the 1880s, according to one observer, "the Federal brigadier was almost as prominent in the iron world of the South as the Confederate brigadier was in the political world at Washington."9 Northern domination of the industry intensified in 1907, when U.S. Steel gained control of Tennessee Iron and Coal, the South's largest company.

Northern Perceptions of the New South

Southern proponents of industrialization welcomed this invasion of Yankee dollars. The South was still too poor to generate sufficient capital itself for heavy industry. The industrial "expositions" held in various Southern cities during the 1880s were designed primarily to attract the favorable attention of Northern and

European investors. The rhetoric of some Yankee prophets of a New South outdid even that of their Southern counterparts. Edward Atkinson of Massachusetts, a textile manufacturer and antebellum free soiler, said in 1881 that the new Southern spirit of "vigor and energy" was "creating new conditions" of prosperity and racial comity that would soon excise the "cancer of slavery" and guide the New South "in the direction of peace, order, stability, and prosperity." In 1886 William D. Kelley of Pennsylvania, a former radical Republican congressman, published a book entitled *The Old South and the New* that pulled out all the stops. "Wealth and honor are in the pathway of the New South," wrote Kelley. "Her impulses are those which are impelling the advance of civilization. . . . She is the coming El Dorado of American adventure."[10]

Atkinson and Kelley represented a significant slice of Republican opinion in the 1880s. Both had been active in the antislavery movement. Both had supported a radical reconstruction policy. Political reconstruction having fallen short of unqualified success, however, they now placed their hopes in economic reconstruction. As they saw it, the modernization of the North had raised the standard of living for all classes and had promoted a progressive ethos; they hoped that Southern modernization would improve material conditions for both races, soften racial asperities, and give blacks the leverage for upward mobility that politics had never done. The South might even become like New England, said a Boston radical. "With railroads and telegraphs traversing its domain should go schools, factories, shops, a better family and community feeling." In 1885, a Massachusetts Republican concluded that "work and money have brought into vogue new ideals, new tests and new ambitions in Southern society. Capital is, after all, the greatest agent of civilization . . . and the two races will move kindly together when wealth is more evenly divided between them."[11]

Education in the New South

The South experienced significant educational as well as economic growth in the 1880s. Although black higher education was still supported mainly by Northern missionary societies, several Southern states established their own black colleges or industrial institutes during the decade. Virginia provided some state aid to Hampton Institute, while Alabama appropriated a modest sum to help Booker T. Washington found Tuskegee Institute. The number of black students enrolled in secondary schools and colleges doubled during the 1880s, while enrollments in black elementary schools grew faster than the population.

But in many respects the Southern educational landscape remained bleak. In 1880, 20 percent of the whites and more than 70 percent of the blacks were still illiterate. Fewer than three-fifths of the white children and two-fifths of the black children of school age attended school. The South spent less than one-third as much per pupil as the North. In the rural South, the average school term was three months or less. "The typical Southern free school," wrote a sympathetic Northern observer in 1888, "is kept in a log house, with dirt or puncheon floor, without desks or blackboards." Millions of children were growing up without adequate schooling. "It is desperately important that those children should be educated. The

North is rich and can educate its children. The South is poor and cannot."[12]

From this concern arose a movement for federal aid to education, with the funds to be apportioned among the states on the basis of illiteracy. This would channel three-quarters of the funds to the South. The idea of federal support for Southern schools had persisted since 1867, when Senator Charles Sumner had introduced legislation for this purpose. In 1872, the House had passed a bill to appropriate the proceeds from public land sales for public schools. But the Senate had failed to act, and the economic depression discouraged further efforts during the 1870s. The revelation by the 1880 census that more than six million Americans aged ten or older could not read and write revived the movement. The 1880 Republican platform pledged the party to work for federal aid. Surviving abolitionists urged generous appropriations for Southern education. "The North," said an antislavery veteran, "shared the responsibility for the sin of slavery, is responsible for emancipation and enfranchisement, and is therefore under a triple obligation to share the duty and the burden of equipping the emancipated Negro race for the duties of citizenship."[13]

In 1884, the Senate passed a bill introduced by Henry W. Blair of New Hampshire to grant the states $77 million (about $700 million at 1981 prices) over seven years for public schools. The money would be apportioned on the illiteracy ratio, and each state would be required to match it with additional appropriations to its own school funds. Lower-South Democrats—whose states would benefit most—as well as Republicans voted for this bill. But the House, controlled by the Democrats from 1883 to 1889, refused to pass it. The Democratic opposition sprang from the party's commitment to states' rights, from fears that the bill would insert an opening wedge for the revival of Reconstruction, and from the suspicions of low-tariff Democrats that the measure was a protectionist trick to maintain high duties.* Although the Republican Senate passed the Blair bill a second time in 1886 and a third in 1888, the margin of passage was reduced in 1888, and the House as usual refused to consider it. When Blair brought his bill before the Senate a fourth time in 1890, three Republicans and four Southern Democrats switched their previous affirmative votes to negative, thereby killing the measure for good. Thus ended one of the more promising efforts to improve Southern schools.

Politics in the New South

Nevertheless, the mood of New South prophets both above and below the Potomac remained upbeat. Editor George William Curtis of *Harper's Weekly* in 1886 expressed the widely shared conviction that "political differences and the friction of races are yielding to the beneficent touch of healthy industrial enterprise."[14]

---

*During most of the 1880s the federal budget ran a surplus. Most Democrats wished to lower the tariff (a major form of taxation then) in order to bring the government's receipts down to the level of its expenditures. Most Republicans opposed tariff reduction. Democrats suspected that one reason for Republican support for federal aid to education was to eliminate the budget surplus and thereby to blunt the movement for lower tariffs.

Although more than a little wishful thinking underlay this belief, some evidence also existed to support it. Racial violence had declined since the heyday of the Klan and the White League. The conservative white supremacists who ruled the South during the 1880s were hardly enlightened by modern standards, but their racism was less virulent than that of the next generation of Southern politicians. Although never allowed to exercise as much power as during Reconstruction, blacks continued to vote and to hold office in considerable numbers during the 1880s and into the 1890s. The Republican share of the two-party vote in the former slave states remained at about 40 percent in the presidential elections of 1884 and 1888. Republican strength in the upper South was impressive: in addition to the successful coalition with Readjusters in Virginia, the party won the Tennessee governorship when the Democrats split on the state debt issue in 1880, and it came within a whisker of winning the North Carolina governorship in 1884. At least one Southern black man served in every Congress from 1881 to 1901. Hundreds of blacks were elected to state legislatures during these years, and thousands to local offices. The complete suppression of black political participation came in the years around 1900, not when federal troops ceased to enforce reconstruction in 1877.

But this point must not be overstated. In the lower South the suppression of Republican votes by intimidation and chicanery prevailed from the 1870s on. In a fair vote, at least South Carolina, Mississippi, and Louisiana would probably have gone Republican. But these were precisely the states that recorded the smallest Republican totals after 1876. Because the threat to white supremacy was greatest there, whites took the strongest steps to eliminate the threat. South Carolina passed an "eight box law" in 1882, which required voters to deposit votes for various offices in separate ballot boxes. This was in effect a literacy test that disfranchised many black voters. Georgia required payment of a poll tax. Several states passed complicated registration laws that discouraged the poor and the poorly informed from voting. Ballot-box stuffing became a fine art. Democrats in South Carolina loaded the boxes with thin "tissue ballots." When counters discovered that the number of ballots exceeded the number of legal voters, they withdrew and discarded the larger, heavier ballots—all Republican.* Similar techniques prevailed elsewhere. White landowners deposited votes on behalf of their black sharecroppers. This helps to explain the large Democratic vote in the black districts of some states. As an Alabamian explained: "Any time it was necessary the black belt could put in ten, fifteen, twenty or thirty thousand Negro votes."[15]

Other Realities in the New South

Other blemishes also marred the New South's image of racial comity. The worst was the convict leasing system. Ironically, this form of neoslavery was a consequence of emancipation. Under the old regime, most slave crimes were punished on the plantation. The Southern prison system was therefore inadequate to accom-

---

*Ballots were then printed by the parties, not by the state. One of the reforms associated with the introduction of the Australian secret ballot system after 1888 was the printing of uniform ballots by the state governments.

modate the increase in convicted criminals after the war. Most states began leasing convicts to private contractors—coal-mining firms, railroad construction companies, planters, and so on. This practice proved so successful that the post-Reconstruction regimes expanded it. The state not only saved the cost of housing and feeding the prisoners but also received an income for leasing them; the lessees obtained cheap labor whom they could work like slaves. Indeed, the system seemed good for everybody—except the convicts. The cruelty and exploitation they suffered soon made convict leasing a national scandal. Ninety percent of the convicts were black, the result in part of discriminatory law enforcement practices. The convicts were ill fed, ill clothed, victimized by sadistic guards, and worked almost to death. The annual death rate among Mississippi convicts in the 1880s was about 11 percent; in Arkansas it was 25 percent. A group of convict laborers building a railroad in South Carolina suffered a death rate of 50 percent in 1878 and 1879. A grand jury investigation of a convict hospital in Mississippi in 1887 reported that most patients had "their backs cut in great wales, scars, and blisters, some with the skin peeling off in pieces as the result of severe beatings. . . . They were lying there dying, some of them on bare boards, so poor and emaciated that their bones almost came through their skin."[16]

Northerners who were otherwise friendly to the New South condemned "this newest and most revolting form of slavery" as "a state of things hardly credible in a civilized community." Thoughtful Southerners agreed; an official investigation in Georgia pronounced convict leasing "barbaric," "worse than slavery," "a disgrace to civilized people."[17] Reform groups, many of them led by women, sprang up in the South to work for the abolition of convict leasing. But the practice proved difficult to reform. Too many powerful people profited from it. Part of the New South's industrial progress was based on it. Only in the first two decades of the twentieth century did Southern reformers gradually manage to overturn the system.

In other respects also, the glitter of the New South turned out to be more gilt than gold. While certain industries grew impressively, the Southern economy remained in colonial dependence on the North. Southern textile mills produced the coarser grades of yarn and cloth, often sending them to New England mills for higher-grade finishing. Northern ownership of Southern steel mills and railroads sometimes brought pricing and rate structures that discriminated against the South. Although the ex-Confederate states doubled their share of the national manufacturing capacity from 5 percent in 1880 to 10 percent in 1900, the latter figure was virtually the same as it had been in 1860. New South industrial progress had done no more than restore the region's antebellum standing relative to the North. In per capita income, the New South did not even do this well. Although Southern per capita income grew by 21 percent between 1880 and 1900, this barely kept pace with Northern growth and left the Southern average only two-fifths of the Northern—the same proportion it had been in 1880 and well below the two-thirds of 1860.

One reason for this failure to gain on the North was the low wages that prevailed in Southern industry. Another reason was the persistent anemia of Southern agriculture. The vicious cycle of debt and overproduction continued to drive down the price of cotton and to impoverish its growers. Except for occasional lip service to the virtues of crop diversification, most New South prophets said little and did less about agriculture. Nearly all new investment went into the nonagricultural sector. While manufacturing capital per capita increased by 300 percent in the ex-Confederate states between 1880 and 1900, the amount per capita invested in agriculture increased by only 29 percent.

The destitution of Southern agriculture produced explosive political consequences after 1890. The Populist movement and other "redneck revolts" overthrew several conservative regimes and permanently altered the Southern political landscape. Meanwhile an attempt to revive federal enforcement of voting rights fell just short of success. With its failure, the last lingering legacy of Reconstruction faded away.

FAREWELL TO THE BLOODY SHIRT

After the collapse of the Readjusters and of other independent movements in 1883, Northern Republicans pursued various and sometimes contradictory courses toward the South. In 1884, presidential nominee James G. Blaine at first hoped to win votes in the industrializing portions of the region on the tariff issue. When this hope proved illusory, Blaine unfurled the bloody shirt and charged that the suppression of Southern Republican votes had cost him the election, which he lost narrowly to Democrat Grover Cleveland. But a good many Republicans had become tired of the bloody shirt, especially since the party seemed to be able to do little to protect black voters even when it held national power. In 1888, still hoping that the presumed legions of old Southern Whigs could be won over on economic issues, the Republican National Committee concentrated almost exclusively on the tariff. Whatever the potency of this issue, the party's presidential nominee Benjamin Harrison won the presidency by carrying 233 of 248 Northern electoral votes, and even came close to cracking the solid South: a switch of less than one-half of one percent of the popular votes in Virginia and West Virginia would have put these states in the Republican column.

But in Mississippi, Louisiana, and South Carolina, the Republicans won respectively only 27, 26, and 17 percent of the vote. Such outrageous results constituted "an open attack on the Constitution," declared a Republican newspaper. "We dare not ignore the challenge."[18] Having won control of both houses of Congress as well as the presidency in 1888, some Republicans wished to respond to the challenge with new enforcement legislation. When Congress met in December 1889, seventeen contested Southern election cases confronted the lawmakers. The House decided eleven of them in favor of the Republican claimants. The testimony in these cases convinced many congressmen of the need for a new federal elections law based on the constitutional right of Congress to regulate the time, place, and manner of electing its members (Article I, Section 4).

Congressman Henry Cabot Lodge of Massachusetts took charge of the numerous bills introduced in the House and fashioned them into a single comprehensive measure. The Lodge bill authorized federal district judges to appoint election supervisors in any congressional district upon petition by 100 voters. The supervisors would have the power to inspect registration books, observe the voting, and advise voters of election procedures. Federal circuit courts were to appoint canvassing boards to certify the results of an election (the board's decision was to be final even if it conflicted with results reported by state boards) and to initiate proceedings against anyone charged with intimidation or fraud. Although this was a strong bill, it applied only to congressional elections and would do nothing to protect black voters in state and local contests, where matters vital to their interests were decided—schools, labor legislation, criminal punishments, and so on. Nevertheless, Democrats mounted a hysterical campaign against this "Force Bill," which, they said, would bring back the darkest days of "Black Reconstruction." Despite the furor, the House passed Lodge's bill by a straight party vote on July 2, 1890.

In the Senate, however, other legislation crowded the Lodge bill aside. Congress had already enacted a new pensions act, an anti-trust law, and an expanded silver coinage act. Still on the Senate docket was the McKinley tariff—the most comprehensive upward revision of import duties since the war. For many Republicans this complicated measure took precedence over an elections law. The Senate Republican caucus decided to postpone the latter until the next session in order to complete work on the tariff. This loss of momentum proved fatal to the Lodge bill. At the next session a group of Western Republican senators, desiring still more generous silver coinage legislation, agreed to abandon the elections bill in return for Southern support of their silver bill. Unable to impose cloture to stop a Democratic filibuster, the Republican managers of the elections bill were compelled to give it up.

The death of the Lodge bill marked the end of an era. The abandonment of legislation on the "Southern question" in favor of bills dealing with tariffs, trusts, and silver symbolized the transformation of American concerns. The sectional and racial issues that had dominated every presidential election for the past half-century faded into insignificance for the next half-century. The generation that had fought the Civil War was passing away, and a new generation with no memories of the war and little interest in its issues was emerging to leadership. The Lodge bill was the last black rights measure to come so close to passage until the Civil Rights Act of 1957. In 1894, the Democratic Congress repealed much of the 1870–1871 enforcement legislation. The era of Reconstruction died an unmourned death.

Epilogue

Southern Democrats correctly interpreted the failure of the Lodge elections bill as a signal of final Northern surrender. Before they could act on this signal, however, the emergence of Populism created a new crisis. The People's party, or Populists, grew out of the agricultural depression and rural unrest in Southern and Western states. When cotton prices plummeted nearly 50 percent in four years, to an all-time low of 4.5 cents a pound in 1894, farmers became desperate. The Southern Farmers' Alliance mobilized hundreds of thousands of farmers into a powerful political force. In several states—South Carolina, Tennessee, Florida, and Arkansas—the farmers movement gained power within the Democratic party and did not form an independent party. But in other states, the farmers bolted the Democrats and in 1892 joined with rebellious Westerners to form the People's party—the largest third party since the Civil War.

In 1896, the national Democratic party absorbed the Populists and nominated William Jennings Bryan for president on a platform advocating the unlimited coinage of silver as a means to reverse declining farm prices and to end the depression that had begun with the Panic of 1893. Although Bryan carried every ex-Confederate state and most trans-Mississippi states, Republican William McKinley swept the North and also won Maryland, Kentucky, West Virginia, and Delaware. The Populist party was dead, while the Democratic party outside the South would appear moribund throughout the next fifteen years.

During its short life, however, Populism caused turmoil in the politics of a half-dozen Southern states. Republican/Populist coalitions won control of North Carolina for four years and fell short of success in a couple of other states only because of wholesale Democratic frauds. Democrats once again pulled out all the stops on the themes of "Negro domination" and "revival of Black Reconstruction" to discredit the Populist/Republican alliance. The viciousness of racist propaganda reached a new low, and violence rose almost to Reconstruction levels. When the dust settled after 1896, the Democrats had regained firm control of Southern politics and had crushed what turned out to be the last serious challenge to one-party rule in the South for the next sixty years.

As part of this process, Southern states disfranchised black voters. Democrats professed several motives for this action: it would purify Southern politics from chaos and corruption; it would eliminate illiterate and unqualified voters; it would make "normal" politics possible once more without the destructive specter of black rule. But the underlying purpose was a Democratic determination to consolidate one-party rule by disfranchising the opposition. Between 1889 and 1902, every ex-Confederate state followed Georgia's example and imposed a poll tax as a prerequisite for voting. In 1890 Mississippi established a literacy qualification, and other states followed suit: South Carolina in 1895, Louisiana in 1898, North Carolina in 1900, Alabama in 1901, Virginia in 1902, and Georgia in 1908. The last five of these states allowed illiterates to vote if they owned property assessed at $300 or more. Since a good many white men could meet neither the literacy nor property qualifications, four states (Mississippi, South Carolina, Virginia, and Georgia) adopted "understanding" clauses, which allowed a registrar to enroll illiterate, propertyless men if they could demonstrate an understanding of a section of the state constitution when read to them. In effect, this gave registrars *carte blanche* to grant the ballot to whites and deny it to blacks—which is precisely what they did. Four states—Louisiana, North Carolina, Alabama, and Georgia— also enacted "grandfather" clauses, allowing men to vote if they could prove that they or their ancestors had voted before 1867—the year blacks were enfranchised. This barefaced violation of the federal Constitution was nullified by the Supreme Court—but not until 1915. The Supreme Court upheld the other suffrage provisions of Southern constitutions, for the Fifteenth Amendment forbade denial of the franchise only on grounds of race or color—not literacy, property, or tax paying. In *Williams* v. *Mississippi* (1898) the Court approved the Mississippi franchise restrictions and the understanding clause because they did not "on their face discriminate between the races."*

Two years earlier, in *Plessy* v. *Ferguson,* the Supreme Court had also sanctioned another dimension of the second-class citizenship fastened on blacks during this period—Jim Crowism. *Plessy* concerned a Louisiana statute requiring separate racial accommodations on railroad passenger cars. Before 1890, segregation in public accommodations was widespread but not universal in the South. Some railroads made blacks ride in "second-class" cars (usually the smoking car) even if they paid full fare. Challenges to this policy came before the newly created Interstate Commerce Commission, which ruled in 1889 that railroads must provide equal accommodations for both races. The ruling, however, did not require

---

*For good measure, after virtually eliminating black voters the Democrats established the "white primary," restricting the franchise to whites in primary elections to nominate party candidates. Since disfranchisement had all but destroyed the Republican party, the primary became the only meaningful election in the South.

the *same* accommodations. This opened the floodgates for Jim Crow legislation. By 1891, seven states had passed laws mandating "separate but equal" railroad coaches. Although such accommodations were rarely equal in fact, the Supreme Court's ruling in *Plessy* legitimated the separate but equal doctrine and thereby put the stamp of approval on Jim Crow. Segregation by law soon prevailed in almost every aspect of Southern public life—streetcars, water fountains, restaurants, recreational facilities, and so on.

While Jim Crow laws formally placed blacks in a separate caste, disfranchisement virtually eliminated black voters as a factor in Southern politics for half a century. Poor white voters also got caught in the disfranchisement net. The poll tax and other restrictive measures reduced the white electorate by a quarter, and the absence of a two-party system lowered voter turnouts still more. Not until the last third of the twentieth century did a two-party system reemerge in the South. And not until the civil rights movement of the 1950s and 1960s produced a second Reconstruction did Southern blacks again achieve the rights and power they had possessed during the first.

Notes

CHAPTER 26

1. James L. Roark, *Masters Without Slaves: Southern Planters in the Civil War and Reconstruction* (New York, 1977), p. 86; John T. Trowbridge, *A Picture of the Desolated States and the Work of Restoration, 1865–1868* (Hartford, 1868), p. 577.

2. Eric L. McKitrick, *Andrew Johnson and Reconstruction* (Chicago, 1960), p. 40.

3. James P. Shenton (ed.), *The Reconstruction: A Documentary History* (New York, 1963), p. 18; Robert M. Myers (ed.), *The Children of Pride: A True Story of Georgia and the Civil War* (New York, 1972), p. 1273.

4. Trowbridge, *A Picture of the Desolated States*, p. 291; Leon F. Litwack, *Been in the Storm So Long: The Aftermath of Slavery* (New York, 1979), p. 108.

5. Whitelaw Reid, *After the War: A Tour of the Southern States 1865–1866* (Cincinnati, 1866), p. 296; Sidney Andrews, *The South Since the War* (Boston, 1866), p. 95.

6. McKitrick, *Andrew Johnson and Reconstruction*, p. 20; John Hope Franklin, *Reconstruction: After the Civil War* (Chicago, 1961), p. 27.

7. McKitrick, *Andrew Johnson and Reconstruction*, p. 87.

8. Kenneth M. Stampp, *The Era of Reconstruction* (New York, 1965), pp. 52–53.

9. Michael Les Benedict (ed.), *The Fruits of Victory: Alternatives in Restoring the Union, 1865–1877* (Philadelphia, 1975), pp. 93–94.

10. Clifton Hall, *Andrew Johnson, Military Governor of Tennessee* (Princeton, 1916), p. 221; LaWanda Cox and John H. Cox, *Politics, Principle, & Prejudice: Dilemma of Reconstruction America* (New York, 1963), p. 163.

11. Howard K. Beale, *The Critical Year: A Study of Andrew Johnson and Reconstruction* (New York, 1930), pp. 63–64.

12. McKitrick, *Andrew Johnson and Reconstruction*, p. 78 and n.

13. Edward McPherson, *The Political History of the United States During the Period of Reconstruction* (Washington, D.C., 1875), p. 19.

14. McKitrick, *Andrew Johnson and Reconstruction*, p. 167.

15. *Boston Commonwealth,* October 7, 1865.

16. Michael Perman, *Reunion Without Compromise: The South and Reconstruction 1865–1868* (Cambridge, 1973), p. 82; Andrews, *The South Since the War,* p. 391.

17. Michael Les Benedict, *A Compromise of Principle: Congressional Republicans and Reconstruction, 1863–1869* (New York, 1974), p. 120.

18. McKitrick, *Andrew Johnson and Reconstruction,* p. 211.

19. Perman, *Reunion Without Compromise,* p. 100; *Boston Commonwealth,* September 30, 1865.

20. Perman, *Reunion Without Compromise,* pp. 170–71; McKitrick, *Andrew Johnson and Reconstruction,* p. 73.

21. McKitrick, *Andrew Johnson and Reconstruction,* pp. 173, 183.

22. *Ibid.,* p. 173.

23. Litwack, *Been in the Storm So Long,* p. 296.

24. Reid, *After the War,* p. 564; Thomas Wentworth Higginson, Journal, entry of November 21, 1863, Higginson Papers, Houghton Library, Harvard University.

25. *Congressional Globe,* 39th Cong., 1st sess., (1866) 1309.

26. George R. Bentley, *A History of the Freedmen's Bureau* (Philadelphia, 1955), p. 93.

27. James M. McPherson, *The Struggle for Equality: Abolitionists and the Negro in the Civil War and Reconstruction* (Princeton, 1964), pp. 411–12.

28. Samuel Thomas to Oliver O. Howard, September 21, 1865, Freedmen's Bureau Records, National Archives, Record Group 105, Box 3, Vol. 1; Andrews, *The South Since the War,* p. 398.

29. Samuel Thomas to Oliver O. Howard, September 21, 1865, *loc. cit.*

30. Bentley, *A History of the Freedmen's Bureau,* pp. 104, 159; Walter Lynwood Fleming (ed.), *Documentary History of Reconstruction,* 2 vols. (Cleveland, 1906), I, 368; Roark, *Masters Without Slaves,* p. 154.

31. Bentley, *A History of the Freedmen's Bureau,* p. 151.

32. *Ibid.,* p. 159.

33. *Chicago Tribune,* December 1, 1865.

CHAPTER 27

1. *Congressional Globe,* 39th Cong., 1st sess., (1865) Appendix, 2–3.

2. Edward McPherson, *The Political History of the United States During the Period of Reconstruction* (Washington, D.C., 1875), pp. 68–72.

3. Eric McKitrick, *Andrew Johnson and Reconstruction* (Chicago, 1960), p. 292.

4. McPherson, *Political History,* pp. 58–63.

5. McKitrick, *Andrew Johnson and Reconstruction,* p. 297n.

6. Michael Les Benedict (ed.), *The Fruits of Victory: Alternatives in Restoring the Union, 1865–1877* (Philadelphia, 1975), p. 22.

7. McPherson, *Political History,* pp. 74–78.

8. LaWanda Cox and John H. Cox, *Politics, Principle, and Prejudice: Dilemma of Reconstruction America* (New York, 1963), pp. 212, 202; Michael Les Benedict, *A Compromise of Principle: Congressional Republicans and Reconstruction* (New York, 1974), p. 164.

9. Cox and Cox, *Politics, Principle, and Prejudice,* p. 206; Benedict, *Compromise of Principle,* p. 165.

10. James M. McPherson, *The Struggle for Equality* (Princeton, 1964), pp. 352, 354, 365; Kenneth M. Stampp, *The Era of Reconstruction* (New York, 1965), p. 142.

11. McKitrick, *Andrew Johnson and Reconstruction,* pp. 318–19.

12. *New York Tribune,* May 22, 1866.

13. Edward McPherson, *Political History*, p. 135; McKitrick, *Andrew Johnson and Reconstruction*, p. 432.

14. McKitrick, *Andrew Johnson and Reconstruction*, p. 451n.; Michael Perman, *Reunion Without Compromise: The South and Reconstruction 1865–1868* (Cambridge, 1973), pp. 238, 239.

15. Cox and Cox, *Politics, Principle, and Prejudice*, p. 230.

16. Benedict, *Fruits of Victory*, p. 31.

17. David Donald, *The Politics of Reconstruction 1863–1867* (Baton Rouge, 1965), pp. 62–63.

18. Benedict, *Fruits of Victory*, pp. 111–12.

19. Stampp, *Era of Reconstruction*, p. 170.

CHAPTER 28

1. *New York Tribune*, October 27, 1866.

2. Michael Les Benedict, *The Impeachment and Trial of Andrew Johnson* (New York, 1973), p. 25.

3. *Ibid.*, p. 56.

4. Edward McPherson, *The Political History of the United States During the Period of Reconstruction* (Washington, D.C., 1875), p. 307.

5. Benedict, *Impeachment*, pp. 58–59.

6. Parker Pillsbury to Gerrit Smith, November 27, 1867, Gerrit Smith Papers, Syracuse University Library.

7. Georges Clemenceau, *American Reconstruction 1865–1870*, trans. Margaret MacVeagh (New York, 1928), p. 131.

8. Michael Perman, *Reunion Without Compromise: The South and Reconstruction 1865–1868* (Cambridge, 1973), pp. 320–21; C. Vann Woodward, "Seeds of Failure in Radical Race Policy," in Harold Hyman (ed.), *New Frontiers of the American Reconstruction* (Urbana, Ill., 1966), p. 137; Ira Brown, "Pennsylvania and the Rights of the Negro, 1865–1887," *Pennsylvania History*, 28 (January 1961), 51.

9. *Independent*, November 14, 21, 1867; *New York Tribune*, December 9, 1867.

10. Perman, *Reunion Without Compromise*, p. 317.

11. Hans L. Trefousse, *Impeachment of a President: Andrew Johnson, the Blacks, and Reconstruction* (Knoxville, 1975), p. 119; Eric McKitrick, *Andrew Johnson and Reconstruction* (Chicago, 1960), p. 500n; Michael Les Benedict, *A Compromise of Principle: Congressional Republicans and Reconstruction, 1863–1869* (New York, 1974), p. 290.

12. Benedict, *Compromise of Principle*, p. 299.

13. *The Trial of Andrew Johnson . . . for High Crimes and Misdemeanors*, 3 vols. (Washington, D.C., 1868), I, 88.

14. *House Reports*, No. 7, 40th Cong., 1st sess., (1867) 2; William R. Brock, *An American Crisis: Congress and Reconstruction 1865–1867* (London, 1963), p. 260.

15. Benedict, *Impeachment*, p. 179.

16. Brock, *American Crisis*, p. 262.

17. Perman, *Reunion Without Compromise*, p. 317.

18. Kenneth M. Stampp, *The Era of Reconstruction 1867–1877* (New York, 1965), p. 170; Joe Gray Taylor, *Louisiana Reconstructed, 1863–1877* (Baton Rouge, 1974), p. 148; John Hope Franklin, *Reconstruction: After the Civil War* (Chicago, 1961), p. 105.

19. Benedict, *Compromise of Principle*, p. 317.

20. *Ibid.*, p. 319.

CHAPTER 29

1. *Independent,* May 4, 1868.

2. *Springfield Republican,* quoted in *The Revolution,* April 23, 1868.

3. Charles Sumner to Frank Bird, May 28, 1868, Bird Papers, Houghton Library, Harvard University; *Independent,* May 28, 1868.

4. John Hope Franklin, "Election of 1868," in Arthur M. Schlesinger, Jr. (ed.), *History of American Presidential Elections,* 4 vols. (New York, 1971), II, 1269; *Independent,* July 16, 1868.

5. Edward McPherson, *The Political History of the United States During the Period of Reconstruction* (Washington, D.C., 1875), pp. 381, 382; Charles H. Coleman, *The Election of 1868* (New York, 1933), p. 155; Franklin, "The Election of 1868," p. 1259; *La Crosse Democrat,* quoted in *National Anti-Slavery Standard,* March 7, 1868.

6. Franklin, "The Election of 1868," p. 1262.

7. Allen W. Trelease, *White Terror: The Ku Klux Klan Conspiracy and Southern Reconstruction* (New York, 1971), pp. xlv, 46.

8. *Zion's Herald,* December 10, 1868.

9. *National Anti-Slavery Standard,* November 14, 1868.

10. Michael Les Benedict, *A Compromise of Principle: Congressional Republicans and Reconstruction, 1863–1869* (New York, 1974), p. 332.

11. *Northwestern Christian Advocate,* February 9, 1870; *New York Tribune,* April 18, 1870.

12. Allan Nevins, *Hamilton Fish: The Inner History of the Grant Administration* (New York, 1936), p. 271.

13. Edward L. Pierce, *Memoir and Letters of Charles Sumner,* 4 vols. (Boston, 1877–1893), IV, 448.

14. Howard N. Meyer, *Let Us Have Peace: The Story of Ulysses S. Grant* (New York, 1966), p. 202.

15. William B. Hesseltine, *Ulysses S. Grant, Politician* (New York, 1935), p. 218.

16. *Speeches, Correspondence, and Political Papers of Carl Schurz,* 6 vols. (New York, 1913), II, 359.

CHAPTER 30

1. John Hope Franklin, *Reconstruction: After the Civil War* (Chicago, 1961), p. 87.

2. James S. Pike, *The Prostrate State: South Carolina Under Negro Government* (New York, 1874), pp. 15, 12.

3. Franklin, *Reconstruction,* pp. 93, 98, 101; E. Merton Coulter, *The South During Reconstruction* (Baton Rouge, 1947), pp. 124–26.

4. Carl N. Degler, *The Other South: Southern Dissenters in the Nineteenth Century* (New York, 1974), pp. 218, 226.

5. *Ibid.,* pp. 217–18.

6. *Ibid.,* pp. 208–9.

7. *Ibid.,* p. 254.

8. Otto H. Olsen, "Reconsidering the Scalawags," *Civil War History,* 12 (December 1966), 314; Degler, *Other South,* p. 233.

9. Thomas Holt, *Black Over White: Negro Political Leadership in South Carolina During Reconstruction* (Urbana, Ill., 1977), pp. 106–7.

10. Degler, *Other South,* p. 258.

11. Holt, *Black Over White,* p. 104.

12. Degler, *Other South,* pp. 256, 257.

13. Holt, *Black Over White,* pp. 59–60.

14. *Ibid.*, p. 123.

15. James Bryce, *The American Commonwealth*, 3rd ed., 2 vols. (New York, 1895), II, 476–77; Coulter, *South During Reconstruction*, p. 148.

16. Richard N. Current, *Three Carpetbag Governors* (Baton Rouge, 1967), p. 60; Roger W. Shugg, *Origins of Class Struggle in Louisiana* (Baton Rouge, 1939), p. 227.

17. Coulter, *South During Reconstruction*, 153.

18. *Harper's Weekly*, November 11, 1871.

19. Allen W. Trelease, *White Terror: The Ku Klux Klan Conspiracy and Southern Reconstruction* (New York, 1971), pp. 296, 354, and *passim.*

20. *Ibid.*, p. 259.

21. *Ibid.*, pp. 369, 327.

22. *Ibid.*, p. 268–69.

23. William Gillette, "Election of 1872," in Arthur M. Schlesinger, Jr., (ed.), *History of American Presidential Elections*, 4 vols. (New York, 1971), II, 1335–36.

24. Lawrence Grossman, *The Democratic Party and the Negro: Northern and National Politics, 1868–1892* (Urbana, Ill., 1976), p. 26.

25. Gillette, "Election of 1872," p. 1336.

26. *Ibid.*, pp. 1358–59.

27. James M. McPherson, "Grant or Greeley? The Abolitionist Dilemma in the Election of 1872," *American Historical Review*, 71 (October 1965), 49, 51.

CHAPTER 31

1. Leon F. Litwack, *Been in the Storm So Long: The Aftermath of Slavery* (New York, 1979), pp. 472–73.

2. *American Freedman*, I (April 1866), 2–6.

3. *Independent*, June 4, 1874.

4. Robert Higgs, *Competition and Coercion: Blacks in the American Economy 1865–1914* (Cambridge, 1977), p. 49.

5. Table adapted from data in Roger L. Ransom and Richard Sutch, "Growth and Welfare in the American South of the Nineteenth Century," *Explorations in Economic History*, 16 (1979), 225.

6. Samuel M. Browne to Samuel L. M. Barlow, January 26, April 9, 1868, S. L. M. Barlow Papers, Henry E. Huntington Library.

7. Ransom and Sutch, *One Kind of Freedom*, p. 161.

8. Allan Nevins, *The Emergence of Modern America, 1865–1878* (New York, 1927), p. 189.

CHAPTER 32

1. William Gillette, *Retreat From Reconstruction 1869–1879* (Baton Rouge, 1979), p. 107.

2. William B. Hesseltine, *Ulysses S. Grant: Politician* (New York, 1935), p. 348.

3. James M. McPherson, *The Abolitionist Legacy: From Reconstruction to the NAACP* (Princeton, 1975), pp. 46, 40–41.

4. *Congressional Record*, 43rd Cong., 2nd sess., (1875) 367.

5. Vincent P. De Santis, *Republicans Face the Southern Question: The New Departure Years, 1877–1897* (Baltimore, 1959), pp. 39–40.

6. *Washington National Republican*, January 24, 1874; Hesseltine, *Grant*, p. 358.

7. Vernon Lane Wharton, *The Negro in Mississippi, 1865–1890* (Chapel Hill, N.C., 1947), p. 183.

8. *Ibid.*, pp. 187, 190.

9. Richard N. Current, *Three Carpetbag Governors* (Baton Rouge, 1967), p. 88.

10. Wharton, *Negro in Mississippi*, p. 195.

11. Everette Swinney, "Enforcing the Fifteenth Amendment," *Journal of Southern History*, 27 (1962), 208.

12. 25 *Fed. Cas.* 707, p. 210; 92 *U.S. Reports*, 542.

13. Arthur Schlesinger, Jr. (ed.), *History of American Presidential Elections 1789–1968*, 4 vols. (New York, 1971), II, 1437–40.

14. *Ibid.*, p. 1441.

15. De Santis, *Republicans Face the Southern Question*, p. 54; Schlesinger, *American Presidential Elections*, II, 1449–50.

16. Hesseltine, *Grant*, p. 409.

17. Keith I. Polakoff, *The Politics of Inertia: The Election of 1876 and the End of Reconstruction* (Baton Rouge, 1973), pp. 115, 145–46.

18. C. Vann Woodward, *Reunion and Reaction: The Compromise of 1877 and the End of Reconstruction*, rev. ed. (New York, 1956), p. 23; Harry Barnard, *Rutherford B. Hayes and His America* (Indianapolis, 1954), p. 343.

19. Hans L. Trefousse, *The Radical Republicans: Lincoln's Vanguard for Racial Justice* (New York, 1969), p. 469; McPherson, *Abolitionist Legacy*, 89–90.

20. De Santis, *Republicans Face the Southern Question*, p. 113.

21. McPherson, *Abolitionist Legacy*, p. 93.

22. *Ibid.*, p. 95; Michael Les Benedict, *The Fruits of Victory: Alternatives in Restoring the Union, 1865–1877* (Philadelphia, 1975), p. 74.

CHAPTER 33

1. Stanley P. Hirshson, *Farewell to the Bloody Shirt: Northern Republicans and the Southern Negro, 1877–93* (Bloomington, Ind., 1962), p. 49.

2. *Ibid.*

3. *Independent*, December 12, 1878.

4. Mary R. Dearing, *Veterans in Politics: The Story of the G.A.R.* (Baton Rouge, 1952), pp. 257–58, 262–63.

5. Carl N. Degler, *The Other South: Southern Dissenters in the Nineteenth Century* (New York, 1974), p. 271.

6. *Boston Commonwealth*, June 11, 1881; James Tice Moore, *Two Paths to the New South: The Virginia Debt Controversy, 1870–1883* (Lexington, Ky., 1974), pp. 85–86; Degler, *Other South*, p. 287.

7. Paul M. Gaston, *The New South Creed: A Study in Southern Mythmaking* (New York, 1970), p. 25.

8. *Ibid.*, pp. 42, 108; Joel Chandler Harris (ed.), *Life of Henry W. Grady, Including His Writings and Speeches* (New York, 1890), p. 88.

9. C. Vann Woodward, *Origins of the New South, 1877–1913* (Baton Rouge, 1951), p. 128.

10. James M. McPherson, *The Abolitionist Legacy: From Reconstruction to the NAACP* (Princeton, 1975), pp. 108–9.

11. *Ibid.*

12. *Ibid.*, p. 130.

13. *Independent*, June 11, 1891.

14. *Harper's Weekly*, December 25, 1886.

15. J. Morgan Kousser, *The Shaping of Southern Politics: Suffrage Restriction and the Establishment of the One-Party South, 1880–1910* (New Haven, Conn., 1974), p. 47.

16. Woodward, *Origins of the New South*, p. 214.

17. McPherson, *Abolitionist Legacy*, p. 115; Woodward, *Origins of the New South*, p. 424.

18. McPherson, *Abolitionist Legacy*, p. 134.

Bibliography

ABBREVIATIONS

AH   *Agricultural History*
AHR   *American Historical Review*
CWH   *Civil War History*
JAH   *Journal of American History*
JEH   *Journal of Economic History*
JNH   *Journal of Negro History*
JSH   *Journal of Southern History*
MVHR *Mississippi Valley Historical Review*
SAQ   *South Atlantic Quarterly*

BIBLIOGRAPHIES ON THE CIVIL WAR–RECONSTRUCTION ERA

The number of books and articles on the era of the Civil War and Reconstruction is so enormous that the following essay can provide only a selective listing of the most important and useful of them. Students desiring a more detailed bibliography should consult the following: Don E. Fehrenbacher (ed.), *Manifest Destiny and the Coming of the Civil War* (1970); David Donald (ed.), *The Nation in Crisis, 1861–1877* (1969); and the relevant portions of Frank Freidel (ed.), *Harvard Guide to American History*, rev. ed. (1974). The bibliography of James G. Randall and David Donald, *The Civil War and Reconstruction*, 2nd ed. rev. (1969), contains a rich listing of items published before 1969. The December issue each year through 1977 of the quarterly journal *Civil War History* (1954–) classifies articles dealing with the Civil War era published in other journals during the previous year. Each issue of the *Journal of American History* and the May issue each year of the *Journal of Southern History* list articles published in other journals, including many articles on the Civil War era. The ongoing volumes of *Writings in American History* and *America: History and Life*, contain classified listings of books and articles on all aspects of American history.

GENERAL WORKS ON THE CIVIL WAR–RECONSTRUCTION ERA

Two eminent historians writing a half-century apart have produced magisterial multivolume narratives of America's sectional trauma: James Ford Rhodes, *History of the United States From the Compromise of 1850 to the McKinley-Bryan Campaign of 1896*, 8 vols. (1892–1919); and Allan Nevins, *Ordeal of the Union*, covering the years 1847–1857, 2 vols. (1947); *The Emergence of Lincoln*, covering 1857–1861, 2 vols. (1950), and *The War for the Union*, 4 vols. (1959–1971). In addition to James G. Randall and David Donald, *The Civil War and Reconstruction*, cited in the first section of this bibliography, other important one-volume studies covering all or part of this period include Peter J. Parish, *The American Civil War* (1975) and William R. Brock, *Conflict and Transformation: The United States 1844–1877* (1973), both by British historians who offer valuable perspectives on the American experience; David M. Potter, *Division and the Stresses of Reunion, 1845–1876* (1973); Robert H. Jones, *Disrupted Decades: The Civil War and Reconstruction Years* (1973); David Herbert Donald, *Liberty and Union* (1978); Arthur C. Cole, *The Irrepressible Conflict 1850–1865* (1934); Elbert B. Smith, *The Death of Slavery: The United States, 1837–1865* (1967); Donald M. Jacobs and Raymond H. Robinson, *America's Testing Time 1848–1877* (1973); Emory M. Thomas, *The American War and Peace 1860–1877* (1973); David Lindsey, *Americans in Conflict: The Civil War and Reconstruction* (1974); Ludwell H. Johnson, *Division and Reunion: America 1848–1877* (1978); Thomas H. O'Connor, *The Disunited States: The Era of Civil War and Reconstruction*, 2nd ed. (1978); and George T. McJimsey, *The Dividing and Reuniting of America: 1848–1877* (1981).

Charles A. Beard and Mary A. Beard's sweeping survey of American history, *The Rise of American Civilization*, 2 vols. (1927), interprets the Civil War as a "Second American Revolution," by which an industrializing North destroyed the agrarian civilization of the Old South. Refinements and modifications of this interpretation can be found in Barrington Moore, *Social Origins of Dictatorship and Democracy* (1966) chap. 3: "The American Civil War: The Last Capitalist Revolution"; Margaret Shortreed, "The Anti-Slavery Radicals, 1840–1868," *Past and Present*, no. 16 (1959), 65–87; and Raimondo Luraghi, *The Rise and Fall of the Plantation South* (1978). Carl N. Degler, "The Two Cultures and the Civil War," in Stanley Coben and Lorman Ratner (eds.), *The Development of an American Culture* (1970), pp. 92–119, emphasizes cultural differences between North and South.

Wilbur J. Cash, *The Mind of the South* (1941), evokes the impact of the sectional conflict on the South; while Robert Penn Warren, *The Legacy of the Civil War* (1964), a book published during the centennial commemoration of the conflict, critically appraises the war's meaning. Several essays in Arthur S. Link and Rembert W. Patrick (eds.), *Writing Southern History: Essays in Historiography in Honor of Fletcher M. Green* (1965), evaluate historical writing about the South during the middle decades of the nineteenth century. Carl N. Degler, *The Other South: Southern Dissenters in the Nineteenth Century* (1974), offers a fresh and enlightening account of Southern whites who resisted the dominant institutions and developments in their region. Roger W. Shugg, *Origins of Class Struggle in Louisiana 1840–1875* (1939), focuses on nonelite whites in one state during the era. Superb insights into the mentality of the South's planter elite can be found in the massive collection of letters from the Jones family of Georgia, Robert M. Myers (ed.), *The Children of Pride* (1972).

Hans L. Trefousse, *The Radical Republicans: Lincoln's Vanguard for Racial Justice* (1969), analyzes the group in the North most committed to an overthrow of the Old South's institutions; while George M. Fredrickson, *The Black Image in the White Mind: The Debate Over Afro-American Character and Destiny, 1817–1914* (1972), traces the evolution of racial ideologies during the era.

Several individual historians have published collections of important and stimulating essays on the Civil War and related themes: C. Vann Woodward, *The Burden of Southern History*, rev. ed. (1968), and *American Counterpoint: Slavery and Racism in the North-South Dialogue* (1971); David M. Potter, *The South and the Sectional Conflict* (1968); David Donald, *Lincoln Reconsidered: Essays on the Civil War Era*, 2nd ed., enl. (1961); Stephen B. Oates, *Our Fiery Trial: Abraham Lincoln, John Brown, and the Civil War Era* (1979); and Eric Foner, *Politics and Ideology in the Age of the Civil War* (1980). The literary critic Edmund Wilson has written a number of provocative essays in *Patriotic Gore: Studies in the Literature of the American Civil War* (1962).

Anthologies of essays and articles by various historians include: Charles Crowe (ed.), *The Age of Civil War and Reconstruction, 1830–1900*, rev. ed. (1975); George M. Fredrickson (ed.), *A Nation Divided: Problems and Issues of the Civil War and Reconstruction* (1975); Robert P. Swierenga, (ed.), *Beyond the Civil War Synthesis: Political Essays on the Civil War Era* (1975); Irwin Unger (ed.), *Essays on the Civil War and Reconstruction* (1970); and Harold D. Woodman (ed.), *The Legacy of the American Civil War* (1973).

The history of political parties and presidential elections during the era is ably covered by several historians in Winifred E. A. Bernhard (ed.), *Political Parties in American History* (1973); Arthur M. Schlesinger, Jr. (ed.), *History of U. S. Political Parties*, 4 vols. (1973), vols. I and II; and Arthur M. Schlesinger, Jr. (ed.), *History of American Presidential Elections*, 4 vols. (1971), vol. II. The maps in Charles O. Paullin, *Atlas of the Historical Geography of the United States* (1932), provide a wealth of important data on the social, economic, and political history of this period. *Historical Statistics of the United States* (1975) and Donald B. Dodd and Wynette S. Dodd (eds.), *Historical Statistics of the South* (1973), are indispensable.

The large literature on Abraham Lincoln provides penetrating insights on the antebellum as well as the war years. The fullest and most scholarly study of Lincoln's career is James G. Randall, *Lincoln the President*, 4 vols. (1945–1955; vol. IV completed by Richard N. Current). Randall published several essays on Lincoln and his times, in *Lincoln the Liberal Statesman* (1947). Two other multivolume biographies of the sixteenth president are John G. Nicolay and John Hay, *Abraham Lincoln: A History*, 10 vols. (1890), by Lincoln's wartime private secretaries; and Carl Sandburg, *Abraham Lincoln: The Prairie Years*, 2 vols. (1926), and *Abraham Lincoln: The War Years*, 4 vols. (1939). Both the Nicolay-Hay and Sandburg biographies perpetuate a number of myths and apocryphal stories about Lincoln that have been discredited by subsequent scholarship. To separate fact from fiction in Lincoln's life, two books are useful: Lloyd Lewis, *Myths After Lincoln* (1929); and Richard N. Current, *The Lincoln Nobody Knows* (1958). Among the many one-volume biographies of Lincoln, the following are the best: Benjamin P. Thomas, *Abraham Lincoln: A Biography* (1952); Reinhard H. Luthin, *The Real Abraham Lincoln* (1960); and Stephen B. Oates, *With Malice Toward None: The Life of Abraham Lincoln* (1977). Three anthologies of essays about Lincoln also contain material of value: Norman Graebner (ed.), *The Enduring Lincoln* (1959); Don E. Fehrenbacher (ed.), *The Leadership of Abraham Lincoln* (1970); and Cullom Davis et al. (eds.), *The Public and Private Lincoln: Contemporary Perspectives* (1979). The historical scholarship on Lincoln is summarized and analyzed in Don E. Fehrenbacher, *The Changing Image of Lincoln in American Historiography* (1968). The student of this period will also wish to read Lincoln's own words, which have been published in Roy P. Basler (ed.), *The Collected Works of Abraham Lincoln*, 9 vols. (1953–1955), and *The Collected Works of Abraham Lincoln—Supplement, 1832–1865* (1974). One-volume editions of Lincoln's selected writings and speeches include Roy P. Basler (ed.), *Abraham Lincoln: His Speeches and Writings* (1946); and Paul M. Angle and Earl Schenck Miers (eds.), *The Living Lincoln* (1955).

RECONSTRUCTION

General Works

For good introductions to the issues and the historiography of Reconstruction, read Eric McKitrick, "Reconstruction: Ultraconservative Revolution," in C. Vann Woodward (ed.), *The Comparative Approach to American History* (1968), pp. 146–59; and Bernard A. Weisberger, "The Dark and Bloody Ground of Reconstruction Historiography," *JSH*, 25 (1959), 427–47. Also useful are Larry G. Kincaid, "Victims of Circumstance: An Interpretation of Changing Attitudes Toward Republican Policy Makers and Reconstruction," *JAH*, 57 (1970), 48–66; Gerald Grob, "Reconstruction: An American Morality Play," in George A. Billias and Gerald N. Grob (eds.), *American History: Retrospect and Prospect* (1971); Herman Belz, "The New Orthodoxy in Reconstruction Historiography," *Reviews in American History*, 1 (1973), 106–13; and Michael Les Benedict, "Equality and Expediency in the Reconstruction Era: A Review Essay," *CWH*, 23 (1977), 322–35.

For the "Dunning" school of Reconstruction historiography, which sympathized with Southern whites and viewed the Republicans as vengeful or partisan oppressors, the best examples are William A. Dunning, *Reconstruction: Political and Economic* (1907); and Walter L. Fleming, *The Sequel of Appomattox* (1919). Even more extreme in its pro-Southern interpretation is Claude G. Bowers, *The Tragic Era* (1929).

For articles representative of the more pro-Republican "revisionist" interpretation, which emerged to maturity in the 1960s, see Kenneth M. Stampp and Leon F. Litwack (eds.), *Reconstruction: An Anthology of Revisionist Writings* (1969); and Edwin C. Rozwenc (ed.), *Reconstruction in the South*, 2nd ed. (1972). Still the best single book representing the revisionist viewpoint is Kenneth M. Stampp, *The Era of Reconstruction* (1965). Also valuable are John Hope Franklin, *Reconstruction: After the Civil War* (1961); Harold M. Hyman (ed.), *New Frontiers of the American Reconstruction* (1966); Rembert W. Patrick, *The Reconstruction of the Nation* (1967); and Avery O. Craven, *Reconstruction: The Ending of the Civil War* (1969). One of the earliest revisionists was the black scholar William E. B. Du Bois; see his "Reconstruction and Its Benefits," *AHR*, 15 (1910), 781–99. For a more radical, detailed, and Marxist interpretation by Du Bois, read his *Black Reconstruction . . . in America 1860–1880* (1935). A concise Marxist study is James S. Allen, *Reconstruction: The Battle for Democracy 1865–1876* (1937); and a more recent account from a black power perspective is Lerone Bennett, *Black Power U.S.A.: The Human Side of Reconstruction* (1967).

The basic laws and other major government documents concerning Reconstruction are published in Edward McPherson (ed.), *The Political History of the United States During the Period of Reconstruction* (1975). Fascinating insights by a young French newspaper correspondent who later became famous as France's premier during World War I are contained in the articles published together as Georges Clemenceau, *American Reconstruction 1865–1870*, trans. Margaret MacVeagh (1928). Other collections of contemporary documents and primary sources include Walter L. Fleming (ed.), *A Documentary History of Reconstruction*, 2 vols. (1906; reprinted 1966); James P. Shenton (ed.), *The Reconstruction: A Documentary History* (1963); Richard N. Current (ed.), *Reconstruction* (1965); Staughton Lynd (ed.), *Reconstruction* (1967); Harold M. Hyman (ed.), *The Radical Republicans and Reconstruction 1861–1870* (1967); Robert W. Johanssen (ed.), *Reconstruction: 1865–1877* (1970); Michael Les Benedict (ed.), *The Fruits of Victory: Alternatives in Restoring the Union* (1975), which contains an excellent introduction; and Hans L. Trefousse and Louis L. Snyder (eds.), *Reconstruction: America's First Effort at Racial Democracy* (1979), which also includes a fine introduction.

Presidential Reconstruction and the Congressional Challenge
1865–1868

For many years Howard K. Beale, *The Critical Year: A Study of Andrew Johnson and Reconstruction* (1930), which sympathizes with Johnson and attributes self-serving economic motives to Congressional Republicans, stood as the accepted interpretation of presidential reconstruction. But since 1960 this viewpoint has been severely and successfully challenged by an outpouring of books and articles that, while they do not uncritically champion the sincerity and wisdom of the Republicans, are invariably and sometimes strongly critical of Johnson: Eric L. McKitrick, *Andrew Johnson and Reconstruction* (1960); LaWanda Cox and John H. Cox, *Politics, Principle, and Prejudice 1865–1866* (1963); William R. Brock, *An American Crisis: Congress and Reconstruction 1865–1867* (1963); David Donald, *The Politics of Reconstruction 1863–1867* (1965); LaWanda Cox and John H. Cox, "Negro Suffrage and Republican Politics: The Problem of Motivation in Reconstruction Historiography," *JSH*, 33 (1967), 303–30; Glen M. Linden, *Politics or Principle: Congressional Voting on the Civil War Amendments and Pro-Negro Measures* (1976); Michael Les Benedict, "Preserving the Constitution: The Conservative Basis of Radical Reconstruction," *JAH*, 61 (1974), 65–90; Michael Les Benedict, *A Compromise of Principle: Congressional Republicans and Reconstruction* (1974); and Patrick W. Riddleberger, *1866: The Critical Year Revisited* (1979). J. Michael Quill, *Prelude to the Radicals: The North and Reconstruction in 1865* (1980), surveys Northern public opinion. For a provocative interpretation of the South's manipulation of Andrew Johnson and the political system to soften reconstruction and lay the basis for the revival of Democratic power, read Michael Perman, *Reunion Without Compromise: The South and Reconstruction 1865–1868* (1975). Most of Andrew Johnson's early biographers were sympathetic. For a sampling of their writings, plus some of the subsequent critical interpretations, consult Eric L. McKitrick (ed.), *Andrew Johnson: A Profile* (1960). Two recent biographies blend critical insights with an appreciation of Johnson's virtues and accomplishments: Albert Castel, *The Presidency of Andrew Johnson* (1979); and James Sefton, *Andrew Johnson and the Uses of Constitutional Power* (1979).

A number of specialized monographs have enlarged our understanding of the presidential reconstruction years. Harold Hyman, *The Era of the Oath* (1954), and Jonathan Dorris, *Pardon and Amnesty Under Lincoln and Johnson* (1953), unravel the complexities of loyalty oaths and presidential pardons. For the context of Northern politics in which congressional Republicans acted, see James C. Mohr (ed.), *Radical Republicans in the North* (1976), and James C. Mohr, *The Radical Republicans and Reform in New York During Reconstruction* (1973). The details of Southern black codes that provoked Northern anger are set forth in Theodore B. Wilson, *The Black Codes of the South* (1965). Mary Frances Berry, *Military Necessity and Civil Rights Policy: Black Citizenship and the Constitution 1861–1868* (1977), maintains that the government's need for black troops was an important factor in Republican policy after as well as during the war. The complex origins of the Fourteenth and Fifteenth Amendments are described in the following three studies: Jacobus ten Broek, *The Antislavery Origins of the Fourteenth Amendment* (1951); Joseph B. James, *The Framing of the Fourteenth Amendment* (1956); and William Gillette, *The Right to Vote: Politics and Passage of the Fifteenth Amendment* (1965). The question of white disfranchisement under the Reconstruction Acts is considered in William A. Russ, "Registration and Disfranchisement Under Radical Reconstruction," *MVHR*, 21 (1934), 163–80; and the role of the Supreme Court in the early years of Reconstruction is analyzed in Stanley I. Kutler, *Judicial Power and Reconstruction Politics* (1968).

For the sensitive and crucial role of the army and of General Grant in Reconstruction, two books are important: James Sefton, *The United States Army and Reconstruction* (1967); and Martin E. Mantell, *Johnson, Grant, and the Politics of Reconstruction* (1973). See also Benjamin Thomas and

Harold M. Hyman, *Stanton* (1962). An old study of Andrew Johnson's impeachment, still valuable for the detail it provides, is David M. De Witt, *Impeachment and Trial of Andrew Johnson* (1903). Two modern studies whose sympathies lean toward the impeachers are Michael Les Benedict, *The Impeachment and Trial of Andrew Johnson* (1973); and Hans L. Trefousse, *Impeachment of a President: Andrew Johnson, the Blacks, and Reconstruction* (1975). Charles H. Coleman, *The Election of 1868* (1933), is still the fullest study of the subject.

The South During Reconstruction

After the war, as before, the South attracted many visitors who described the conditions of life and politics for readers back home. For an annotated bibliography of such writings, see Thomas D. Clark (ed.), *Travels in the New South*, 2 vols. (1962). Four books made up of collected articles by Northern journalists who toured the postwar South did much to shape Northern attitudes and policy: Sidney Andrews, *The South Since the War* (1866; reprinted 1970, with introduction by David Donald); John Richard Dennett, *The South as It Is 1865–1866* (1866; reprinted 1965, with introduction by Henry M. Christman); Whitelaw Reid, *After the War: A Tour of the Southern States 1865–1866* (1866; reprinted 1965, with introduction by C. Vann Woodward); and John T. Trowbridge, *A Picture of the Desolated States and the Work of Restoration 1865–1868* (1868). These writers generally presented a critical view of the racial attitudes of Southern whites; by the 1870s, however, the most widely read of the Northern journalists who visited the South sympathized with the plight of white Southerners, and their articles, also collected into books, did much to influence the Northern retreat from Reconstruction. Especially important in this respect were Edward King, *The Great South* (1875; reprinted 1969, with introduction by James M. McPherson); Charles Nordhoff, *The Cotton States in the Spring and Summer of 1875* (1875); and James Shepherd Pike, *The Prostrate State: South Carolina Under Negro Government* (1874; reprinted 1968, with introduction by Robert F. Durden). For an analysis of this last book and of its author, see Robert F. Durden, *James Shepherd Pike: Republicanism and the American Negro 1850–1882* (1957).

There is a large scholarly literature on the South and on individual Southern states during Reconstruction. Books and articles published before 1960 generally reflect the conservative Dunning viewpoint sympathetic to Southern whites and critical of Republicans, while those published since 1960 are usually "revisionist" of this viewpoint: E. Merton Coulter, *The South During Reconstruction* (1947); Jack B. Scroggs, "Carpetbagger Constitutional Reform in the South Atlantic States, 1867–1868," *JSH*, 27 (1961), 475–93; Otto H. Olsen (ed.), *The Reconstruction and Redemption of the South: An Assessment* (1979); Walter L. Fleming, *Civil War and Reconstruction in Alabama* (1905); George H. Thompson, *Arkansas and Reconstruction* (1976); Jerrell Shofner, *Nor Is It Over Yet: Florida and the Era of Reconstruction* (1974); Alan Conway, *The Reconstruction of Georgia* (1966); Joe Gray Taylor, *Louisiana Reconstruction 1863–1877* (1974); James W. Garner, *Reconstruction in Mississippi* (1901); William C. Harris, *Presidential Reconstruction in Mississippi* (1967); William C. Harris, *The Day of the Carpetbagger: Republican Reconstruction in Mississippi* (1979); William McKee Evans, *Ballots and Fence Rails: Reconstruction on the Lower Cape Fear* (1966); Francis B. Simkins and Robert H. Woody, *South Carolina During Reconstruction* (1932); Thomas B. Alexander, *Political Reconstruction in Tennessee* (1950), which despite its early date, reflects much of the revisionist viewpoint; and Jack P. Maddex, *The Virginia Conservatives 1867–1879* (1970). For modern studies of the border states, see especially Richard O. Curry (ed.), *Radicalism, Racism, and Party Realignment: The Border States During Reconstruction* (1969); and William E. Parrish, *Missouri Under Radical Rule* (1965).

Most of the monographs on blacks and Republicans during Reconstruction express one variety or another of revisionism, whatever their date of publication: Robert Cruden, *The Negro in Reconstruction* (1969); Otis Singletary, *Negro Militia and Reconstruction* (1957); Horace Mann Bond,

Negro Education in Alabama: A Study in Cotton and Steel (1939); Peter Kolchin, *First Freedom: The Responses of Alabama's Blacks to Emancipation and Reconstruction* (1972); Loren Schweninger, *James T. Rapier and Reconstruction* (1978), about an Alabama black leader; Joe M. Richardson, *The Negro in the Reconstruction of Florida 1865–1877* (1965); Elizabeth Studley Nathans, *Losing the Peace: Georgia Republicans and Reconstruction* (1964); John W. Blassingame, *Black New Orleans 1860–1880* (1973); Charles Vincent, *Black Legislators in Louisiana During Reconstruction* (1976); Vernon Lane Wharton, *The Negro in Mississippi 1865–1890* (1947); Alrutheus A. Taylor, *The Negro in South Carolina During the Reconstruction* (1924); Joel Williamson, *After Slavery: The Negro in South Carolina During Reconstruction 1861–1877* (1965); Thomas Holt, *Black Over White: Negro Political Leadership in South Carolina During Reconstruction* (1977); Alrutheus A. Taylor, *The Negro in Tennessee 1865–1880* (1941); Carl Moneyhon, *Republicanism in Reconstruction Texas* (1979); Alrutheus A. Taylor, *The Negro in the Reconstruction of Virginia* (1926); and Robert F. Engs, *Freedom's First Generation: Black Hampton, Virginia, 1869–1902* (1980).

For excellent revisionist writings on the carpetbaggers, see Richard N. Current, "Carpetbaggers Reconsidered," in David Pinkney and Theodore Ropp (eds.), *A Festschrift for Frederick B. Artz* (1964), pp. 139–57; Richard N. Current, *Three Carpetbag Governors* (1967); Sarah Van Woolfolk, "Carpetbaggers in Alabama: Tradition Versus Truth," *Alabama Review*, 15 (1962), 133–44; and Otto H. Olsen, *Carpetbagger's Crusade: The Life of Albion W. Tourgee* (1965). Albert Morgan, *Yazoo* (1884), is a fascinating autobiography by a Mississippi carpetbagger.

Two articles debate the role of former Southern Whigs, some of whom became Republicans, in the postwar era: Thomas B. Alexander, "Persistent Whiggery in the Confederate South, 1860–1877," *JSH*, 27 (1961), 305–29; and John V. Mering, "Persistent Whiggery in the Confederate South: A Reconsideration," *SAQ*, 69 (1970), 124–43. For the question of the social origins and previous political affiliations of scalawags, see the following four articles: David Donald, "The Scalawag in Mississippi Reconstruction," *JSH*, 10 (1944), 447–60; Allen W. Trelease, "Who Were the Scalawags?" *JSH*, 29 (1963), 445–68; Otto H. Olsen, "Reconsidering the Scalawags," *CWH*, 12 (1966), 304–20; and Warren A. Ellem, "Who Were the Mississippi Scalawags?" *JSH*, 38 (1972), 217–40. Sarah Woolfolk Wiggins, *The Scalawag in Alabama Politics 1865–1881* (1977), is a fine monograph on a state with significant scalawag strength; while Gordon B. McKinney, *Southern Mountain Republicans 1865–1900: Politics and the Appalachian Community* (1978), analyzes the single most persistent group of Southern white Republicans. For the violent counterrevolution of Southern Democrats against Republicans and Reconstruction, see Allen W. Trelease's exhaustive *White Terror: The Ku Klux Klan Conspiracy and Southern Reconstruction* (1972).

Social and Economic Reconstruction

A partly outdated but still valuable study of the Freedmen's Bureau is George R. Bentley, *A History of the Freedmen's Bureau* (1955). William McFeely, *Yankee Stepfather: General O. O. Howard and the Freedmen* (1968), is critical of the bureau and its leaders for failure to promote and protect the freedmen's interests with more vigor and egalitarianism. Donald G. Nieman, *To Set the Law in Motion: The Freedmen's Bureau and the Legal Rights of Blacks 1865–1868* (1979), presents an incisive analysis of the bureau's mixed record in protecting freedmen's legal rights. Two good state studies of the bureau are Martin Abbott, *The Freedmen's Bureau in South Carolina* (1967); and Howard Ashley White, *The Freedmen's Bureau in Louisiana* (1970).

Henry Lee Swint, *The Northern Teacher in the South 1862–1870* (1941), is a relatively fair-minded study that nevertheless portrays the Yankee teachers as disruptive and naive egalitarians who needlessly alienated Southern whites. On the other hand Donald Spivey, *Schooling for the New Slavery: Black Industrial Education 1868–1915* (1978), and to a lesser extent Ronald E. Butchart,

Northern Schools, Southern Blacks, and Reconstruction: Freedmen's Education 1862–1875 (1980), and Robert C. Morris, *Reading, 'Riting,' and Reconstruction: Freedmen's Education in the South, 1865–1870* (1981), are critical of Northern educators for almost the opposite reason—their alleged paternalism and attitudes of racial superiority toward blacks. James M. McPherson, *The Abolitionist Legacy: From Reconstruction to the NAACP* (1975), and Jacqueline Jones, *Soldiers of Light and Love: Northern Teachers and Georgia Blacks 1865–1873* (1980), explore sympathetically but not uncritically the contribution of Northern whites to freedmen's education. William Preston Vaughan, *Schools for All: The Blacks & Public Education in the South 1865–1877* (1974), focuses primarily on the question of segregation and desegregation in education. Roger A. Fischer, *The Segregation Struggle in Louisiana 1862–1877* (1974), deals with this issue in all aspects of public life including education. Of several articles on the Civil Rights Act of 1875, perhaps the most comprehensive is Alfred H. Kelly, "The Congressional Controversy Over School Segregation, 1867–1875," *AHR*, 54 (1959), 537–63. The most influential study of the segregation question in the Reconstruction and post-Reconstruction South is C. Vann Woodward, *The Strange Career of Jim Crow*, 3rd rev. ed. (1974). For a fresh perspective on this issue, see Howard N. Rabinowitz, *Race Relations in the Urban South 1865–1890* (1977).

During the 1970s, a large number of books and articles appeared on the economic consequences of emancipation and the evolution of a new agricultural labor system to succeed slavery. Valuable summaries and critiques of this literature can be found in Harold D. Woodman, "Sequel to Slavery: The New History Views the Postbellum South," *JSH*, 43 (1977), 523–54; and Jonathan Wiener, Robert Higgs, and Harold Woodman, "Class Structure and Economic Development in the American South, 1865–1955," *AHR*, 84 (1979), 970–1006. The fullest and most persuasive analysis of the postwar Southern economy and the freedmen's place in it is Roger L. Ransom and Richard Sutch, *One Kind of Freedom: The Economic Consequences of Emancipation* (1977). See also Roger L. Ransom and Richard Sutch, "Growth and Welfare in the American South of the Nineteenth Century," *Explorations in Entrepreneurial History*, 16 (1979), 207–35. Two studies that present an even more optimistic picture of Southern agriculture and the freedmen's economic gains are Stephen J. DeCanio, *Agriculture in the Postbellum South* (1974); and Robert Higgs, *Competition and Coercion: Blacks in the American Economy 1865–1914* (1977). Two Marxian-oriented studies that portray a persistence of planter domination and of quasi-slavery for blacks are Jonathan M. Wiener, *Social Origins of the New South: Alabama 1860–1885* (1978); and Jay Mandle, *The Roots of Black Poverty: The Southern Plantation Economy After the Civil War* (1978). On the face of it, much of the legislation passed in the post-Reconstruction South supports the quasi-slavery thesis, though questions remain concerning the degree of enforcement of these laws: See Harold D. Woodman, "Post-Civil War Southern Agriculture and the Law," *AH*, 53 (1979), 319–37; William Cohen, "Negro Involuntary Servitude in the South, 1865–1940: A Preliminary Analysis," *JSH*, 42 (1976), 31–60; and Daniel A. Novak, *The Wheel of Servitude: Black Forced Labor After Slavery* (1978). Other useful articles on Southern agriculture include: Theodore Saloutos, "Southern Agriculture and the Problems of Readjustment, 1865–1877," *AH*, 30 (1956), 58–76; Eugene M. Lerner, "Southern Output and Agricultural Income, 1860–1880," *AH*, 33 (1959), 117–25; Harold D. Woodman, "The Decline of Cotton Factorage After the Civil War," *AHR*, 71 (1966), 1219–36; and Gavin Wright, "Cotton Competition and the Post-Bellum Recovery of the American South," *JEH*, 34 (1974), 610–35. An important study that analyzes the experiences of Northerners who tried their hands at cotton planting after the war is Lawrence N. Powell, *New Masters: Northern Planters During the Civil War and Reconstruction* (1980).

LaWanda Cox, "The Promise of Land for the Freedmen," *MVHR*, 45 (1958), 413–40, discusses the various congressional and executive acts that first opened and then closed the door to significant land reform in the South. Eric Foner, "Thaddeus Stevens, Confiscation, and Reconstruction," in Stanley Elkins and Eric McKitrick (eds.), *The Hofstadter Aegis: A Memorial* (1974), pp. 154–83, describes Stevens's proposals for land reform. For the mixed record of the Freedmen's Bureau in helping blacks achieve land ownership, see Claude F. Oubre, *Forty Acres and a Mule: The Freedmen's Bureau and Black Land Ownership* (1978). Edward Magdol, *A Right to the Land: Essays on the Freedmen's Community* (1977), is a series of uneven but interesting essays on the experiences of the first generation of freedmen. Two institutions that began their work with great hopes but ended with disappointments are treated in Carol Rothrock Bleser, *The Promised Land: The History of the South Carolina Land Commission 1869–1890* (1969); and Carl R. Osthaus, *Freedmen, Philanthropy, and Fraud: A History of the Freedmen's Savings Bank* (1976).

The large hopes but limited achievements of railroad expansion in the postwar South are treated in John F. Stover, *The Railroads of the South, 1865–1900: A Study of Finance and Control* (1955); and Carter Goodrich, "Public Aid to Railroads in the Reconstruction South," *Political Science Quarterly,* 71 (1956), 407–42. The economic history of the whole country, including the South, during the postwar generation is chronicled in the following studies: Edward C. Kirkland, *Industry Comes of Age . . . 1860–1897* (1961); Robert Higgs, *The Transformation of the American Economy 1865–1914: An Essay in Interpretation* (1971); Glenn Porter and Harold C. Livesay, *Merchants and Manufacturers* (1971); Glenn Porter, *The Rise of Big Business* (1973); and Harold G. Vatter, *The Drive to Industrial Maturity: The U.S. Economy 1860–1914* (1975). For a general history of agriculture, consult Fred A. Shannon, *The Farmer's Last Frontier: Agriculture 1860–1897* (1945). Three books offer a fascinating account and important insights about labor movements and industrial conflicts: David Montgomery, *Beyond Equality: Labor and the Radical Republicans 1862–1872* (1967); Wayne G. Broehl, *The Molly Maguires* (1965); and Robert V. Bruce, *1877: Year of Violence* (1959). Four books together provide exhaustive coverage of the tangled financial and monetary question during the era: Robert P. Sharkey, *Money, Class, and Party: An Economic Study of the Civil War and Reconstruction* (1959); Irwin Unger, *The Greenback Era: A Social and Political History of American Finance* (1964); Walter T. K. Nugent, *The Money Question During Reconstruction* (1967); and Allen Weinstein, *Prelude to Populism: Origins of the Silver Issue 1867–1878* (1970). An older but still useful social history of the postwar decade is Allan Nevins, *The Emergence of Modern America 1865–1878* (1927).

National Politics and the Retreat from Reconstruction in the 1870s

For a broad survey of changes in Northern opinion about the "Southern Question," read Paul H. Buck, *The Road to Reunion 1865–1900* (1937). A more comprehensive and up-to-date study of the Reconstruction years themselves is William Gillette, *Retreat from Reconstruction: A Political History 1867–1878* (1979). While William B. Hesseltine's study of the Grant Presidency, *Ulysses S. Grant, Politician* (1935), contains material of value, it has been superseded in many respects by William S. McFeely, *Grant: A Biography* (1981). Domestic as well as foreign affairs during the Grant administration are also treated in Allan Nevins, *Hamilton Fish: The Inner History of the Grant Administration* (1936). An exhaustive treatment of the most important foreign policy issue is Adrian Cook, *The Alabama Claims* (1975). For a detailed analysis of state and national politics during the postwar generation, see Morton Keller, *Affairs of State: Public Life in Late Nineteenth Century America* (1977). The important role of veterans' organizations in both Northern and Southern politics is described in Mary R. Dearing, *Veterans in Politics: The Story of the G.A.R.* (1952); and William W. White, *The Confederate Veteran* (1962).

The civil service reformers and Liberal Republicans are treated in Ari A. Hoogenboom, *Outlawing the Spoils: A History of the Civil Service Reform Movement* (1961); and John G. Sproat, *"The Best Men": Liberal Reformers in the Gilded Age* (1968). For the Liberals and the 1872 election, see Earle Dudley Ross, *The Liberal Republican Movement* (1919); Matthew T. Downey, "Horace Greeley and the Politicians: The Liberal Republican Convention of 1872," *JAH,* 53 (1967), 727–50; and

Richard A. Gerber, "The Liberal Republicans of 1872 in Historiographical Perspective," *JAH*, 62 (1975), 40–73. An older study of the 1876 presidential election and its aftermath, still serviceable for its factual detail, is Paul L. Haworth, *The Hayes-Tilden Disputed Presidential Election of 1876* (1906). For a provocative interpretation of the negotiations by which the electoral dispute was settled, read C. Vann Woodward, *Reunion and Reaction*, rev. ed. (1956). But consult also Allan Peskin, "Was There a Compromise of 1877?" *JAH*, 60 (1973), 63–73; and C. Vann Woodward, "Yes, There was a Compromise of 1877," *JAH*, 60 (1973), 215–23. Challenges to Woodward's interpretation can also be found in Keith I. Polakoff, *The Politics of Inertia: The Election of 1876 and the End of Reconstruction* (1973); and Michael Les Benedict, "Southern Democrats in the Crisis of 1876–1877: A Reconsideration of *Reunion and Reaction*," *JSH*, 46 (1980), 489–524. Additional light on the question is shed by George C. Rable, "Southern Interests and the Election of 1876: A Reappraisal," *CWH*, 26 (Dec. 1980), 347–61.

The changing attitudes of various groups in the North toward the role of government in protecting the equal rights of blacks are chronicled in Rayford W. Logan, *The Betrayal of the Negro: From Rutherford B. Hayes to Woodrow Wilson* (1965); James M. McPherson, *The Abolitionist Legacy: From Reconstruction to the NAACP* (1975); and Lawrence Grossman, *The Democratic Party and the Negro: Northern and National Politics, 1868–1892* (1976). The decline in federal efforts to enforce black voting rights is discussed in Everette Swinney, "Enforcing the Fifteenth Amendment," *JSH*, 27 (1962), 202–18.

The New South

The New South ideology of industrial progress and modernization on the Yankee model is dissected in Paul M. Gaston, *The New South Creed* (1970). Gaston expands upon the influential thesis set forth by C. Vann Woodward, *Origins of the New South 1877–1913* (1951), that the economic and political leaders of the New South came from the rising middle class, which had little connection with the antebellum planter regime and its ideology. For a sympathetic evaluation of this thesis, see Sheldon Hackney, "*Origins of the New South* in Retrospect," *JSH*, 38 (1972), 191–216. For a critical evaluation, see James Tice Moore, "Redeemers Reconsidered: Change and Continuity in the Democratic South, 1870–1900," *JSH*, 44 (1978), 357–78. A summary and reflection on this question can be found in George B. Tindall, *The Persistent Tradition in New South Politics* (1975). For the persistence of Old South romanticism after the war, see Rollin G. Osterweis, *The Myth of the Lost Cause 1865–1900* (1973). Monographs containing additional information on economic and political developments in the post-Reconstruction South include Theodore Saloutos, *Farmer Movements in the South 1865–1933* (1960); Robert C. McMath, *Populist Vanguard: A History of the Southern Farmers' Alliance* (1975); Michael Schwartz, *Radical Protest and Social Structure: The Southern Farmers' Alliance and Cotton Tenancy* (1977); and Melton A. McLaurin, *The Knights of Labor in the South* (1978).

Numerous studies of individual Southern states address implicitly if not explicitly the Woodward thesis concerning the discontinuity of Southern leadership and ideology. In addition to Jonathan Wiener's *Social Origins of the New South*, cited in the section on Social and Economic Reconstruction, consult the following: William Warren Rogers, *The One-Gallused Rebellion: Agrarianism in Alabama 1865–1896* (1970); Sheldon Hackney, *Populism to Progressivism in Alabama* (1969); William Ivy Hair, *Bourbonism and Agrarian Protest: Louisiana Politics 1877–1900* (1969); Albert D. Kirwan, *Revolt of the Rednecks: Mississippi Politics 1877–1925* (1951); Dwight D. Billings, *Planters and the Making of a "New South": Class, Politics, and Development in North Carolina 1865–1900* (1979); William Cooper, *The Conservative Regime: South Carolina 1877–1890* (1968); Francis B. Simkins, *Pitchfork Ben Tillman: South Carolinian* (1944); Roger L. Hart, *Redeemers, Bourbons, and Populists: Tennessee 1870–1896* (1975); and Alwyn Barr, *Reconstruction to Reform: Texas Politics 1876–1906* (1971).

James Tice Moore, *Two Paths to the New South: The Virginia Debt Controversy 1870–1883* (1974), analyzes the Mahone movement in Virginia, which seemed to offer Northern Republicans the best opportunity during the 1880s to crack the solid South in alliance with Southern independent political movements. Vincent P. DeSantis, *Republicans Face the Southern Question: The New Departure Years 1877–1897* (1959), and Stanley P. Hirshson, *Farewell to the Bloody Shirt: Northern Republicans and the Southern Negro 1877–1893* (1962), trace the continuing efforts of national Republican leaders to nurture a viable Republican party in the South. For an analysis of the last congressional effort before the 1950s to pass a voting rights bill, see Richard E. Welch, "The Federal Elections Bill of 1890: Postscripts and Prelude," *JAH,* 52 (1965), 511–26. The persistence of Southern Republican-ism and the ultimately successful Democratic counterattack by means of disfranchisement are trenchantly recounted in J. Morgan Kousser, *The Shaping of Southern Politics: Suffrage Restriction and the Establishment of the One-Party South 1880–1910* (1974). Claude H. Nolen, *The Negro's Image in the South: The Anatomy of White Supremacy* (1967), narrates the evolution of a postemanci-pation ideology of white supremacy; while C. Vann Woodward, *The Strange Career of Jim Crow,* 3rd rev. ed. (1974), discusses the hardening code of segregation in the South after 1890.

The politics and ideology of race and racism are also treated in the following state studies: William W. Rogers and Robert D. Ward, *August Reckoning: Jack Turner and Racism in Post–Civil War Alabama* (1973); Margaret Law Callcott, *The Negro in Maryland Politics 1870–1912* (1969); Frenise Logan, *The Negro in North Carolina 1876–1894* (1964); George B. Tindall, *South Carolina Negroes 1877–1900* (1952); Joseph H. Cartwright, *The Triumph of Jim Crow: Tennessee Race Relations in the 1880's* (1976); Lawrence D. Rice, *The Negro in Texas 1874–1900* (1971); Charles E. Wynes, *Race Relations in Virginia 1870–1902* (1961); and William Ivy Hair, *Carnival of Fury: Robert Charles and the New Orleans Race Riot of 1900* (1976). Numerous articles and books address the complex question of the Southern Populists and the race issue. Three of the most important are C. Vann Woodward, *Tom Watson, Agrarian Rebel* (1938); Helen G. Edmonds, *The Negro and Fusion Politics in North Carolina 1894–1901* (1951); and Lawrence C. Goodwyn, "Populist Dreams and Negro Rights: East Texas as a Case Study," *AHR,* 76 (1971), 1435–56. The most comprehen-sive analysis of this question is Gerald H. Gaither, *Blacks and the Populist Revolt: Ballots and Bigotry in the "New South"* (1977).

Index

―――

639

titudes toward Reconstruction, 497; differences with Johnson, 497–98; growing concern at Johnson's policy, 500–1, 502; majority of Republican voters favor black suffrage in Northern states, 501–2, 502n, 529; and question of land confiscation, 509; growing schism with Johnson, 513–16; and Fourteenth Amendment, 517; and first Reconstruction Act, 521–23; and impeachment, 525–26, 528, 529, 531–33; readmission of Southern states by, 538; Fifteenth Amendment, 545–46; and attempt to annex Santo Domingo, 549–51; and civil service reform, 550; schism in, and Liberal Republicans, 553, 567–68; divisions among on monetary questions, 588; and affairs in Louisiana, 591–92; growing disillusionment with Southern policy, 593–94; and scandals of Grant administration, 596; negotiations with Southern Democrats, 602; futile efforts for new enforcement acts, 605; coalitions with Southern independents, 607–8; and federal elections bill of 1890, 615–17. See also Elections; Radical Republicans; Republican party in South

Republican party in South: organization and composition of, 524, 526–27, 535–36, 555; in constitutional conventions, 536–37; gains control of state governments, 538; black leadership and constituency, 555–57, 559; carpetbagger leadership, 557–58; scalawag leadership, 558; divisions within, 558–60; progressive legislation of, 560–61; corruption issue, stereotype and reality, 561–63; schism in Louisiana, 591; schisms in states besides Louisiana, 593; loses control of Mississippi, 594–95; loses control of Louisiana and South Carolina, 603; coalition with Readjusters, 608; coalitions with Populists, 617–18

Rockefeller, John D., 584, 610

Santo Domingo, attempt to annex, 549–51, 553
Saxton, Rufus, 508
Scalawags, 524; stereotype of, 557; reality of, 558; tensions between carpetbaggers and, 559–60
Schofield, John M., as secretary of war, 533
Schurz, Carl: and Sharkey affair, 503; and Santo Domingo, 550; as Liberal Republican leader, 553, 563; denounces army intervention in Louisiana, 593; on Southern question in 1876

election, 597, 598; as secretary of interior under Hayes, 603
Scott, Robert, 562
Segregation: opposed in freedmen's schools, 575; movements against in Northern public schools, 575; issue of in Southern public education, 575–76; Civil Rights Act of 1875, 576–77; and Jim Crow legislation in South, 618–19
Seward, William H.: and National Union party, 518; and purchase of Alaska, 549
Seymour, Horatio: as Democratic presidential nominee in 1868, 541, 542; defeat of, 545
Sharecropping and share tenantry: development of after war, 510, 578–79; and crop lien system, 581
Sharkey, William L., 500–1, 503
Shenandoah, C.S.S., and Alabama claims, 549
Sheridan, Philip H.: and enforcement of Reconstruction, 527; removed by Johnson, 528, 530; on White League, 592
Sherman, John, and specie resumption, 588
Sherman, William Tecumseh, Special Order No. 15 (land for freedmen), 506, 508
Sickles, Daniel, 529
Silver, movement for expanded coinage of, 589–90, 616
Slaughterhouse cases, 517n
Slocum, Henry W., 503
South: chaotic conditions after war, 493; attitudes of white population, 494–95; revival of defiant attitudes, 502–3; and Andrew Johnson, 503–5; refusal to ratify Fourteenth Amendment, 521; response to Reconstruction Acts, 526–27; constitutional conventions in, 535–37; readmission to Congress, 538–39; New South ideology, 609–10, 611; New South realities, 610–15; disfranchisement and segregation of blacks in 1890s, 618–19. See also Reconstruction
South Carolina: destruction in, 493; integration of state university, 575–76; violence in, in 1876 election, 598; disputed election returns of, 599, 600; violence in elections of 1878, 605
South Carolina Land Commission, 537, 580
Specie Resumption Act, 588
Springfield Republican, urges magnanimity toward South, 496
Stanbery, Henry, 527, 532
Stanton, Edwin M.: and land for freedmen, 508;

A Note About the Author

James M. McPherson is Edwards Professor of American History at Princeton University, where he has taught since 1962. He was born in Valley City, North Dakota, in 1936. He received his B.A. from Gustavus Adolphus College in 1958 and his Ph.D. from The Johns Hopkins University in 1963. He has been a Guggenheim Fellow, a National Endowment for the Humanities Fellow, a visiting Fellow at the Henry E. Huntington Library in San Marino, California, and a Fellow at the Center for Advanced Study in the Behavioral Sciences at Stanford. In 1982 he was Commonwealth Fund Lecturer at University College, London.

A specialist in Civil War–Reconstruction history and in the history of race relations, Mr. McPherson is the author of *The Struggle for Equality: Abolitionists and the Negro in the Civil War and Reconstruction* (1964), *The Negro's Civil War* (1965), *Marching Toward Freedom: The Negro in the Civil War* (1968), and *The Abolitionist Legacy: From Reconstruction to the NAACP* (1975).

A Note on the Type

This book was set via computer-driven cathode ray tube in Avanta, a film version of Electra, a type face designed by W. A. Dwiggins. The Electra face is a simple and readable type suitable for printing books by present-day processes. It is not based on any historical model, and hence does not echo any particular time or fashion. Composed by Haddon Craftsmen, Inc. Scranton, Pennsylvania. Printed and bound by R. R. Donnelley & Sons, Co., Crawfordsville, Indiana.

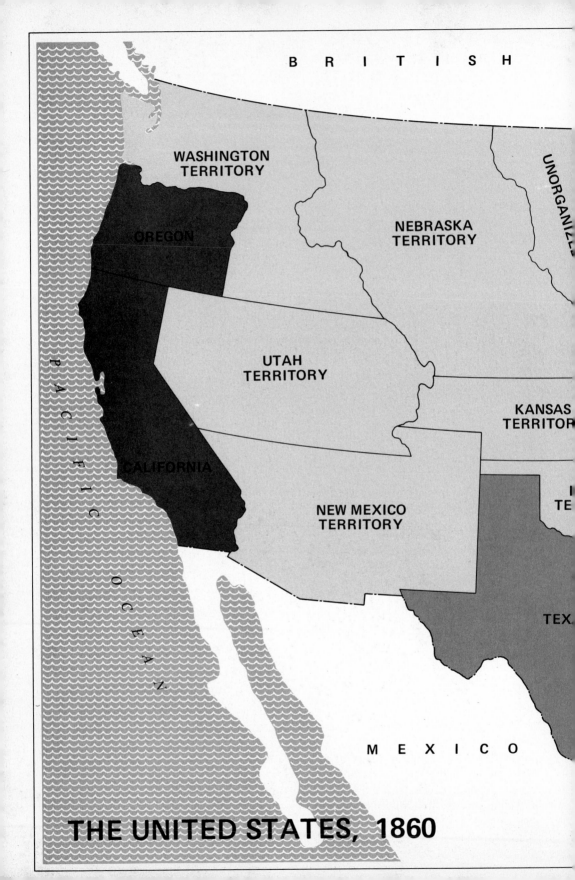

B R I T I S H

WASHINGTON
TERRITORY

OREGON

NEBRASKA
TERRITORY

UNORGANIZE

UTAH
TERRITORY

KANSAS
TERRITOR

CALIFORNIA

I
TE

NEW MEXICO
TERRITORY

TEX.

P A C I F I C   O C E A N

M E X I C O

THE UNITED STATES, 1860

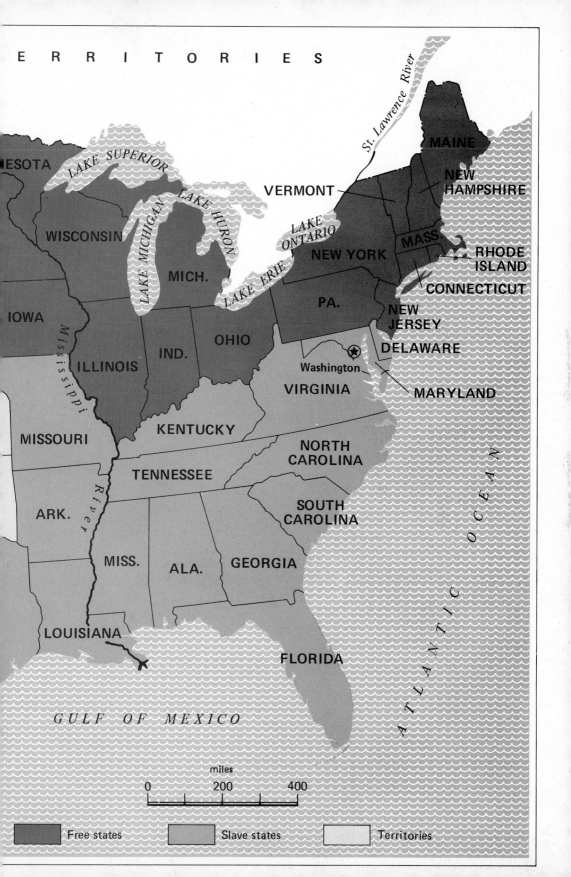

ERRITORIES

St. Lawrence River

MAINE

VERMONT

NEW HAMPSHIRE

LAKE SUPERIOR

MINESOTA

LAKE MICHIGAN

LAKE HURON

WISCONSIN

MICH.

LAKE ONTARIO

NEW YORK

MASS.

LAKE ERIE

RHODE ISLAND

CONNECTICUT

PA.

NEW JERSEY

IOWA

Mississippi

ILLINOIS

IND.

OHIO

DELAWARE

Washington

MARYLAND

VIRGINIA

MISSOURI

KENTUCKY

River

NORTH CAROLINA

TENNESSEE

ARK.

SOUTH CAROLINA

ATLANTIC OCEAN

MISS.

ALA.

GEORGIA

LOUISIANA

FLORIDA

GULF OF MEXICO

miles

0   200   400

Free states   Slave states   Territories